Tax Policy Reforms 2022

OECD AND SELECTED PARTNER ECONOMIES

OECD
BETTER POLICIES FOR BETTER LIVES

Please cite this publication as:
OECD (2022), *Tax Policy Reforms 2022: OECD and Selected Partner Economies*, OECD Publishing, Paris, https://doi.org/10.1787/067c593d-en.

ISBN 978-92-64-32221-9 (print)
ISBN 978-92-64-60057-7 (pdf)
ISBN 978-92-64-40679-7 (HTML)
ISBN 978-92-64-94789-4 (epub)

Tax Policy Reforms
ISSN 2617-3425 (print)
ISSN 2617-3433 (online)

Photo credits: Cover image word cloud ©Tagul.com.

Corrigenda to publications may be found on line at: www.oecd.org/about/publishing/corrigenda.htm.

Foreword

This report was produced by the Tax Policy and Statistics Division of the OECD's Centre for Tax Policy and Administration. It was led by Richard Clarke and written jointly by Richard Clarke, Patrice Ollivaud (Economics Department), Antonia Ramm, Michael Stemmer, and Astrid Tricaud. The report's Special Feature (Chapter 4) is largely based on an OECD Policy Brief written by Kurt Van Dender (OECD Centre for Tax Policy and Administration), Assia Elgouacem (Economics Department), Grégoire Garsous and Hamza Belgroun (Trade and Agriculture Directorate), and Mark Mateo and Amy Cano Prentice (Environment Directorate).

The authors would like to thank the delegates of Working Party No.2 on Tax Policy Analysis and Tax Statistics and the Committee on Fiscal Affairs for their inputs. The authors would also like to thank David Bradbury and Bert Brys for their guidance and acknowledge their helpful contributions and comments. Comments received from Piet Battiau, Stéphane Buydens, Nicolas Miranda, Sarah Perret, Pierce O'Reilly and Kurt Van Dender were also gratefully received. The authors would like to thank Karena Garnier and Natalie Lagorce for their assistance with formatting and communication, Michael Sharratt for his support with data processing and analysis, Céline Colin for her work on health tax design, and Mariona Mas Montserrat and Yannic Rehm for their tax buoyancy analysis.

The report was approved by the Committee on Fiscal Affairs and Working Party No.2 on Tax Policy Analysis and Tax Statistics on 31 August 2022 and prepared for publication by the OECD Secretariat.

Table of contents

FIGURES

TABLES

BOXES

Follow OECD Publications on:

https://twitter.com/OECD

https://www.facebook.com/theOECD

https://www.linkedin.com/company/organisation-eco-cooperation-development-organisation-cooperation-developpement-eco/

https://www.youtube.com/user/OECDiLibrary

https://www.oecd.org/newsletters/

This book has...

StatLinks

A service that delivers Excel® files from the printed page!

Look for the *StatLink* at the bottom of the tables or graphs in this book. To download the matching Excel® spreadsheet, just type the link into your Internet browser or click on the link from the digital version.

Reader's Guide

***Tax Policy Reforms: OECD and Selected Partner Economies (2022)* is an annual publication that provides comparative information on tax reforms across countries and tracks tax policy developments over time**. This year's edition focuses on the tax reforms that were introduced or announced during the calendar year of 2021.

As in previous years, the 2022 edition of the report is based principally upon responses to the OECD's annual tax policy reform questionnaire. The questionnaire requests information on the type of tax; the dates of announcement and introduction; the direction of the rate and/or base change; and a detailed description of the reform. At the November 2010 WP2 meeting, the following criteria were agreed for deciding whether a tax policy measure was sufficiently substantial to be reported in the questionnaire: (1) a significant change in a tax rate; (2) a change in the tax base that is expected to change revenue from that base by more than 5% of total tax revenue or 0.1% of GDP; and (3) a politically important systemic reform. The questionnaire also asks for the rationale behind the reform and estimates of the revenue effects of the tax measures.

The number of countries covered by the report has expanded over time. The first edition of the *Tax Policy Reforms* report in 2016 covered all OECD countries, before being expanded to all OECD countries and "selected partner countries", to include Argentina and South Africa for the 2017 and 2018 editions, and then adding Indonesia in 2019 and the People's Republic of China (China) in 2020. At the request of the G20 Finance Ministers and Central Bank Governors, the previous year's questionnaire was sent to all members of the OECD/G20 Inclusive Framework on Base Erosion and Profit Shifting, of which 66 jurisdictions responded. The 2021 edition of the report covered reforms made by all OECD and G20 countries (other than India), and 21 additional Inclusive Framework jurisdictions. The 21 additional Inclusive Framework members that responded to the OECD questionnaire for the 2021 edition of the Tax Policy Reforms report were: Albania, Andorra, Barbados, Bulgaria, Croatia, Honduras, Jersey, Macau, Mauritius, Nigeria, Republic of North Macedonia, Panama, Paraguay, Peru, Seychelles, Singapore, Thailand, Trinidad and Tobago, Tunisia, Turks and Caicos, and Uruguay.

This year, the questionnaire was sent out to all delegates of Working Party 2 in its Inclusive Framework format. The intention was to have greater country coverage than in previous years, which is aligned with the Centre for Tax Policy & Administration's goal of expanding the number and type of countries that the Directorate supports, to a greater number of low- and middle-income countries that are more geographically diverse.

The 2022 report has a wider country coverage than previous editions of the report, with 71 jurisdictions responding to the questionnaire. In addition to all OECD members, the report covers the following Inclusive Framework jurisdictions: Albania, Andorra, Argentina, Armenia, Bosnia and Herzegovina, Brazil, Brunei Darussalam, Bulgaria, Cabo Verde, the Cook Islands, Croatia, Georgia, Honduras, Indonesia, Kenya, Malaysia, Malta, Mauritius, Monaco, Morocco, Nigeria, Pakistan, Peru, Romania, Saudi Arabia, Senegal, Seychelles, South Africa, Togo, Ukraine, the United Arab Emirates, Uruguay, and Viet Nam.

The report is comprised of three chapters. Its principal chapter, Chapter 3, describes the tax policy reforms implemented by the 71 jurisdictions that responded to the questionnaire. Chapter 3 is split into five sections depending on the category of tax reform reported: personal income taxes and social security contributions (Section 3.1), corporate income taxes and other corporate taxes (Section 3.2), taxes on goods and services, including value added taxes, sales taxes and excise duties (Section 3.3), environmentally related taxes (Section 3.4) and property taxes (Section 3.5).

To better understand the context for the tax reforms described in Chapter 3, Chapter 1 provides an overview of the macroeconomic environment and Chapter 2 the tax revenue context. Tax policy developments are closely connected with economic trends: tax revenues are affected by changes in macroeconomic conditions and economic developments are important factors behind tax reforms. Chapter 1 therefore, covers trends in growth, inflation, productivity, investment, the labour market, public finances, and inequality, while Chapter 2 describes the latest tax revenue trends, analysing both changes in total tax-to-GDP ratios and tax structures.

The report includes a fourth Chapter, which is a Special Feature on government responses to the rising energy prices experienced in the second half of 2021 and the first half of 2022. This *Special Feature* is based on a joint Policy Brief produced by the Centre for Tax Policy and Administration, the Economics Department, the Environment Directorate and the Trade and Agriculture Directorate. The fourth Chapter of the Report draws on data collected by the OECD on government support measures implemented in 89 jurisdictions, including 74 member jurisdictions of the OECD/G20 Inclusive Framework on Base Erosion and Profit Shifting.

There are several differences in the data used for each Chapter of the Report. Chapter 1 is primarily based on the *OECD's Economic Outlooks (Issues 1 and 2) for 2021*, which predominantly uses 2020 and 2021 data from OECD countries and other selected Inclusive Framework jurisdictions (Argentina, Brazil, China, India, Indonesia, and South Africa). As in previous editions of the Tax Policy Reforms Report, Chapter 2 uses the Tax Revenue Statistics Database as its primary source and covers all OECD countries and other selected Inclusive Framework jurisdictions (Argentina, Brazil, China, Indonesia and South Africa) who report annual tax revenue data across tax categories to the OECD. Notably, Chapter 2 draws heavily on the *2021 OECD Revenue Statistics report* that provides an assessment of the initial impact of COVID-19 on OECD Tax Revenues. At the time of the publication of this Report, not all OECD countries had reported on their preliminary tax revenue data for 2020. Therefore, tax revenue data are not available for certain tax categories for some countries, such as Australia and New Zealand, but also Greece and Japan on occasion.

Chapter 3 uses a wider variety of data sources, with notable differences in country coverage across sections. As described above, Chapter 3 is predominantly based on the questionnaire responses provided by 71 Inclusive Framework members. The number and type of the reforms implemented by jurisdictions therefore determines the extent to which they feature in each Section of Chapter 3. However, tax revenue and tax policy analysis data are also used throughout the Chapter to complement the tax reforms described. In most cases, tax revenue data has the same country coverage as in Chapter 2 – all OECD countries as well as Argentina, Brazil, China, Indonesia, and South Africa. The country coverage of the tax policy analysis data, such as marginal and effective tax rates on labour (Section 3.1), corporations (Section 3.2) and carbon (Section 3.4), varies more widely, however, and depends on which jurisdictions provide data to the OECD. Differences in country coverage are described in the notes below all the figures used, while references to country coverage in the text are often explained in more detail in the footnotes.

Executive Summary

Tax Policy Reforms: OECD and Selected Partner Economies is an annual publication that provides comparative information on tax reforms across countries. It tracks tax policy developments over time and gives an overview of the latest tax reform trends. This year's edition focuses on the tax reforms that were introduced or announced during the calendar year of 2021.

The 2022 Edition has the largest country coverage in its seven-year history. This year's report covers the tax policy reforms made in 71 member jurisdictions of the OECD/G20 Inclusive Framework on Base Erosion and Profit Shifting, including all OECD countries, for the 2021 calendar year. The greater country coverage than in previous editions reflects the OECD Centre for Tax Policy and Administration's efforts to expand the number and diversity of countries it provides support to.

This Report contains four chapters. Chapter 1 discusses the macroeconomic background within which changes in tax policy have been made, providing an overview of developments in the global economy. Chapter 2 presents the latest trends in tax revenues and in the composition of taxes, identifying how these were affected by the COVID-19 pandemic in 2020. Chapter 3 provides a detailed description of the tax reforms that were implemented or announced in the calendar year 2021 across tax categories. Chapter 4 is a Special Feature that examines the measures countries have introduced in response to rising energy prices and offers policy recommendations if prices remain elevated.

The Report identifies several common themes driving tax policy decisions. Exposure to the COVID-19 pandemic and vaccination rates continued to be key determinants of the type of tax policy governments introduced in 2021, as well as the speed at which certain measures were implemented, retracted, or replaced, as countries sought to stimulate recovery in consumption and investment whilst limiting infection rates. Countries' fiscal space and policymakers' ability to use their tax and transfer systems to target measures has also played a key role in tax policy decisions. Those with more advanced fiscal and welfare systems were better able to adapt the duration of measures and the sectors (and in some cases, specific types of firms) that continued to require support. As energy prices rose steeply in the second half of the year, countries with greater exposure to natural gas and oil markets sought to shield households and businesses from their impact through temporary fiscal support measures, and taper existing stimulus measures that could add to inflation.

The report identifies the following policy trends by tax category:

- **Personal income taxes (PIT) and social security contributions (SSCs)** were reduced in most countries as policy makers sought to boost economic growth and promote equity. PIT rate changes were less common than in previous years while PIT base narrowing measures were widespread, with measures targeted towards low- and middle-income households, and particularly those with children, to promote employment and provide in-work benefits. A very limited number of changes in the taxation of household capital income were introduced. SSC rate reductions and base narrowing measures were largely temporary.
- Statutory **corporate income tax (CIT)** rates were cut in four countries, while five countries reduced SME CIT and IP regime rates, leading to further convergence in CIT rates across countries. Many

countries increased the generosity of corporate tax incentives to stimulate investment and innovation, particularly to promote environmental sustainability. However, the most important development was the significant strengthening of international tax cooperation as 137 jurisdictions agreed to a two-pillar solution to reform the international taxation rules and ensure that multinational enterprises pay a fair share of tax wherever they operate and generate profits.

- The **Value Added Tax (VAT)** base was subject to many changes in 2021, but rates were mostly untouched. Standard VAT rates were maintained in almost all countries, continuing the trend observed for the last six years. However, VAT bases underwent significant alterations through the reversal of most temporary VAT rate reductions for specific sectors that were introduced in 2020, and countries applying reduced VAT rates to a range of goods and services on a permanent basis in 2021. Most countries kept zero rate or VAT exemptions for COVID-19 related medical products from 2020, whilst some also temporarily applied reduced VAT rates to fuel sources during the third and fourth quarters. The largest reforms centered on e-commerce, including an enormous growth in e-invoicing and digital reporting requirements.
- Progress on **environmentally related taxes** continued in 2021, though at a slower pace than in previous years. Promoting environmental sustainability has become increasingly central to the policy goals of taxing energy and vehicle use and eexplicit carbon taxes on fuel were expanded over the year. Of the small number of countries that increased or introduced carbon taxes, some did so as part of a policy package that balanced these tax rises with compensatory lower taxes on personal incomes and corporate revenues. However, effective carbon prices remain low overall, contributed to by temporary cuts in energy taxes towards the end of 2021.
- **Property tax** measures focused on promoting progressivity and fairness in 2021, though reforms were less common than in previous years. Property tax reforms predominantly involved tax rises, through either increases in tax rates or tax base broadening measures, often targeted at individuals or entities that use properties predominantly as an investment vehicle as well as at higher net worth individuals. These measures often sought to promote the efficient use of the existing housing stock as well as the fairness of property taxation more generally.

The Special Feature examines the support measures introduced by governments to shield households and firms from the impacts of high energy prices. It cautions that while the measures introduced up to May 2022 were relatively simple to implement and communicate, many that have sought to lower the price of energy have not been targeted and weaken incentives to reduce energy use when supply is tight. The Special Feature also provides policy recommendations to governments if prices remain elevated, suggesting a shift towards more targeted measures, which may require improvements to existing transfer and social welfare systems.

1 Macroeconomic background

This Chapter provides background information on macroeconomic conditions up until 2021. Tax policy developments are closely connected with economic trends: tax revenues are affected by changes in macroeconomic conditions and economic developments are important factors behind tax reforms. This Chapter covers recent trends in growth, inflation, productivity, investment, the labour market, public finances, and inequality.

1.1. Global growth, labour market and investment trends

This section provides background information on macroeconomic conditions up until 2021 to help better understand the tax policy changes described in Chapter 3. It covers recent trends in growth, inflation, productivity, investment, the labour market, public finances, and inequality. Tax policy developments are closely connected with economic trends: tax revenues are affected by changes in macroeconomic conditions and economic developments are important factors behind tax reforms.

1.1.1. Global growth recovered strongly in 2021 from the COVID-19 crisis

Global GDP growth reached 5.8% in 2021 after a decline of 3.4% in 2020, reflecting a rebound from the deep COVID-19 crisis (Figure 1.1). Most economies experienced output declines in 2020. Unlike the Global Financial Crisis (GFC) of 2008, when many emerging-market economies were less affected by falling output relative to advanced economies, with COVID-19, macroeconomic changes were more similar across the world, and may have lasting costs.[1]

The quarterly profile of global GDP growth since the pandemic began has been volatile. The COVID-19 pandemic hit economies mostly in the second quarter of 2020, before rebounding (Figure 1.1). By the end of 2021 real GDP was back above pre-pandemic levels in most economies. However, despite the swift recovery, the effect of the crisis was still visible at the end of 2021 (Figure 1.2). In Q4 of 2021, the gap between the GDP level recorded and the GDP level projected before the pandemic was still significant at the global level (above 2%) and, to a smaller extent, the OECD as a whole (less than 1.5%).

However, foregone growth to date has not been distributed equally. The loss has been greater for middle-income emerging-market economies than for advanced economies, and greatest of all for low-income developing countries (OECD, 2021[1]). Amongst major emerging-market economies, the gap between the GDP level recorded and pre-pandemic projections is especially large for India and Indonesia, and to a lesser extent for Brazil and South Africa. In those countries that recorded relatively slow recoveries, this has often been due to delays in vaccinations, the greater size and importance of the informal sector and international tourism, poorer quality health systems and more limited fiscal space. There is a risk that scarring results from the crisis, notably due to lasting income losses and to education disruptions affecting the future of many children. In contrast, there was a quick return to the output path projected before the pandemic in China, helped by ample policy space, although the zero-COVID policy has continued to cause occasional disruptions to activity.

The pace of recovery has also varied across the OECD economies (Figure 1.3). By the end of 2021, output in some OECD countries was in line with a pre-pandemic counterfactual – for Colombia, Costa Rica, Finland, Lithuania, the Netherlands, Poland, Switzerland, and the United States. For the United States, the large pandemic-related fiscal stimulus, including the American Rescue Plan in early 2021, helped to boost GDP growth as well as the global outlook (OECD, 2021[2]). However, many OECD countries lagged behind, especially in Europe. In Q4 of 2021, the GDP of the euro area and the United Kingdom was still more than 2% below pre-pandemic expectations. Policies implemented to mitigate COVID-19 consequences notably diverged between the United States and the euro area, shaping a different recovery (Boone, 2022[3]), where the different size and timing of pandemic waves, as well as the diverse speed of vaccination campaigns during 2021 also partly explain different outcomes across countries. Similar to emerging economies, the pre-existing size of the travel and tourism sector, which suffered from restrictions on international mobility, also played a role (Rusticelli and Turner, 2021[4]). Differences in the measurement of non-market activities contributed to the output differences recorded across countries too (OECD, 2021[5]; Mitchell et al., 2022[6]). Overall, GDP growth in the OECD as a whole was 5.5% in 2021 after a decline of 4.6% in 2020.

Figure 1.1. Real GDP growth

Year-on-year percentage changes

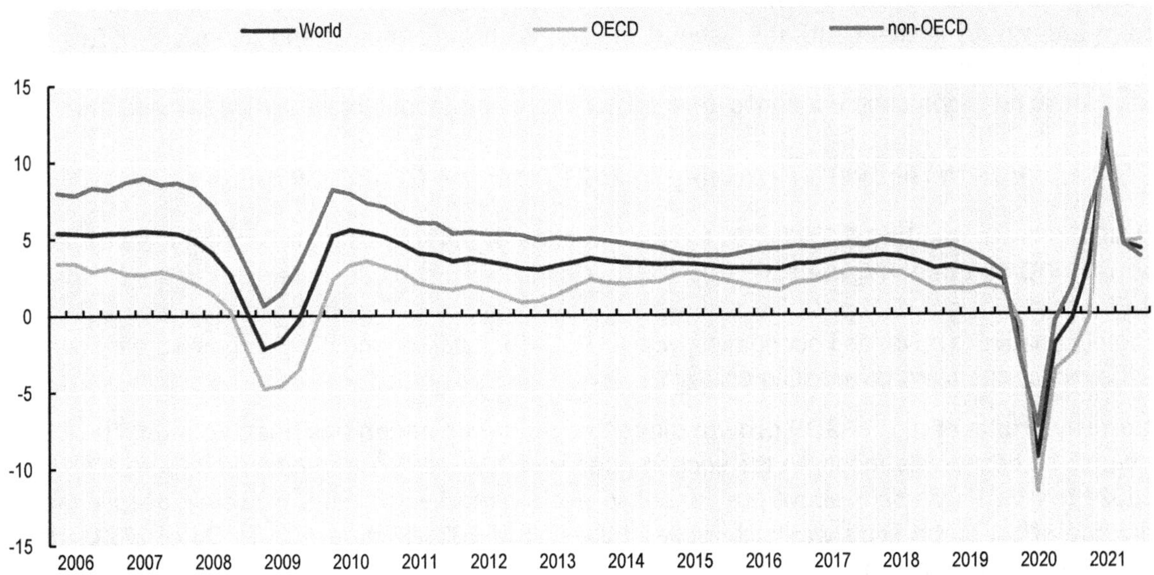

Note: Aggregates using weights in purchasing power parities.
Source: OECD Economic Outlook 111 database.

StatLink https://stat.link/95wyhp

Figure 1.2. Comparison of GDP with its pre-pandemic expected level

Index 2019 Q4=100

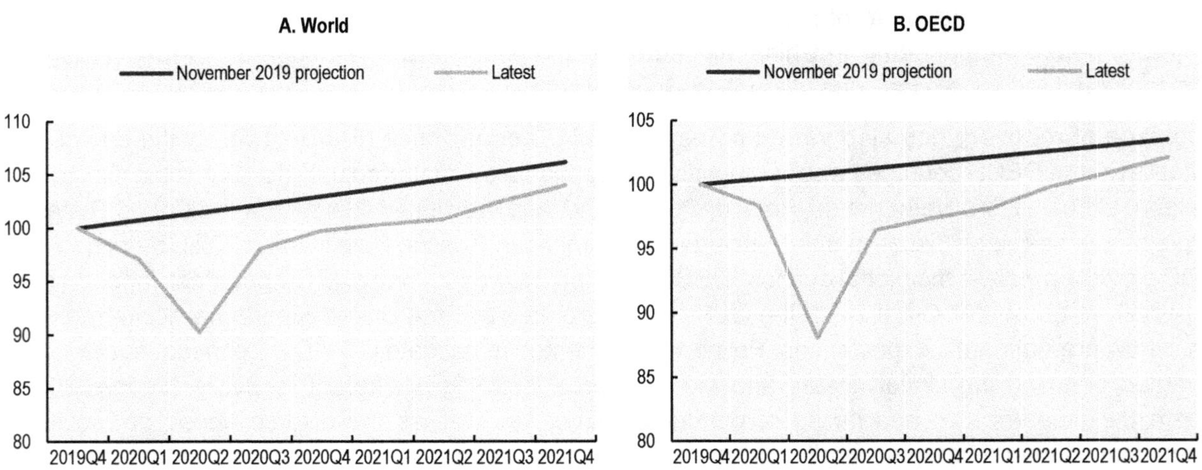

Source: OECD Economic Outlook 111 database; OECD Economic Outlook 106 database; and OECD calculations.

StatLink https://stat.link/otmg8p

Figure 1.3. Real GDP growth in OECD and selected non-OECD countries

Real GDP growth, percentage change

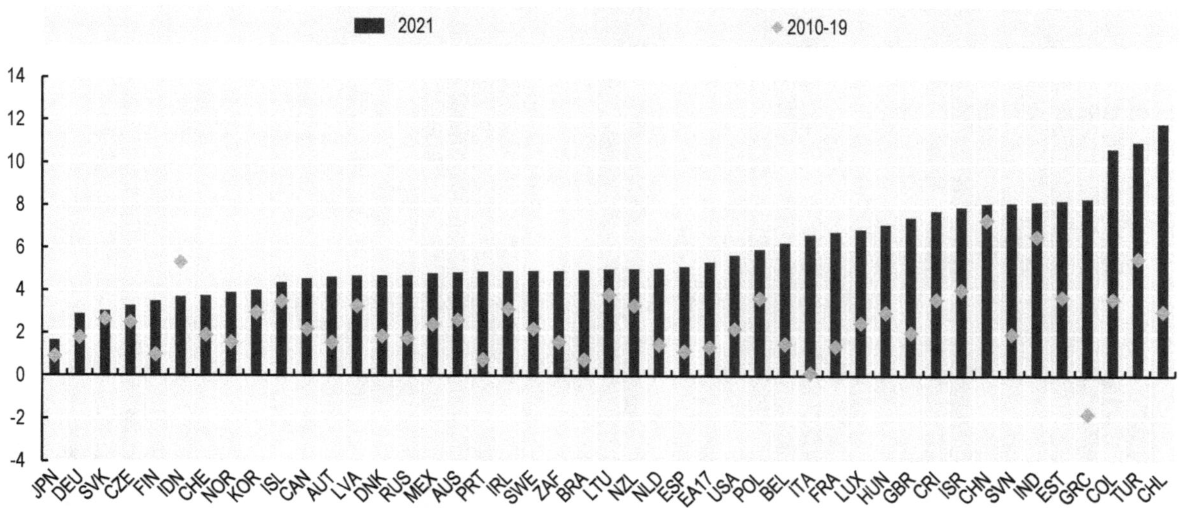

Note: Growth in Ireland was computed using gross value added at constant prices excluding foreign-owned multinational enterprise dominated sectors.
Source: OECD Economic Outlook 111 database; and OECD calculations.

StatLink https://stat.link/dfke03

1.1.2. Labour market conditions returned towards the pre-crisis situation

The OECD unemployment rate declined to 5.5% of the labour force by the end of 2021, almost returning to pre-pandemic levels (5.4% in 2019). Compared with previous crises, the impact of COVID-19 on aggregate unemployment proved relatively short-lived, especially given that the recovery of labour markets usually lags output. For many countries, the unemployment rate barely moved during 2020 despite a sizeable fall in output (Figure 1.4), reflecting the successful use of job retention schemes. However, the unemployment rate increased significantly in 2020 in Canada, Chile, Colombia, Costa Rica, Greece, and the United States.

In the United States, the unemployment rate increased by nearly 6.5 percentage points (p.p.) over two quarters to reach approximately 13% by mid-2020. Unemployment quickly returned to levels approaching the pre-pandemic level by the end of 2021, but the employment level remained nearly 2 p.p. below its pre-pandemic rate (Figure 1.5, Panel A), despite rising labour shortages in several sectors – notably in leisure and hospitality, transport and warehousing (OECD, 2021[1]). Part of the decline in labour force participation came from early retirements, as well as exits related to the COVID-19 crisis. Real labour income surged in 2020 for those employed, as inflation was low and the newly unemployed had previously been employed in low-wage occupations (Figure 1.5, Panel B), but by the end of 2021, real labour income growth slowed, reflecting higher inflation and the return of low-wage workers to the labour market.

Changes to the euro area labour market were more limited. While output fell sharply at the peak of the pandemic, the unemployment rate increased by approximately 1 p.p. during 2020 and 2021 and was even below its pre-crisis level at the end of 2021. The fall in employment was temporary in the euro area and by the end of 2021 it had already exceeded its pre-pandemic level (although in many countries total hours worked had not fully recovered) (Figure 1.5, Panel A). The situation was very similar in the United Kingdom, where the expansion in job retention schemes supported workers and firms when health-related restrictions prevented economic activities (OECD, 2021[7]). Inside the euro area, Greece and Spain were more affected than other countries due to the larger contribution of tourism to employment. Labour market policies also resulted in a temporary reduction in labour income at the peak of the pandemic, while data for Q4 of 2021 suggest the real wage rate remained flat over the year (Figure 1.5, Panel B).

Figure 1.4. Unemployment rates in OECD countries

As a percentage of labour force

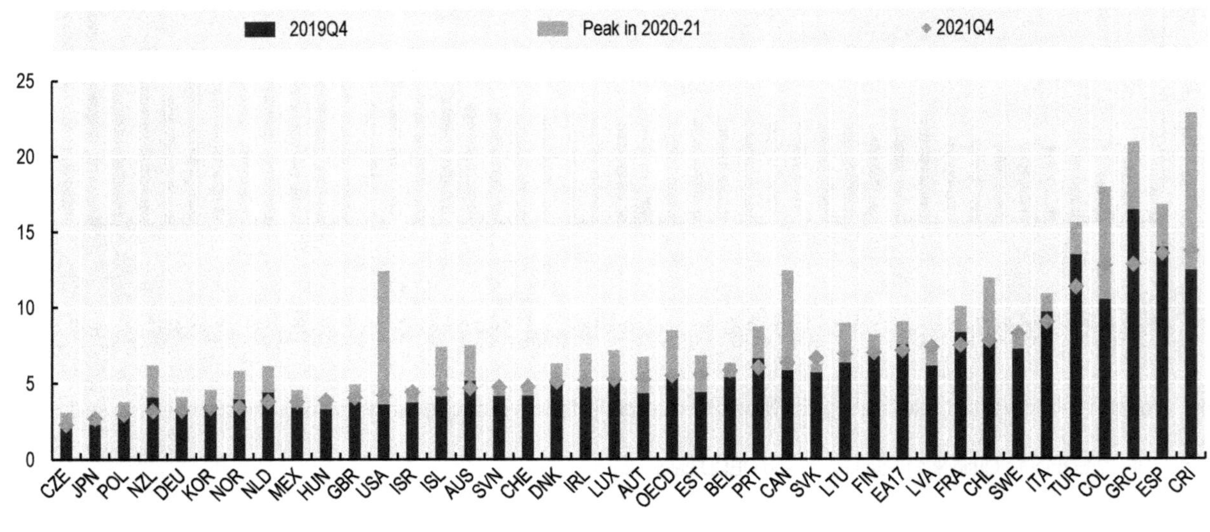

Source: OECD Economic Outlook 111 database; and OECD calculations.

StatLink https://stat.link/87qfp2

Figure 1.5. Employment and real income growth

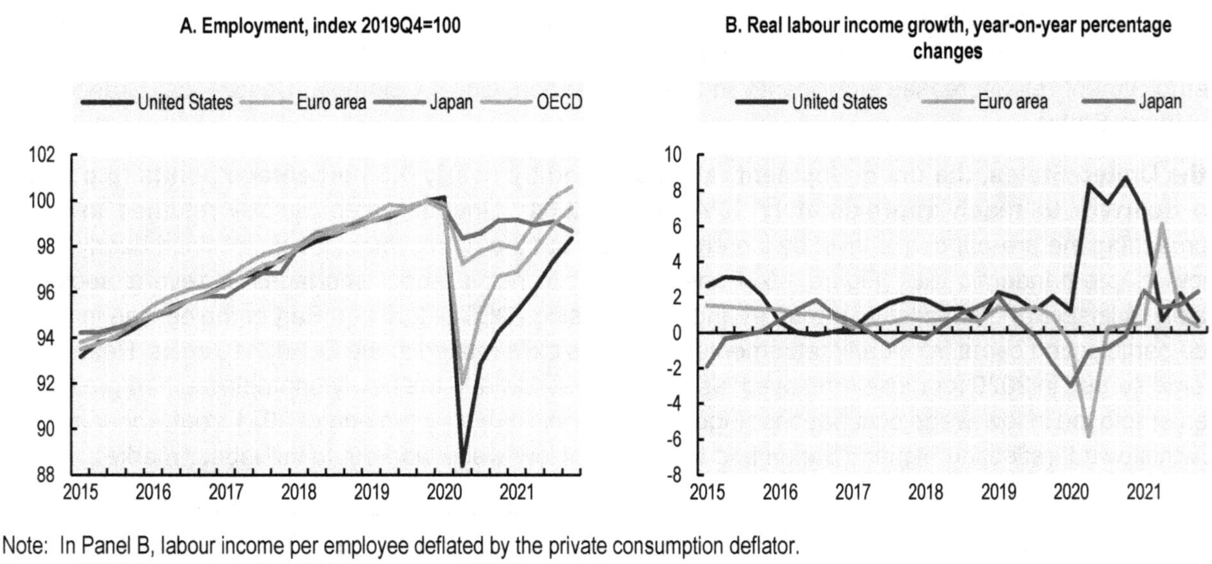

Note: In Panel B, labour income per employee deflated by the private consumption deflator.
Source: OECD Economic Outlook 111 database; and OECD calculations.

StatLink https://stat.link/wier4a

In Japan, the labour market was less affected by the pandemic than in other economies. The unemployment rate barely moved and changes in employment were marginal in 2020, but 2021 proved more difficult as the country's economic recovery was more sluggish than elsewhere in the OECD (OECD, 2021[8]). More sanitary restrictions – partly resulting from the slow start to its vaccination campaign – dampened the recovery in employment. Real labour income growth was depressed in 2020 but grew above its long-term average at the end of 2021 helped by limited consumer price inflation.

Recent labour developments appear quite different from those experienced during the global financial crisis. Labour market transitions (mobility between jobs and in and out of employment) were particularly affected in 2008 and it took more than a decade for the transition from study to unemployment to return to pre-recession levels (Causa, Luu and Abendschein, 2021[9]). The impact of COVID-19 is estimated to be smaller in that regard, but with some variation across countries. The increased use of teleworking over the last two years appears likely to persist (Adrjan et al., 2021[10]).

1.1.3. The rebound in private consumption brought a quick recovery but also contributed to higher inflation

Private consumption growth in the OECD returned to a level approaching its pre-crisis trend in 2021 (Figure 1.6, Panel A). The 6.3% growth recorded was despite some service activities remaining constrained due to health-related restrictions and changes in consumer preferences, following a large decline in 2020 (around -5.5%). Policy support for household incomes and the decline in spending led to a marked rise in household saving rates in 2020. The decline in saving rates from these temporarily very high levels, together with accommodative fiscal and monetary policies, helped to push spending growth well above income growth (OECD, 2021[1]).

Despite a sizeable fall in Q2 of 2020, there was a speedy and strong rebound in private consumption in the United States. This rebound was sufficiently large that for the two-year period to the end of 2021, private consumption increased by a similar magnitude to the two previous years (nearly 2.5% for 2017-2019 vs. nearly 2% for 2019-2021). Meanwhile, the composition of spending changed dramatically – spending on goods represented nearly 35% of consumer expenditure by Q4 of 2021, up from just over 30% in 2019. In the euro area and Japan, private consumption at the end of 2021 remained below pre-crisis levels but still increased by approximately 3.5% and 1.25%, respectively. Spending on goods also picked up relative to spending on services, but the composition change was much smaller than in the United States.

The surge in private spending on goods, in addition to persistent supply disruptions, contributed to the acceleration of inflation in the second half of 2021 (OECD, 2021[1]). Sanitary restrictions and COVID-19-related absences caused delivery times to rise, and inventories were substantially depleted in many industries. Production of cars was particularly affected by semiconductor shortages – in Germany, lower car production is estimated to have reduced GDP by more than 1.5% in 2021 (Guilloux-Nefussi and Rusticelli, 2021[11]). The effect of supply disruptions could also be seen in the surge in shipping costs, which also contributed to rising inflation in OECD countries (OECD, 2021[12]).

Figure 1.6. Private consumption and headline inflation

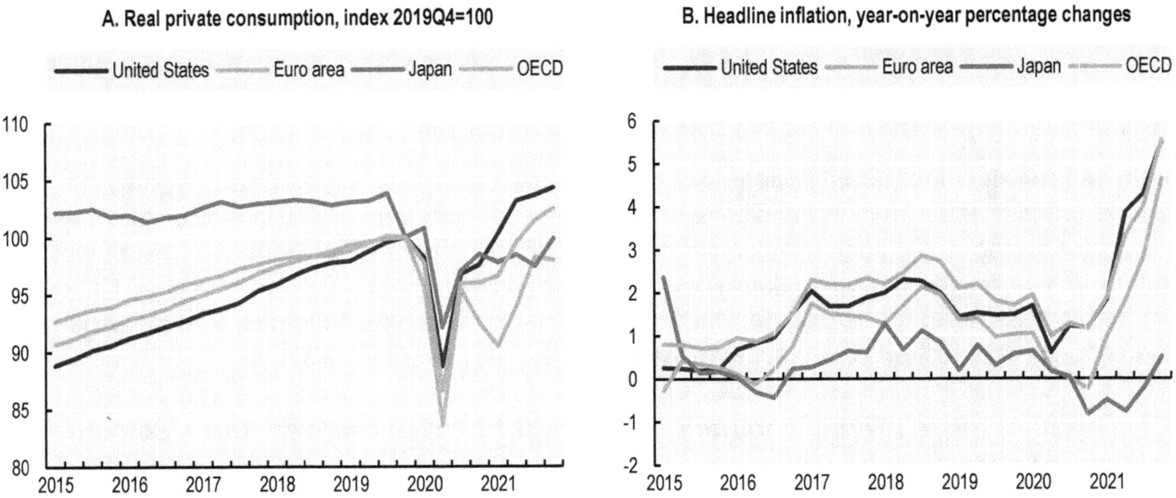

Note: In Panel B, labour income per employee deflated by the private consumption deflator.
Source: OECD Economic Outlook 111 database; and OECD calculations.

StatLink https://stat.link/iyz3tw

Energy prices were another key driver of consumer price inflation during 2021, the result of supply restrictions and resurgent demand (IEA, 2021[13]). In the last quarter of 2021, headline inflation for the OECD reached 5.5% year-on-year, its highest level since the mid-1990s (5.5% in the United States, 4.5% in the euro area 17 and 0.5% in Japan). Even excluding food and energy products, annual consumer price inflation for the OECD as a whole reached 4% in Q4 of 2021. The surge in inflation reduced purchasing power across the population, but the substantial savings accumulated during the pandemic by largely better off households helped partially mitigate their impact on total household demand. Most central banks announced a gradual normalisation of the future monetary stance in 2021 to fight inflation and address the risks of inflation expectations becoming less well anchored, with some central banks in small open advanced economies and emerging-market economies already raising policy rates in the latter part of 2021.

1.1.4. Investment picked up in 2021

With the recovery firming, fixed capital investment rebounded in 2021. For the OECD as a whole, gross fixed capital formation grew 5% in 2021 after a decline of nearly 4.25% in the previous year. Strong output growth, very low interest rates and improvements in business confidence all helped to boost corporate investment. A build-up of corporate raised concerns but did not weigh on investment, notably thanks to strong growth of liquid, short-term investments held by companies (OECD, 2021[1]). While pandemic support measures were partially unwound during 2021, fiscal policy also continued to sustain demand and business investment. Government investment also picked up in some economies.

Figure 1.7. Gross fixed capital formation growth in OECD and selected countries

Percentage change

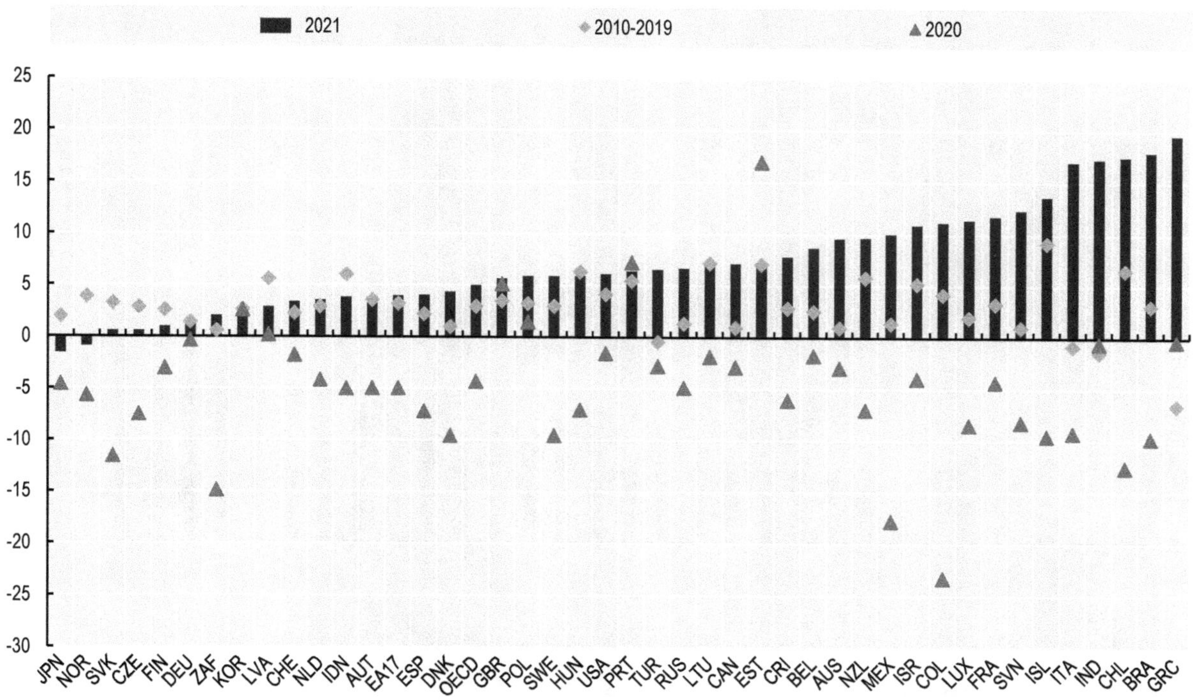

Source: OECD Economic Outlook 111 database; and OECD calculations.

StatLink https://stat.link/57sfqu

OECD estimates indicate that the two-year growth rate of the productive capital stock in 2021 was comparable with the situation before the COVID-19 crisis (Figure 1.8). Nevertheless, the productive capital stock in 2021 is estimated to have been below that in 2019 in some countries, notably Greece, Italy, Japan, and Mexico.

Figure 1.8. Productive capital stock growth

Growth over two years, in percentage

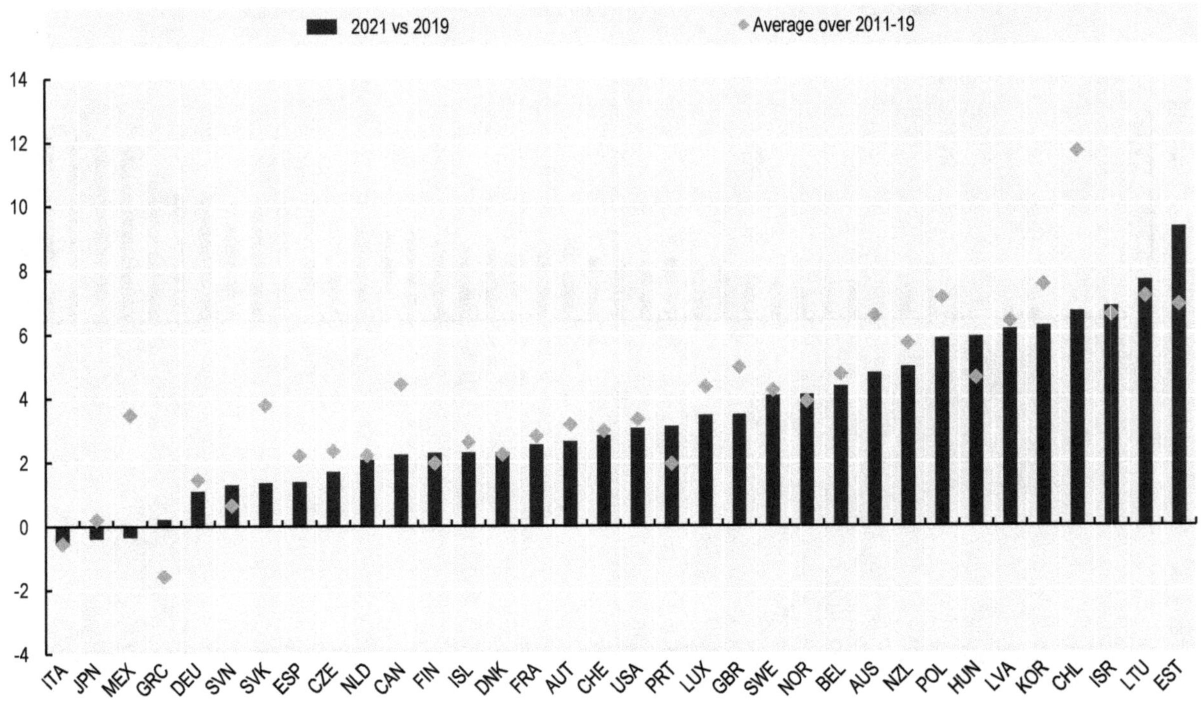

Source: OECD Economic Outlook 111 database; and OECD calculations.

StatLink https://stat.link/3idl8p

1.2. Public debt and budget balances

1.2.1. Budget balances started to normalise in 2021 but public debt ratios remained high

Strong and swift pandemic-related fiscal responses led government expenditures to soar during the pandemic. With revenues declining, borrowing and public debt rose sharply. For the OECD as a whole, general government gross debt increased by more than 20 p.p. in 2020, before declining slightly to an estimated 125% of GDP in 2021 (Figure 1.9, Panel A). In the euro area, the public debt ratio levelled off in 2021 at around 100% of GDP. Across the OECD, there were wide differences with the gross debt ratio ranging from below 30% in Estonia and Luxembourg to above 150% in Italy, Greece, and Japan (Figure 1.10). For all countries, the pandemic-related debt burden has added to existing fiscal pressure from secular trends such as population ageing and the rising relative price of services, implying that most OECD governments will eventually need to undertake fiscal reforms to maintain current public service standards and benefit levels over the longer term (Guillemette and Turner, 2021[14]; OECD, 2021[15]).

Average OECD budget deficits peaked at around -10% of GDP in 2020 and moderated to approximately -7.5% of GDP in 2021 (Figure 1.9, Panel B). The United States recorded a particularly large deterioration in its fiscal balance in 2020, which was maintained in 2021, as the government extended unemployment benefits and sought to support low- and middle-income families and to increase public spending on transport infrastructure, broadband and clean technologies. In the euro area, the fiscal stance remained expansionary in 2021, helped by continued support during successive pandemic waves. Support through the EU-wide recovery plan ("Next Generation EU") will cover several years (OECD, 2021[7]).

In 2021, many countries started to consolidate their deficit, though to varying degrees. A measure which removes the influence of the economic cycle indicates a moderate pace of consolidation for the OECD as a whole (of about 0.75 percentage points (p.p.) of GDP). Using the same metric, there was discretionary consolidation in the United States (of around 1.25 p.p.) but a further fiscal easing in the euro area (by 0.75 p.p.).

Figure 1.9. General government gross debt and budget balance

As a percentage of GDP

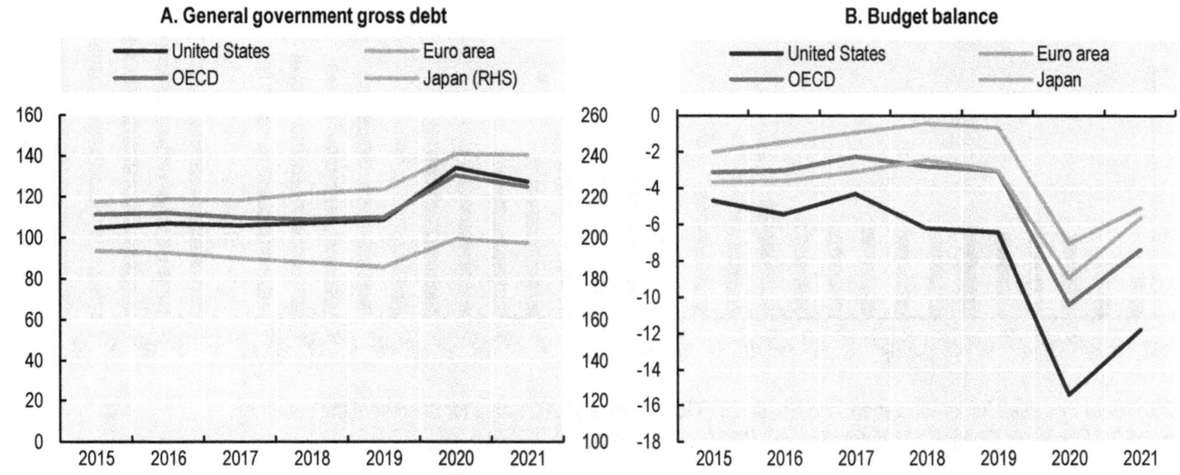

Note: Maastricht definition for general government gross debt of the euro area. The 2021 data for Japan are estimates.
Source: OECD Economic Outlook 111 database; and OECD calculations.

StatLink https://stat.link/hpy7dc

Fiscal policies during the pandemic boosted public investment, but not sufficiently to make up for past shortfalls. It is expected that about three-fifths of OECD countries will experience an increase in the share of public investment in total public expenditure over the next two years (Morgavi, Pina and Sunel, 2022[16]), with a notable share of this investment dedicated to addressing long-term challenges such as the transition towards a greener economy. Nonetheless, this is not enough to compensate for insufficient investment in the past and to make up for shortfalls in GDP per capita. In the ten years before COVID-19, annual growth of potential GDP per capita stood at 1.1% in the median OECD country, about 0.9 p.p. lower than in the decade before the GFC.

Figure 1.10. General government gross debt, 2021 or latest

As a percentage of GDP

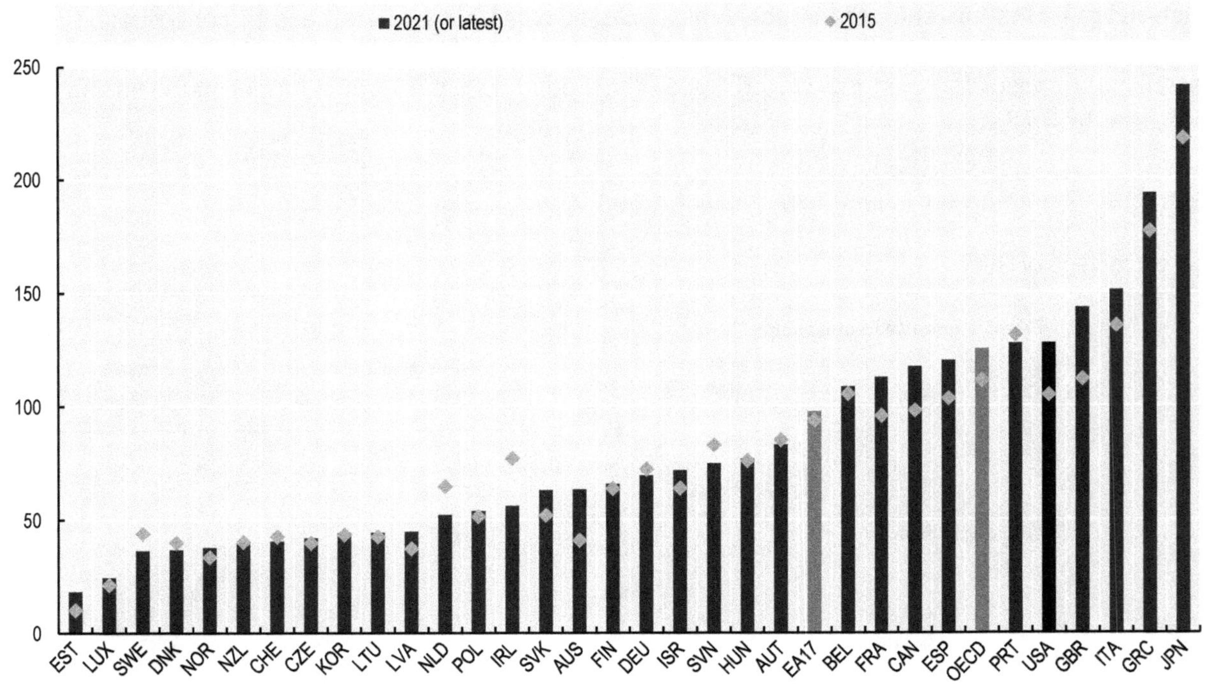

Note: 2020 data was used for Israel, Japan, and Spain; 2019 for Korea; and 2021 data for the rest of the countries.
Source: OECD Economic Outlook 111 database; and OECD calculations.

StatLink https://stat.link/c7fqrz

All countries introduced fiscal measures in response to the economic consequences of COVID-19, contributing to higher budget deficits in 2021 (Figure 1.11). In major emerging-market economies, the fiscal response was usually more limited than amongst OECD countries either because they had less fiscal space or because they were less severely affected by the pandemic. The average OECD headline deficit increased by around 7.5 p.p. of GDP in 2020, a significantly larger rise than the 3 p.p. of GDP recorded by China and India in the same year (OECD, 2022[17]; OECD, 2021[1]).

Figure 1.11. General government budget balance, 2021 or latest

As a percentage of GDP

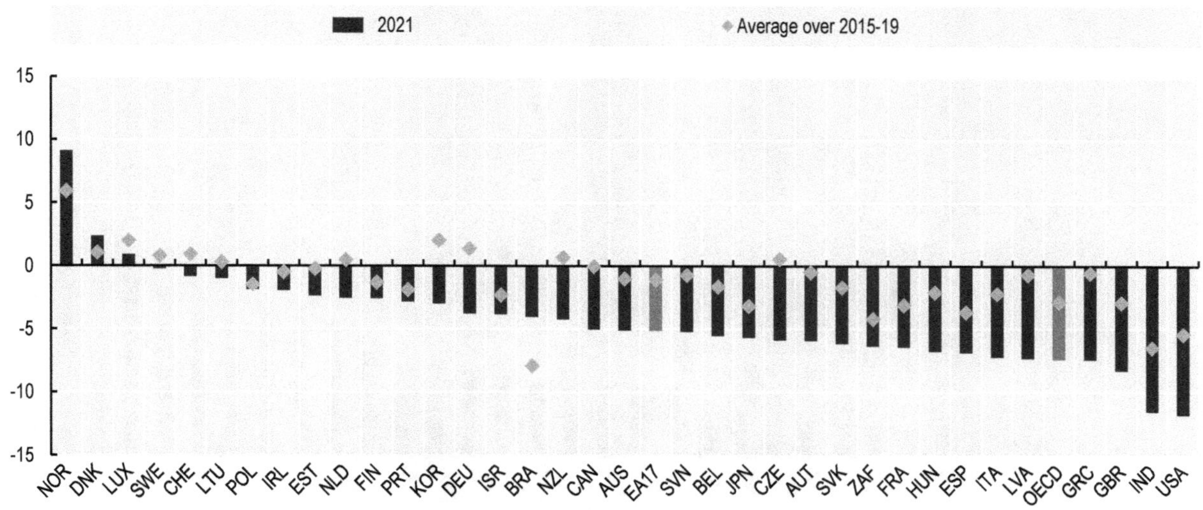

Note: 2021 is an OECD projection for Brazil, Japan, Korea, New Zealand, and Switzerland.
Source: OECD Economic Outlook 111 database; and OECD calculations.

StatLink https://stat.link/z5ecfx

Government bond yields declined substantially over 2020-21 for most countries, supported by accommodative monetary policy by the major central banks (OECD, 2021[1]). The rate on 10-year government bonds was negative on average in both 2020 and 2021 for some countries, including Austria, Belgium, Denmark, Finland, Germany, Luxembourg, the Netherlands, the Slovak Republic, and Switzerland. The increasing share of debt issued at a low interest rate helps to explain a downward trend for overall interest payments on public debt, which were lower in 2021 than in 2015 for all countries, apart from Israel, South Africa, and the United Kingdom, despite higher debt levels. Towards the end of 2021, bond yields started to increase in anticipation of the future normalisation of monetary policy. However, it will take some time for this to be reflected in debt service burdens given the maturity structure of debt.

Figure 1.12. Gross government interest payments in OECD and selected countries, 2020

As a percentage of GDP

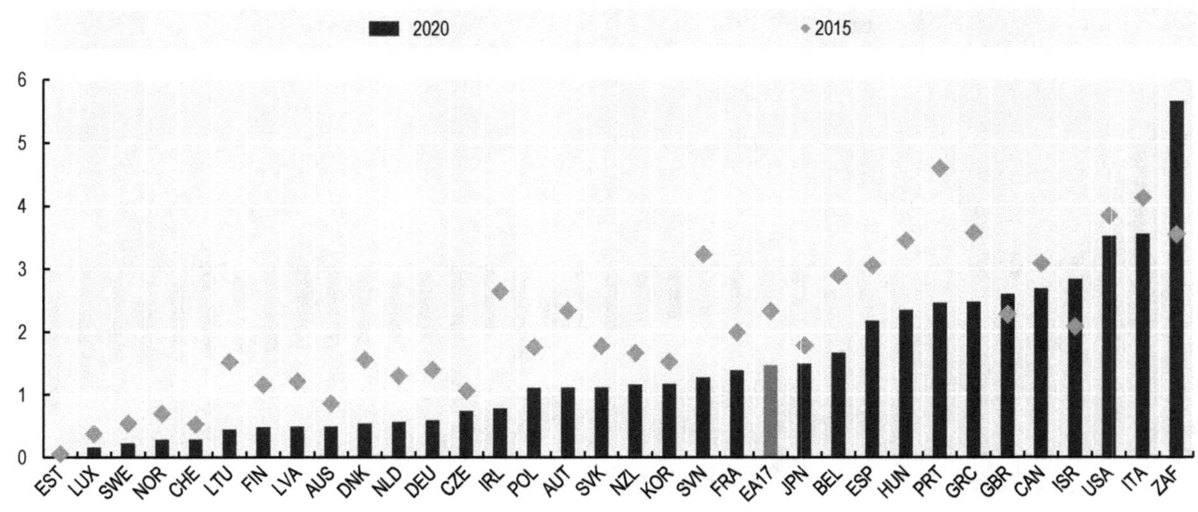

Note: 2020 data used for Korea, Japan, New Zealand, and Switzerland.
Source: OECD Economic Outlook 111 database; and OECD calculations.

StatLink https://stat.link/x7zcdh

1.3. Trends in income inequality

1.3.1. While income inequality had been decreasing before the crisis, the impact of the pandemic on inequality remains uncertain

COVID-19 had a diverse impact on household disposable income (Figure 1.13). In some countries, such as Australia, Canada, Ireland, Lithuania and the United States, extraordinary government support, often in the form of cash transfers and other benefits, resulted in an unusually strong increase in real incomes in 2020. However, in most countries, government support associated with restrictions on the consumption of some services also helped to raise household saving rates to record highs (OECD, 2021[5]) largely to the benefit of the wealthy and those households with higher incomes. Household income for 2021, when available, returned to historical averages, except in a few countries such as Austria, Finland, and Spain.

Figure 1.13. Real household disposable income growth, 2020

Percentage change

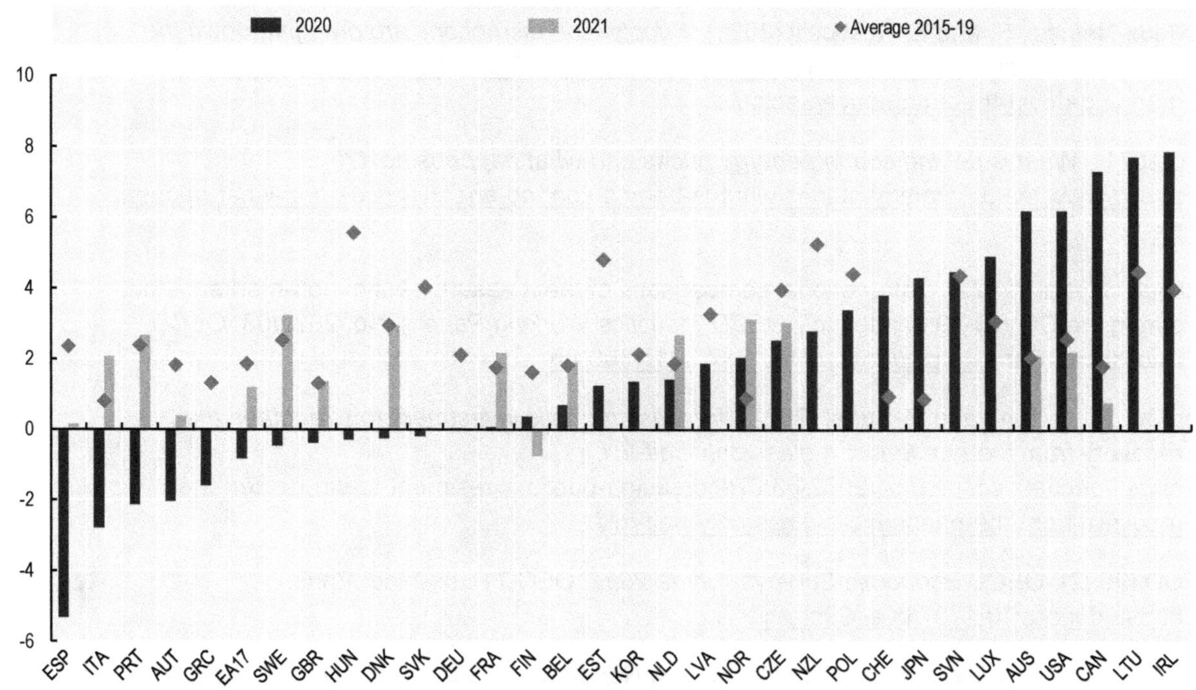

Source: OECD Economic Outlook 111 database; and OECD calculations.

StatLink https://stat.link/mkudfi

In some countries, income support during COVID-19 reduced inequalities. In Canada, household disposable income increased substantially more for the lowest two income quintiles in 2020 compared to other quintiles; it was again the case in 2021 except compared to the highest quintile (as reported by Statistics Canada). Disruptions to schooling during the pandemic, which were not uniform in their impact across locations and social groups, also have the potential to exacerbate earnings disparities in the future (OECD, 2021[18]).

References

Adrjan, P. et al. (2021), "Will it stay or will it go? Analysing developments in telework during COVID-19 using online job postings data", *OECD Productivity Working Papers*, No. 30, OECD Publishing, Paris, https://doi.org/10.1787/aed3816e-en. [10]

Boone, L. (2022), *The EA and the US in the COVID-19 crisis: Implications for the 2022-2023 policy stance*, https://oecdecoscope.blog/2022/01/18/the-ea-and-the-us-in-the-covid-19-crisis-implications-for-the-2022-2023-policy-stance/. [3]

Causa, O., N. Luu and M. Abendschein (2021), "Labour market transitions across OECD countries: Stylised facts", *OECD Economics Department Working Papers*, No. 1692, OECD Publishing, Paris, https://doi.org/10.1787/62c85872-en. [9]

Guillemette, Y. and D. Turner (2021), "The long game: Fiscal outlooks to 2060 underline need for structural reform", *OECD Economic Policy Papers*, No. 29, OECD Publishing, Paris, https://doi.org/10.1787/a112307e-en. [14]

Guilloux-Nefussi, S. and E. Rusticelli (2021), *Supply-side disruptions are dragging down the automotive sector*, https://oecdecoscope.blog/2021/12/22/supply-side-disruptions-are-dragging-down-the-automotive-sector/. [11]

IEA (2021), *What is behind soaring energy prices and what happens next?*, https://www.iea.org/commentaries/what-is-behind-soaring-energy-prices-and-what-happens-next. [13]

Mitchell, J. et al. (2022), "International comparisons of the measurement of non-market output during the COVID-19 pandemic", *OECD Statistics Working Papers*, No. 2022/03, OECD Publishing, Paris, https://doi.org/10.1787/301f1306-en. [6]

Morgavi, H., A. Pina and E. Sunel (2022), *Increasing public investment to strengthen the recovery from the pandemic: A glass only half-full*, https://oecdecoscope.blog/2022/03/07/increasing-public-investment-to-strengthen-the-recovery-from-the-pandemic-a-glass-only-half-full/. [16]

OECD (2022), *OECD Economic Surveys: China 2022*, OECD Publishing, Paris, https://doi.org/10.1787/b0e499cf-en. [17]

OECD (2021), *OECD Economic Outlook, Interim Report March 2021*, OECD Publishing, Paris, https://doi.org/10.1787/34bfd999-en. [2]

OECD (2021), *OECD Economic Outlook, Interim Report September 2021: Keeping the Recovery on Track*, OECD Publishing, Paris, https://doi.org/10.1787/490d4832-en. [12]

OECD (2021), *OECD Economic Outlook, Volume 2021 Issue 1*, OECD Publishing, Paris, https://doi.org/10.1787/edfbca02-en. [5]

OECD (2021), *OECD Economic Outlook, Volume 2021 Issue 2*, OECD Publishing, Paris, https://doi.org/10.1787/66c5ac2c-en. [1]

OECD (2021), *OECD Economic Surveys: Euro Area 2021*, OECD Publishing, Paris, https://doi.org/10.1787/214e9f0a-en. [7]

OECD (2021), *OECD Economic Surveys: Japan 2021*, OECD Publishing, Paris, https://doi.org/10.1787/6b749602-en. [8]

OECD (2021), *Tax and fiscal policies after the COVID-19 crisis*, https://doi.org/10.1787/5a8f24c3-en. [15]

OECD (2021), *The State of Global Education: 18 Months into the Pandemic*, OECD Publishing, Paris, https://doi.org/10.1787/1a23bb23-en. [18]

Rusticelli, E. and D. Turner (2021), "The economic costs of restricting international mobility", *OECD Economics Department Working Papers*, No. 1678, OECD Publishing, Paris, https://doi.org/10.1787/dcad4c73-en. [4]

Notes

[1] Preliminary estimates of medium-term output loss show that annual potential output growth in the median advanced and emerging-market economy could have declined by 0.3 and 0.4 percentage point per year (OECD, 2021[5]).

2 Tax Revenue Trends

This chapter is based on the OECD Global Revenue Statistics Database and its accompanying publications. It describes the latest tax revenue trends, analysing both total tax-to-GDP ratios and tax structures over time, across OECD countries and a selection of inclusive framework jurisdictions for whom data are available. A preliminary analysis of the initial impact of the COVID-19 crisis on tax revenues is also included.

This chapter describes the latest tax revenue trends, analysing both total tax-to-GDP ratios and tax structures over time, across OECD countries and a selection of Inclusive Framework jurisdictions for whom data is available.[1] Where possible, the analysis covers tax revenue trends until 2020 – the last year for which comparable tax revenue data from the OECD Global Revenue Statistics Database are available (see Box 2.1). This overview provides useful background to the subsequent discussion on the latest tax reforms introduced by countries (Chapter 3) and may in part reflect the impact of past reforms discussed in earlier editions of this annual publication.

Overall, this chapter shows that the average OECD and partner countries' tax-to-GDP ratio rose marginally against the background of the COVID-19 pandemic. Although nominal tax revenues fell in the majority of OECD and partner countries in 2020, the falls in GDP levels across countries were often greater, resulting in a 0.1 percentage point (p.p) increase in the average tax-to-GDP ratio to 32.4% in 2020.

This chapter also identifies trends in tax structures and shows the notable impact that the pandemic had on the composition of overall tax revenues. Previous editions of this report have highlighted how the average tax structure has remained relatively stable over time, but the COVID-19 crisis altered this, at least temporarily, having a much stronger impact on direct taxes on income than indirect or property taxes. In 2020, an increase is observed in tax revenues from personal income taxes (PIT) and social security contributions (SSCs) as a share of GDP, on average across the OECD; whereas corporate income taxes (CIT) experienced the largest relative decrease, albeit smaller than that observed during the global financial crisis. No change was seen in property taxes or Value Added Taxes (VAT) as a share of GDP, on average, and a small but widespread decrease in revenues from excise duties was experienced, particularly because of mobility restrictions and reduced fuel use.

The preliminary data for 2020 discussed in this chapter suggests that tax policy measures implemented in OECD countries, as a whole, did not lead to significant declines in tax-to-GDP ratios. In many cases, the fall in GDP was larger than the fall in tax revenues, and a as result, tax-to-GDP levels remained stable or increased slightly. Tax policy changes via deferrals or reductions in tax liabilities, enhanced tax credits and allowances and temporary or permanent reductions in tax rates often directly reduced revenues, and the sharp reduction in economic activity due to lockdowns and other restrictions reduced labour force participation, household consumption and business profits, further affecting tax revenues. However, government support measures may have indirectly supported tax revenues insofar as they were successful in reducing job losses and business closures. These support measures may therefore have contributed to the weaker nominal falls in tax revenues than were seen during the global financial crisis of 2008-2009.

2.1. Trends in tax revenue levels

2.1.1. Variance in tax revenues remains large despite continued narrowing

Tax revenues in 2020 varied significantly across the countries for whom data are available, ranging from just above 10% to more than 46% of GDP. Denmark had the highest tax-to-GDP ratio in 2020 (46.5%), and with the exceptions of 2017 and 2018, in which France was higher, has had the highest tax-to-GDP ratio of all OECD countries since 2002. France had the second-highest tax-to-GDP ratio in 2020 (45.4%). On the other end of the scale, and consistent with data over the last decade, Indonesia (11.6%), Mexico (17.9%) and Colombia (18.7%) had the lowest tax-to-GDP ratios (see Figure 2.1).

Figure 2.1. Trends in tax-to-GDP ratios from 1990 to 2020

Tax revenues as a percentage of GDP

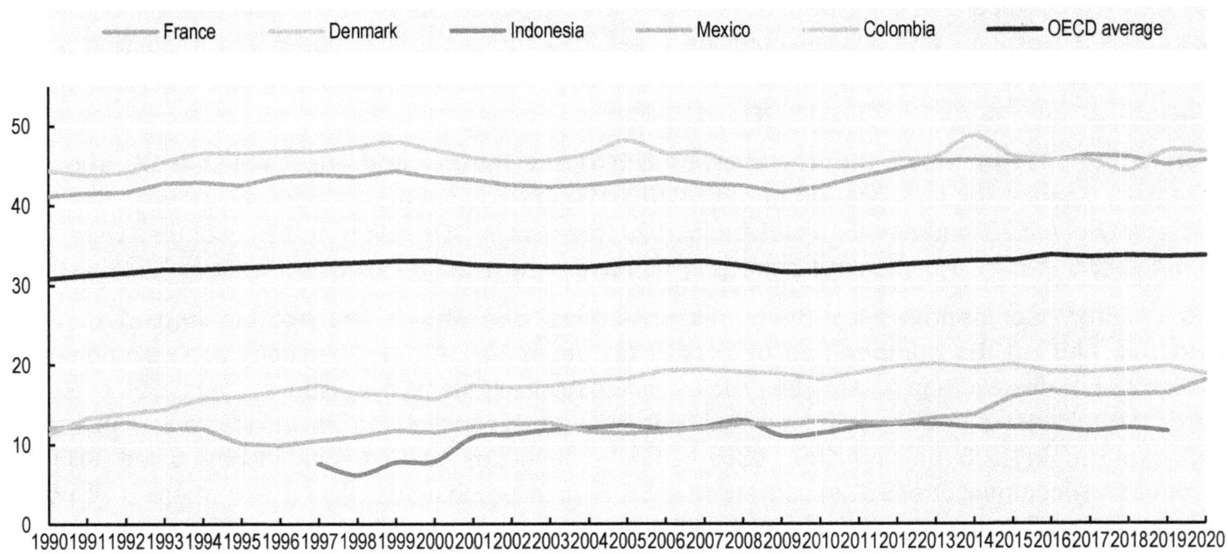

Note: The OECD average in 2020 is calculated by applying the unweighted average percentage change for 2020 in the 36 countries providing data for that year to the overall average tax to GDP ratio in 2019. The additional countries selected are those that represent the lower and upper bounds of tax-to-GDP ratios.
Source: OECD Global Revenue Statistics Database.

StatLink https://stat.link/yqpvzg

Despite the wide range of tax-to-GDP ratios, there is a relatively high concentration of countries with tax-to-GDP ratios around the OECD average. On average across OECD countries, tax revenues amounted to 33.5% of GDP in 2020 (Figure 2.1), with the average falling slightly to 32.4% when the five additional IF jurisdictions are included (see Note 1). Figure 2.2 shows a high concentration of countries that have tax revenues close to that level with 11 countries recording tax revenues between 30% and 35% of GDP and another 10 countries with tax revenues ranging from 35% to 40% of GDP. Canada (34.4%), the Czech Republic (34.4%) and the United Kingdom (32.8%) were the countries closest to the OECD average. A marginally larger number of countries recorded tax-to-GDP ratios further away from the OECD average: 15 had tax-to-GDP ratios below 30%, including all but one of the five partner countries, Brazil (33.1%), and seven countries recorded tax revenues above 40% of GDP.

Figure 2.2. Distribution of tax-to-GDP ratios in 2020

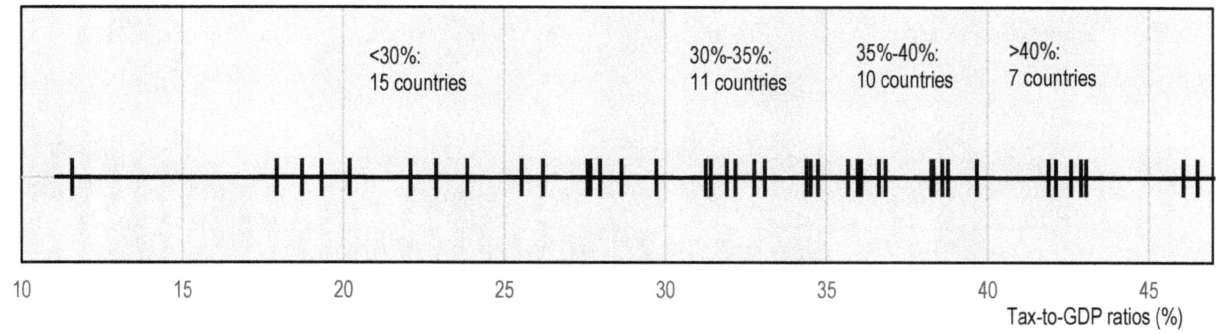

Note: Each + represents the tax-to-GDP ratio of an OECD or partner country in 2020. Partner countries included are Argentina, Brazil, China (People's Republic of), Indonesia and South Africa. 2019 data were used for Argentina, Australia, Brazil, China, Japan, Indonesia, and South Africa.
Source: OECD Global Revenue Statistics Database.

StatLink https://stat.link/fgzei7

Of the 36 countries for which data for 2020 are available, the ratio of tax revenues to GDP compared to 2019 rose in 20 and fell in 16 (Figure 2.3). Between 2019 and 2020, the largest tax ratio increase was in Spain, at 1.9 (p.p.) of GDP. This was largely due to an increase in revenues from SSCs as a share of GDP (1.5 p.p.), following a smaller fall in SSC revenues than in GDP (see Section 2.2 for more information). The second largest increase was in Mexico (1.6 p.p.), with increases in all major tax types both in nominal terms and as a share of GDP. Iceland was the only other country with an increase of over 1 p.p. Ireland experienced the largest fall in the tax-to-GDP ratio between 2019 and 2020, at 1.7 p.p. The decrease in Ireland was in large part due to a fall in VAT revenues following the temporary reduction in VAT rates in 2020 and the impact of the COVID-19 pandemic in decreasing economic activity. Smaller falls in PIT, SSCs, property taxes and excises also contributed. Decreases in the tax-to-GDP ratio of more than one percentage point were observed in Chile (1.6 p.p.) and Norway (1.3 p.p.). In Norway, the fall was due to a sharp decrease in CIT revenues (3.5 p.p.), due to temporary changes in the Petroleum Tax Act to help oil and gas companies introduce planned investments as well as the opportunity to offset losses in 2020 against taxed surpluses from the previous two years. This fall was counterbalanced by increases in all other major tax types. See Figure 2.9 for a more detailed examination of the change in tax revenues as a share of GDP by tax category between 2019 and 2020.

Figure 2.3. Tax revenues as a share of GDP by country in 2019 and 2020

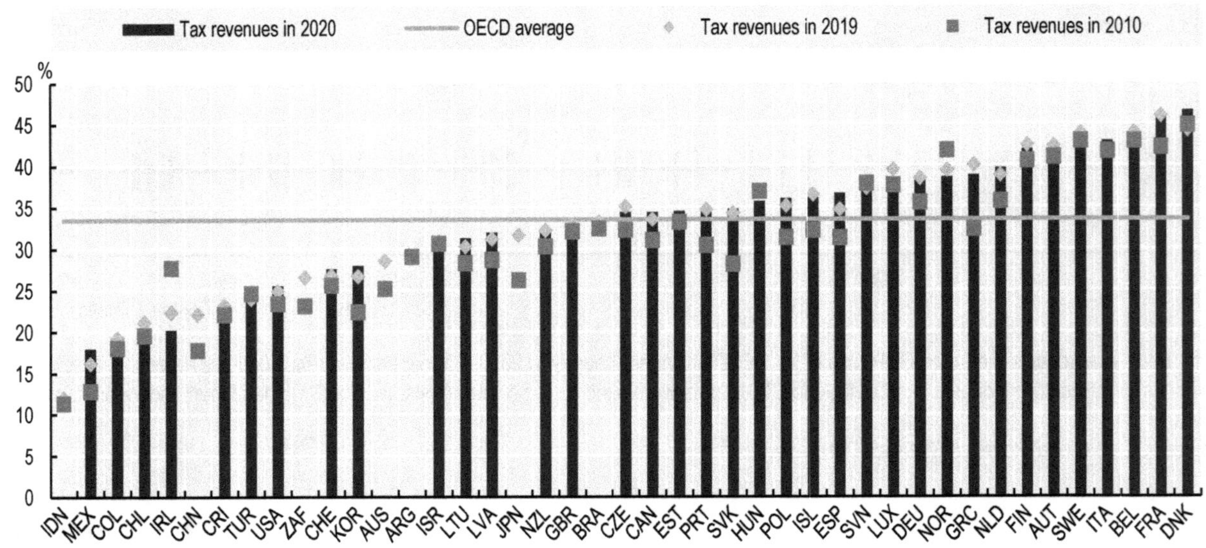

Note: 2020 data are unavailable for Argentina, Australia, Brazil, China, Japan, Indonesia, and South Africa.
Source: OECD Global Revenue Statistics Database.

StatLink https://stat.link/7uckpr

Over the last decade, the average tax-to-GDP ratio was higher in 2020 (32.4%) than in 2010 (30.5%) for the countries for whom data were available. Across countries, the tax-to-GDP ratio was higher in 2020 than in 2010 in 34 countries. The largest increase was seen in the Slovak Republic (6.7 p.p.) and in Greece (6.5 p.p.); increases of over 5 p.p. were also seen in Korea, Spain, Japan (2019 data) and Mexico. Decreases since 2010 were seen in the remaining nine countries. The largest fall has been in Ireland, from 27.7% in 2010 to 20.2% of GDP in 2020, largely due to the exceptional increase in GDP in 2015, although the tax-to-GDP ratio has declined more slowly since 2015.

2.1.2. The COVID-19 pandemic had a notable impact on tax-to-GDP ratios

Changes in tax-to-GDP ratios are driven by relative changes in nominal tax revenues and nominal GDP. If tax revenues rise more than GDP or fall less than GDP from one year to the next, the tax-to-GDP ratio will increase. Conversely, if tax revenues rise less than GDP, or fall more than GDP, there will be a decrease in the tax-to-GDP ratio. Therefore, an increase in the tax-to-GDP ratio should not be immediately interpreted as an increase in tax revenues in nominal, or even real, terms.[2]

In 2020, 20 OECD and partner countries experienced an increase in their tax-to-GDP ratio relative to 2019. However, as shown in Figure 2.4 this was due to an increase in nominal tax revenues in only six of these countries. The slightly higher average tax-to-GDP ratio recorded in 2020 relative to 2019 was therefore the result of marginally larger falls in GDP than tax revenues during the COVID-19 crisis. In the remaining 14 countries in which tax-to-GDP ratios increased in 2020, both tax revenues and GDP fell – with even larger falls in GDP. As shown in Figure 2.5, tax-to-GDP ratios declined in 16 OECD countries, falling by 2.4% on average. Of these 16 countries, only Denmark had higher levels of tax revenues in nominal terms than the preceding year, but this increase was slightly less than the growth in nominal GDP. Eleven of these countries saw declines in both nominal tax revenues and in nominal GDP, with tax revenues decreasing further; and the remaining four countries (Ireland, Chile, Hungary, and Luxembourg) saw decreases in nominal tax revenues concurrent with increases in nominal GDP. The changes for Australia, Brazil, Indonesia, Japan, and South Africa are from 2018 to 2019, as revenue statistics were not available for 2020 at the time of writing.[3] All five countries experienced falls in their tax-to-GDP ratios: in Australia and Japan because nominal tax revenues decreased while GDP increased, and in Brazil, Indonesia, and South Africa because tax revenue growth did not keep pace with GDP growth.

Figure 2.4. Changes in nominal tax and nominal GDP from 2019 to 2020

Year-on-year % change

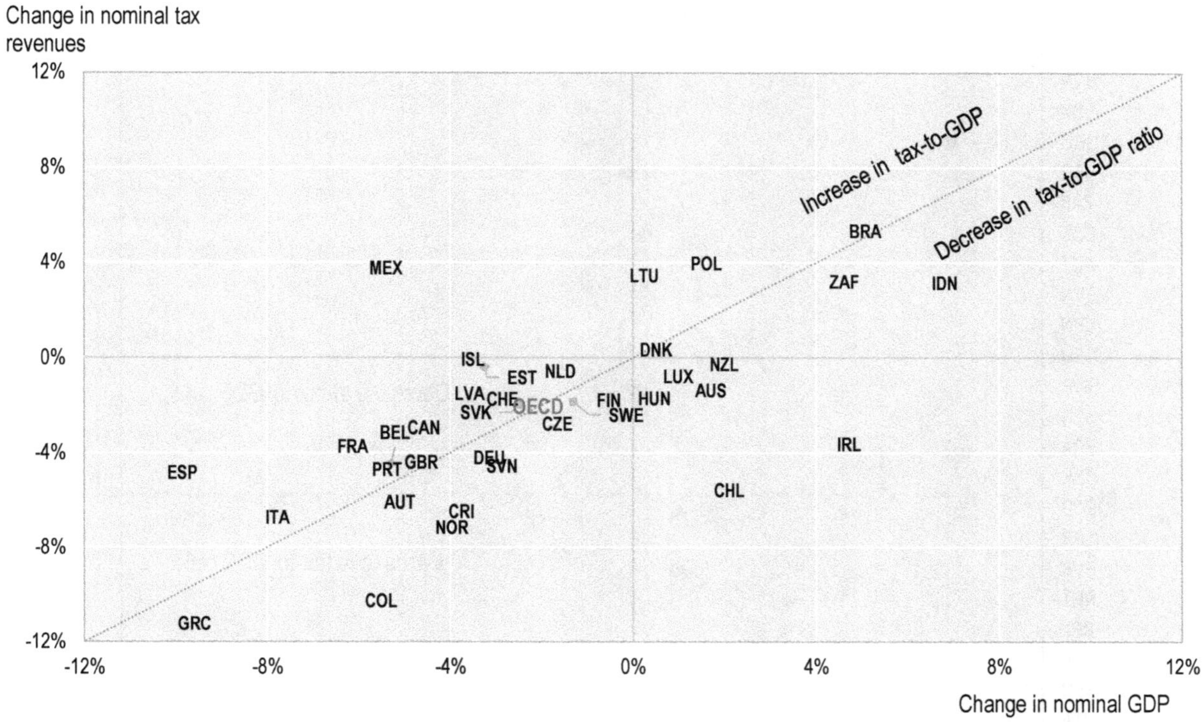

Note: Data for 2020 are preliminary and should be interpreted with caution; please see Box 2.1 for more details. Data for Australia and New Zealand show the change between the fiscal years 2018 and 2019 (as both countries report tax revenues on a fiscal year basis that includes Q2 of 2020 in the 2019 fiscal year); data for Japan are not included as data on SSC revenues is not available. See Box 2.2 for more information. The diagonal line across the graph represents the point at which the change in tax revenues and in GDP were of the same magnitude and therefore the point at which the tax-to-GDP ratio remained unchanged. Countries above the diagonal line had increases in their tax to GDP ratios; countries below it, had falls.
Source: Revenue Statistics (2021[1]).

StatLink https://stat.link/qw56gm

Figure 2.5. Relative changes in nominal tax revenues and nominal GDP in 2019 and 2020

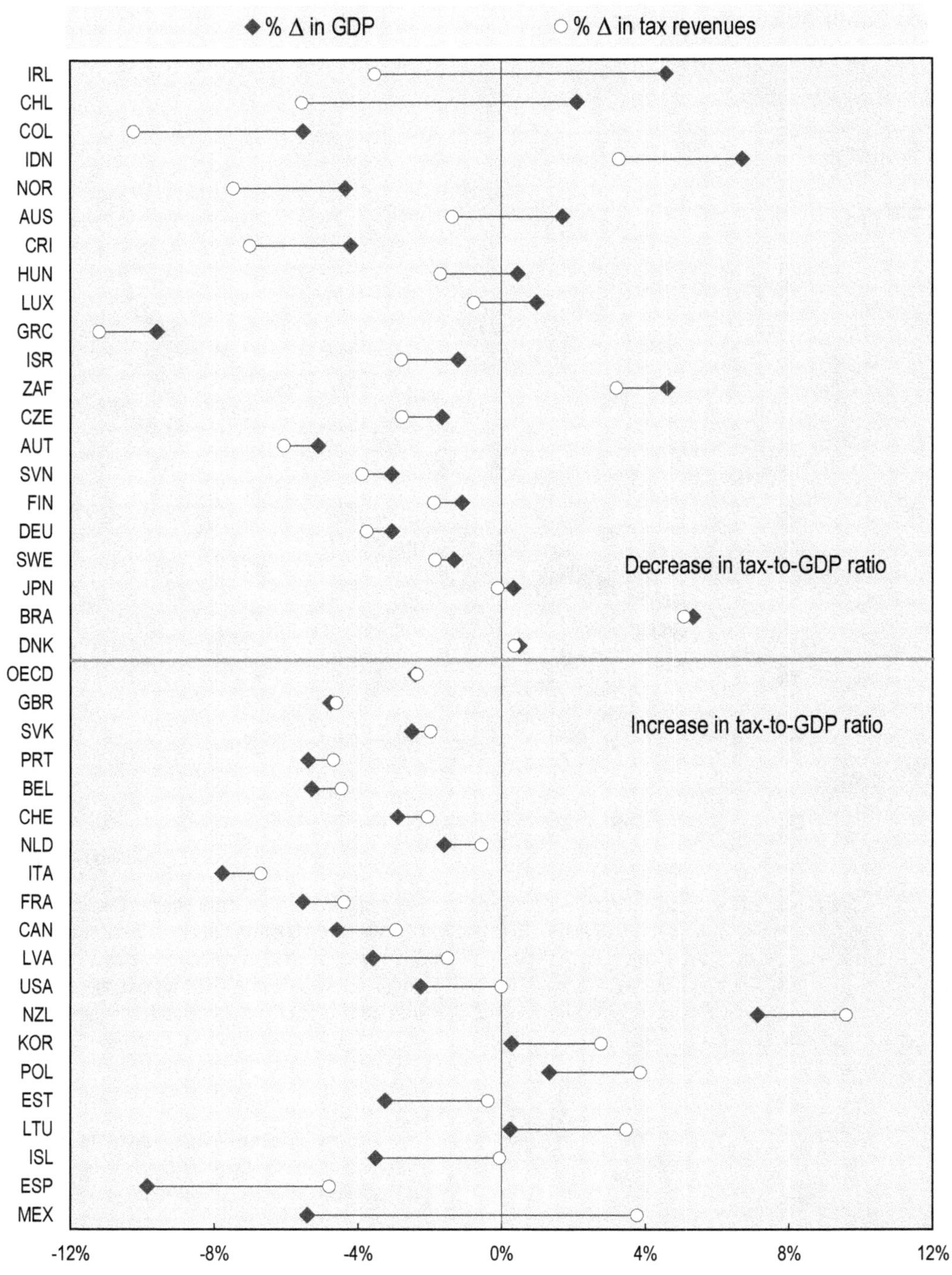

Note: The figure is split into two sections, the first part for those countries that experienced a decrease in their tax-to-GDP ratio, the second for those who experienced an increase. Within these groups, countries are then ordered by those that experienced the largest change in their nominal GDP between 2019 and 2020 relative to their change in nominal tax revenues between 2019 and 2020. For example, Ireland experienced a -3.5% fall in its tax revenues between 2019 and 2020, and a 4.6% increase in its GDP over the same period. Mexico, meanwhile, recorded a 3.8% increase in its tax revenues between 2019 and 2020, and a -5.4% decrease in its GDP. Data for Australia, Brazil, Indonesia, Japan, and South Africa show the change between 2018 and 2019, as preliminary data for 2020 were not available.
Source: OECD Revenue Statistics (2021[1]).

StatLink https://stat.link/9bwk2j

Box 2.1. The OECD Global Revenue Statistics Database

The Global Revenue Statistics Database provides the world's largest public source of harmonised tax revenue data, verified by countries and regional partners. Spanning more than 110 countries in all corners of the world, the database provides a rich and accessible resource for policymakers and researchers, based on the internationally recognised OECD standard. It allows comparisons of the tax burden in these countries, measured by the tax-to-GDP ratio, as well as of the tax structure or tax mix, i.e., the distribution of total tax revenues by the main types of taxes. The database presents tax revenue data in national currency and USD and provides information on the share of tax revenues attributed to different levels of government.

Domestic revenues are critical to efforts to fund sustainable development and to implement the Sustainable Development Goals. The database supports these efforts by measuring progress on domestic resource mobilisation, building statistical capability, and providing country-specific indicators as called for in SDG 17, in the Addis Ababa Action Agenda and by more than 55 countries and international organisations in the Addis Tax Initiative.

The database shows that countries have made strong progress towards mobilising domestic financing for development in the 21st century. Tax revenues are now higher as a percentage of GDP and their levels are more evenly distributed across countries than they were at the turn of the century. With few exceptions, the countries that recorded the lowest level of tax revenues in 2000 have increased their revenues the most.

The Global Revenue Statistics Database is updated several times a year with the latest available data from the regional Revenue Statistics publications, which cover Africa, Asia and the Pacific, Latin America and the Caribbean, and OECD countries.

Data are available for most OECD countries up to the year 2020, while other countries included in the analysis have provided data up to 2019. Notably, the 2020 tax revenue data presented in this Chapter remain provisional until possible revisions following the publication of 2021 data.

The database can be accessed at the following web address:
https://www.oecd.org/tax/tax-policy/global-revenue-statistics-database.htm.

2.2. Trends in the composition of tax revenues

2.2.1. The composition of tax revenues has remained relatively stable

While on average tax levels have generally been rising, the tax structure or tax 'mix' has remained relatively stable over time. Nevertheless, several trends have emerged up to 2019 – the latest year for which data is available for the 38 OECD countries and five partner countries.

Revenues from personal income taxes were 22.3% of total taxes on average in 2019 compared with around 24.2% at the beginning of the 1990s. Corporate income tax revenues rose from around 8.2% of total tax revenues in 1990, on average, to a high of 12.1% in 2007. Following the aftermath of the global financial crisis, they have remained at between 9-10% of total tax revenues over the last decade.

Figure 2.6. Trends in tax structures from 1990 to 2019

Percentage of total tax revenue

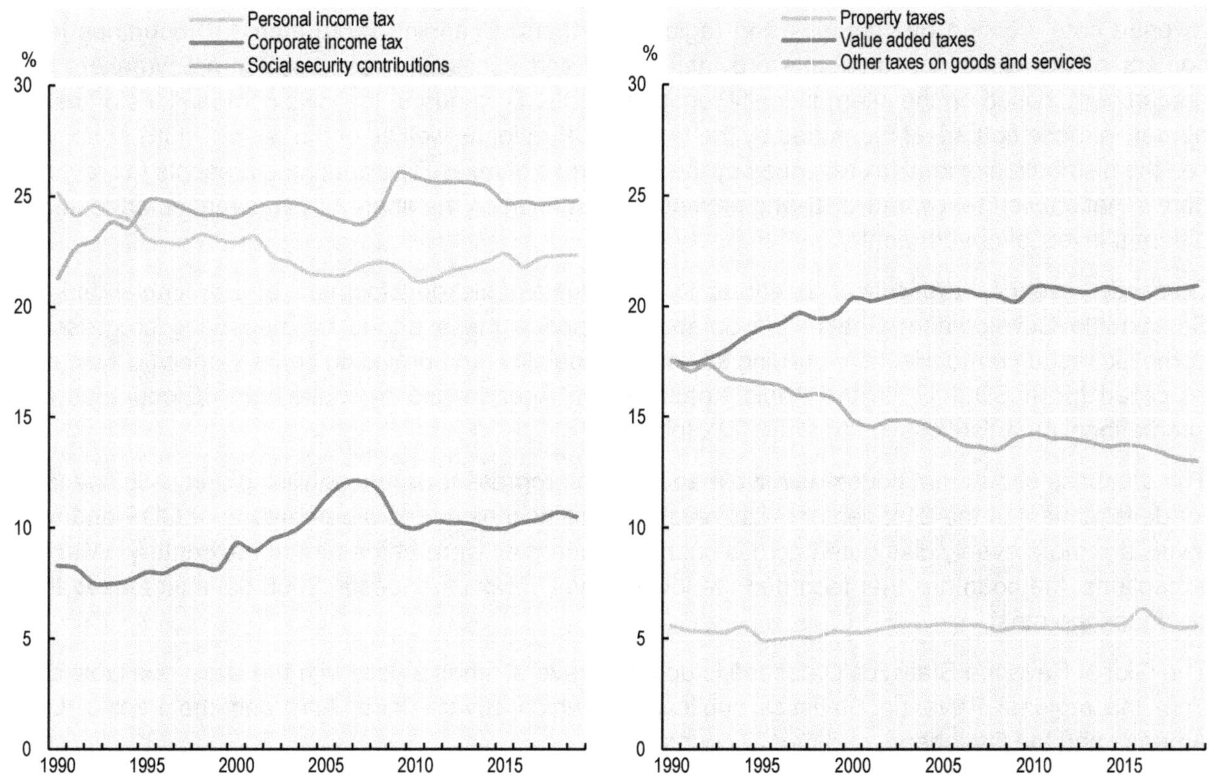

Note: The OECD average tax revenue in 2016 from main categories includes the one-off revenues from stability contributions in Iceland. This predominately affects the average revenues from property taxes, as a percentage of total tax revenues, in that year only.
Source: OECD Global Revenue Statistics Database.

StatLink https://stat.link/0qo65n

The average share of SSCs in total tax revenues has increased more than any other tax type over the last 30 years. SSCs represented 24.7% of the overall tax composition in 2019, having risen from 20.3% in 1990. Notable increases in the proportion of SSCs in total tax revenues were seen following the global financial crisis as rates were increased in a significant number of countries, reflecting governments' desire to raise revenues quickly (OECD, 2016[2]).These trends also highlight the rapid revenue-raising effects of increases in SSCs and consumption tax rates compared to other taxes.

Consumption taxes consistently contributed the largest share to total tax revenues of all major tax category types between 1990 (33.1%) and 2019 (33.9%). However, their composition – between VAT/GST, excise tax and customs duties – has changed considerably. VAT/GST revenues have risen considerably, from 17% of total tax revenues in 1990 to 20.9% in 2019. Similar to SSCs, a particularly large increase in VAT/GST was registered shortly after the global financial crisis given the relatively immediate revenue-raising effects of these taxes. The share of other excise taxes on specific goods and services in total tax revenues fell considerably in OECD and partner countries, from 16.7% to 12.3%, over this period. Customs duties and other trade-related taxes were reduced considerably across countries from 1990 onwards but remain elevated in the five emerging economies for which data are available as compared to OECD countries. These revenue changes reflected a global trend to remove trade barriers, as well as the general shift from specific consumption taxes to general consumption taxes – the VAT in most cases.

Between 1990 and 2019, the share of taxes on property has remained relatively constant within the overall tax composition. Taxes on property as a proportion of total tax revenues have remained between 5.2% and 5.4% for all but one year over this period on average across OECD and partner countries. As noted under Figure 2.6, the average tax revenue from property in 2016 was notably affected by one-off revenues from stability contributions in Iceland.

2.2.2. There is notable variation in the composition of countries' tax revenues

There are significant differences between countries' tax structures across OECD members and emerging economies. Seventeen countries raised the largest proportion of their total tax revenues from income taxes (both corporate and personal), while ten relied most heavily on SSCs, and 16 countries recorded consumption taxes (including VAT) as the largest contributor – the last group containing all five non-OECD partner countries. Taxes on property and payroll taxes played a smaller role in the revenue systems of most countries in 2019, both in most countries and, on average, across those countries for which data is available.

Figure 2.7. Tax structures by country in 2019

Revenues from each tax type as a percentage of total tax revenue

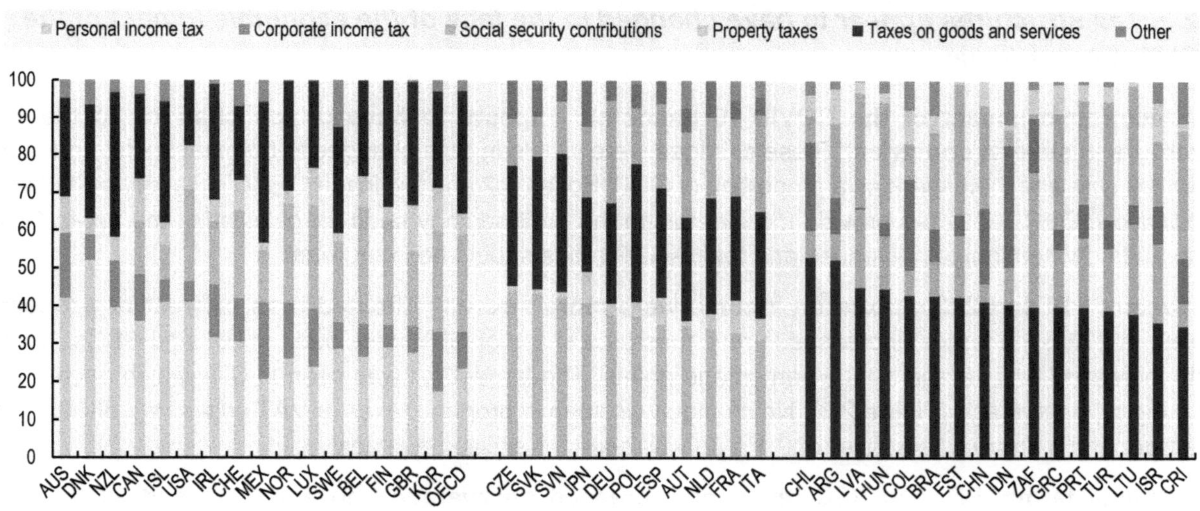

Note: Countries are grouped and ranked by those where income tax revenues (personal and corporate) form the highest share of total tax revenues, followed by those where social security contributions, and, subsequently, taxes on goods and services, form the highest share.
Source: OECD Global Revenue Statistics Database.

StatLink https://stat.link/eswyp1

As shown in Figure 2.7, OECD and partner countries collected 32.8% of their tax revenues through taxes on income and profits – of both individuals and companies – on average in 2019. There are ten countries in which taxes on personal and corporate incomes represent 40% of total tax revenues – Australia, Canada, Denmark, Iceland, Ireland, Mexico, New Zealand, Norway, Switzerland, and the United States. Of these countries, Australia, Denmark, and New Zealand received over 50% of their total tax revenues in taxes on income, as only a very small proportion (Denmark) or no SSCs are collected these countries.

The variation in the share of income taxes (i.e., PIT and CIT) between countries is considerable. In 2019, it ranged from lows of 4.8% in China, 6.1% in Costa Rica and 6.8% in Colombia to 41% in the United States, 42% in Australia and 52.1% in Denmark. The share of the CIT in total tax revenues varied considerably across countries in 2019, from less than 5% (France, Hungary, Italy, and Latvia) to over 20% in Chile (23.4%), Colombia (24%) and Indonesia (32.3%). In addition to differences in statutory corporate income tax rates, these differences are at least partly explained by institutional and country specific factors, including variations in incorporation rates, the breadth of the corporate income tax base, and the degree of cyclicality of the corporate tax system (given its implications for loss-offset provisions).

In 2019, SSCs accounted for 24.8% of total tax revenues on average across OECD countries and the emerging economies covered. In 11 countries, including Central European countries and large Western European countries, SSCs are the primary source of tax revenues. In the Slovak Republic, the Czech Republic, Lithuania, and Slovenia, SSCs account for over 40% of total tax revenues.

Tax revenues from consumption taxes represented 33.9% of the average OECD and partner countries' tax composition and were the primary source of revenues in 16 countries in 2019. Argentina and Chile collected over 45% of their tax revenues from consumption taxes in 2019 while personal income taxes accounted for 7.1% and 7.2%[4] respectively – the lowest shares among the 43 countries analysed (see footnote 1 at the beginning of this chapter). Property tax revenues also vary widely across countries: Canada, Israel, Korea, the United Kingdom, and the United States had property tax revenues that amounted to more than 10% of total tax revenues, but in Estonia and Lithuania property taxes accounted for less than 1% of total revenues.

2.2.3. Tax structures appear to have changed in the face of the economic impact of the COVID-19 pandemic

The economic impact of the COVID-19 pandemic appears to have driven changes to the tax structure in several countries. These changes were visible in both changes to nominal tax revenues by each tax type and their share as a proportion of GDP. Boxes 1.2 and 2.1 in the OECD's *Revenue Statistics* publication (OECD, 2021[1]) provide more detail on the methodology used for calculating the tax-to-GDP ratio and how nominal tax revenues and tax-to-GDP ratios should be interpreted.

Between 2019 and 2020, taxes on income were more strongly affected than indirect or property taxes. In 2020, the largest increases in revenues as a share of GDP were seen in PIT and SSCs, which both increased on average by 0.3 percentage points. The largest fall was seen in CIT, which decreased by 0.4 p.p., on average (Figure 2.8). No change was seen in property taxes or VAT as a share of GDP, on average, and a smaller decrease (of 0.1 p.p.) was seen for excise revenues.

In nominal terms, PIT and SSC revenues increased on average between 2019 and 2020. In its *Revenue Statistics* publication (2021[1]), the OECD shows that country-level changes in PIT and SSCs were only weakly correlated with changes in nominal GDP. This suggests that the respective tax bases remained relatively stable considering broader GDP fluctuations, or that policy changes limited the impact of economic changes on revenues from these tax bases, for example, by stabilising the base, or increasing the effective tax rate. Seventeen OECD countries recorded increases in nominal PIT revenues and twenty saw increases in SSCs in nominal terms. In those countries that experienced a nominal fall in PIT and SSCs, many recorded a smaller decrease than that of nominal GDP.

Approximately a quarter of countries (9) experienced decreases in PIT revenues as a share of GDP from 2019 to 2020, while half (18) saw increases of between zero and 0.5 p.p. The remaining quarter (10 countries) recorded increases of more than 0.5 p.p. year-on-year. The country that saw the largest fall in PIT revenues as a share of GDP was Türkiye (-0.6 p.p.), followed by Austria and Latvia (both by -0.4 p.p.). At the other end of the scale, Denmark registered the largest increase in PIT revenues as a share of GDP (1.0 p.p.). Seven OECD countries experienced decreases in SSC revenues as a share of GDP, while 29 countries saw increases, 13 of which were greater than 0.5 p.p. Hungary recorded the largest decrease in SSCs at -0.7 p.p., while the largest increase was seen in Spain (1.5 p.p.); the latter was a consequence of a much sharper fall in nominal GDP (-9.9%, the largest contraction across the OECD) than in SSC revenues (4.8%).

Figure 2.8. Changes in tax revenues by category as a share of GDP from 2019 to 2020

Share of GDP

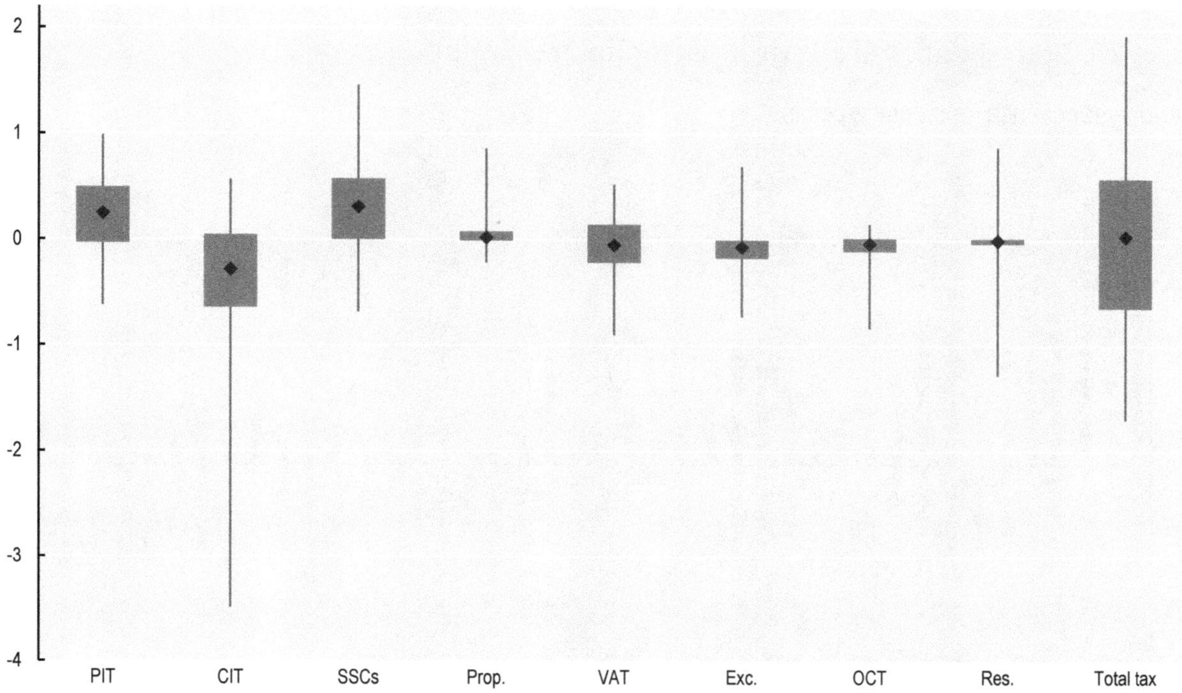

Note: In the figure, the lowest point represents the minimum country change for the tax type between 2019-2020; the box represents the changes for countries between the lower and upper quartiles (i.e., 50% of countries had changes within the range shown by each box); and the upper point for each tax type represents the maximum country change. The line in each box represents the median country change (i.e., half of countries were both above and below this line). The tax category "Prop." refers to property taxes, "Exc." to excise taxes, "OCT" to other consumption taxes, and "Res." to Residual. Note that the figure contains only data for OECD countries who had preliminary data available for 2020 – it therefore does not cover partner countries Argentina, Brazil, China, Indonesia, and South Africa.
Source: OECD Revenue Statistics (2021[1]).

StatLink https://stat.link/b16uoh

Corporate income taxes, as a share of GDP, fell widely across OECD countries in 2020. The average fall in CIT revenues as a proportion of GDP was -0.37 p.p., with 26 countries recording falls. The largest decrease was seen in Norway (-3.5 p.p.), while the Czech Republic also experienced a decrease of over -1 p.p. Thirteen countries saw increases in CIT revenues as a percentage of GDP in 2020 relative to 2019, the largest of which was experienced in Latvia.

Revenues from excise taxes decreased slightly as a share of GDP on average in 2020 and this tax category saw the most widespread reductions in revenues of all tax types, with falls in 28 countries. Most decreases were caused by reduced sales of transport fuels leading to falls in fuel excises due to COVID-19-related mobility restrictions and lockdowns. The largest fall was seen in Estonia (-0.7 p.p.) and the largest increase was seen in Türkiye (0.7 p.p.). Other than Estonia and Türkiye, the range of changes across countries was comparatively small, reflecting in part the smaller size of excises as a share of total tax revenues. No other changes in excise revenues exceeded 0.5 p.p. of GDP in 2020.

Revenues from the CIT and excise taxes were the most heavily impacted by the crisis, both on average and in terms of the number of countries affected. Nominal CIT revenues fell by 12.1%, with 30 countries experiencing falls, whereas excise tax revenues fell by 5.4% on average, with 31 countries experiencing falls. The sharp fall in CIT revenues can be attributed to the impact of COVID-19 on general economic activity, while changes in nominal excise tax revenues across OECD countries were primarily due to COVID-19-related restrictions on mobility, which in turn limited fuel excise revenues (OECD, 2021[1]).

Figure 2.9. Decomposition of change in tax-to-GDP ratio by tax category, 2019-2020

Year-on-year change, percentage points

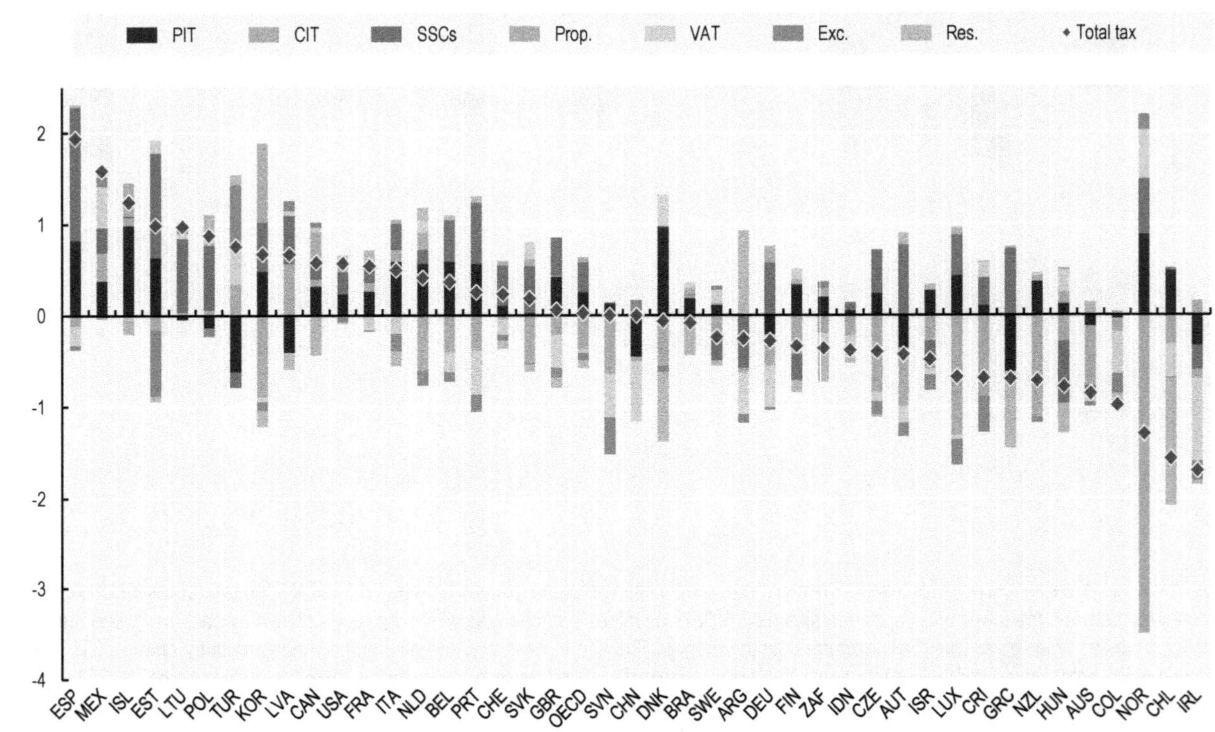

Note: This graph includes the change between years 2018 and 2019 for Argentina, Australia, Brazil, China, Indonesia, New Zealand, and South Africa, as tax revenues for the full 2020 fiscal year were not available at the time of writing. Due to data availability, the average excludes Japan for SSCs (category 2000) and for total tax revenues; it excludes Greece for PIT (category 1100), CIT (category 1200), VAT (category 5111) and excises (5111) due to disaggregated data for these categories not being available.
Source: OECD Global Revenue Statistics Database.

StatLink https://stat.link/2ln5z8

Only a small change was observed in the average share of property tax revenues to GDP in 2020 relative to 2019 – an increase of 0.05 p.p. of GDP. Twenty-nine OECD countries saw increases in the share of property tax revenues, with 18 of these between 0 and 0.7 p.p. The largest increase was seen in Korea (0.9 p.p.). Of the nine OECD countries where property tax revenues fell as a share of GDP, the largest falls (0.2 p.p.) were seen in the Czech Republic and the United Kingdom.

Similarly, no significant change was observed in the average share of VAT to GDP in 2020 – a very small decrease of 0.04 p.p. was recorded by countries overall. VAT revenues decreased as a share of GDP in 19 countries and increased in the other 17 countries that apply a VAT, half of these changes being between -0.2 and +0.1 p.p. of GDP. The largest fall was seen in Ireland (0.9 p.p.) due to the temporary

VAT rate cut during the COVID-19 pandemic as well as a decrease in economic activity. The largest increase was seen in Norway, at 0.5 p.p.

Revenues from VAT decreased slightly on average across OECD countries between 2019 and 2020. However, as described above, as a share of GDP, VAT/GST revenues remained relatively stable as this fall was more muted than the average fall in nominal GDP. Twenty-four OECD countries saw decreases in nominal VAT revenues in 2020. Country changes in VAT revenues were more closely correlated to changes in GDP, contributing to their relative stability as a share of GDP on average.

Box 2.2. Using tax buoyancy estimates to assess whether changes in tax revenues in 2020 were smaller or larger than expected

Alongside tax revenue elasticity, tax revenue buoyancy is one of the key measures that captures the sensitivity of government revenue to economic activity. For instance, an overall tax revenue buoyancy of 1.2 suggests that when GDP grows by 1%, total tax revenues would be expected to grow by 1.2%. Buoyancy estimates thus capture the total response of tax revenues to changes in GDP, including the impact of tax policy changes. In contrast, revenue elasticities control for tax policy reforms to isolate the impact of economic growth on tax revenue, i.e., in the absence of policy changes.

As tax buoyancy incorporates the impact of policy changes on tax revenues, it can be used to evaluate how the overall response of tax revenues to changes in economic growth in 2020 may have differed from previous years. Furthermore, decomposing the tax revenue impact into its individual components can suggest whether tax policy changes have been able to limit (or have exacerbated) the impact of macroeconomic conditions on particular tax categories, relative to earlier periods. Comparing real changes in tax revenues following an economic contraction with the estimates of tax revenue changes predicted by tax buoyancy calculations can thus shed light on the role of economic stabilizers and the nature of discretionary policy choices, such as increasing expenditure on furlough schemes and reducing revenue through tax cuts during the pandemic.

This box provides estimates of the short-term revenue buoyancy of different tax types between two consecutive years for OECD countries over the 2010-2019 period. The calculations are based on data from the OECD Global Revenue Statistics database and the methodology employed by Belinga et al. (2014[3]) who estimate short-run and long-run revenue buoyancy for OECD countries in their widely cited paper. As depicted below, the results suggest an average short-run revenue buoyancy over the 2010-2019 period of below 1 for total tax revenues and for all individual taxes components other than the CIT. Short-run buoyancy estimates are the lowest for property taxes, followed by PIT, SSCs, excise taxes, and VAT/GST.

Figure 2.10 compares OECD estimates of the *expected* tax revenue response (according to tax buoyancy estimates) against the *actual* experience recorded by countries in 2020. The expected response is calculated by multiplying the average short-run buoyancy estimate with average GDP growth in 2019-2020. Hence, it refers to the expected change in tax revenues had the response to the recession in 2020 been governed by the average short-run buoyancy over the 2010-2019 period. It is important to note that the results in Figure 2.10 may appear different to those described earlier in the Chapter, such as in Figure 2.8 and Figure 2.9. However, these differences reflect in large part the different values and calculations that are referred to, i.e., the difference between percentage changes (as in Figure 2.10) and percentage point changes (as in Figure 2.8 and Figure 2.9), as well as some small variances in the country data coverage.

Figure 2.10. Average inflation-adjusted change in tax revenue in 2019-2020 vs. expected change

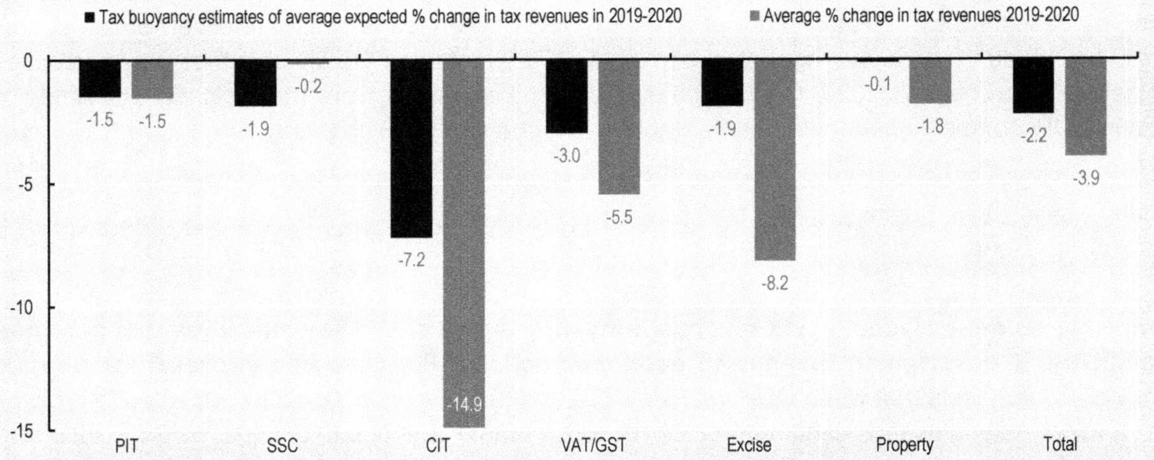

Note: Based on 32 OECD countries with available data. Excludes countries without tax revenue data for 2020 and outliers (Iceland, Latvia, and Mexico) that record very large relative revenue changes for some taxes and years that significantly distort the results. Tax-specific short-run buoyancy indicators are estimated for the 2010-2019 period through a log-log single error correction panel regression, following the methodology in Belinga et al. (2014[3]). Property tax short-run buoyancy estimates have been included but the average is not statistically significant. All variables are adjusted for inflation.
Source: OECD Global Revenue Statistics Database and OECD calculations.

StatLink https://stat.link/zm6p3u

As illustrated in Figure 2.10, the decline in total tax revenues (-3.9%) in 2019-2020 was stronger than would have been expected - based on tax buoyancy estimates - given the size of the economic contraction (-4% real GDP). The decline in revenues also exceeded the expected reduction for most individual tax components, namely for CIT, VAT/GST, excise taxes and property taxes. On the contrary, the PIT and SSCs stand out because revenues in 2020 declined by less than or in line with the estimated short-run buoyancy.

The larger than expected decline in total tax revenues suggests that the specific nature of the pandemic shock and/or additional discretionary tax policies played a role. This was in addition to the functioning of automatic stabilizers and the potential replication of past policy choices, which are already represented by the expected reduction in tax revenues. Notably, the reduction of total revenues points to an implicit tax buoyancy of just less than 1 in 2020 (-3.9% average fall in tax revenues divided by a -4% fall in GDP).

The corporate income tax is known to be the most buoyant tax that fluctuates strongly with GDP growth (Dudine and Tovar Jalles, 2017[4]). However, in 2020, the implicit short-run buoyancy (3.7) surpassed the already large estimate for the 2010-2019 period (1.8) – the actual fall in CIT revenues (-14.9%) was therefore almost double its expected size (-7.2%). This large decline in CIT revenues is likely the result of a combination of lower profits due to the pandemic shock and the introduction of generous tax measures sought to provide relief to businesses, such as tax payment deferrals and the reduction of tax prepayments. Furthermore, the pandemic shock resulted in a large decline in excise tax revenues, even though the tax buoyancy estimates suggest that excise tax revenue usually does not respond strongly to changes in GDP. This anomalously large reduction was likely the result of the unprecedented policy response to the health crisis (lockdowns, mobility restrictions), resulting, for example, in reduced revenue from fuel excise taxes.

Though stronger than expected the reduction in VAT and property tax revenues remained closer to the expected contraction. The implicit short-run buoyancy for property taxes in 2020 is smaller than 0.5 (-1.8% fall in average property tax revenues divided by -4% fall in GDP), which compares against a short-run buoyancy that is, in statistical terms, not significantly different from zero over the 2010-2019 period. The somewhat larger buoyancy of property taxes in 2020 could be the result of policies that deferred or waived business and residential property tax payments or reduced property transaction taxes during the pandemic (OECD, 2021[5]). Similarly, the previous edition of the Tax Policy Reforms Report found that more than 80% of OECD countries introduced VAT payment deferrals. In addition, temporary VAT rate reductions, such as for medical supplies, were widespread. These discretionary choices together with changes in the tax bases driven by the pandemic shock elevated the implicit VAT short-run buoyancy in 2020 to a value above one (1.4).

The subdued decline in PIT and SSC revenues demonstrates the importance of automatic stabilizers as well as further unprecedented tax policy choices made in 2019-2020. In particular, the very small decline in PIT and SSC revenues relative to the contraction in GDP appears to reflect the success of large-scale and generous discretionary expenditure programmes such as furlough schemes and job subsidy programmes that were able to prevent widespread layoffs.

References

Belinga, V. et al. (2014), "Tax Buoyancy in OECD Countries", *IMF Working Papers*, Vol. 14/110, p. 1, https://doi.org/10.5089/9781498305075.001. [3]

Dudine, P. and J. Tovar Jalles (2017), "How Buoyant is the Tax System? New Evidence from a Large Heterogeneous Panel", *IMF Working Papers*, Vol. 17/4, p. 1, https://doi.org/10.5089/9781475569797.001. [4]

OECD (2021), *Revenue Statistics 2021: The Initial Impact of COVID-19 on OECD Tax Revenues*, OECD Publishing, Paris, https://doi.org/10.1787/6e87f932-en. [1]

OECD (2021), *Tax Policy Reforms 2021: Special Edition on Tax Policy during the COVID-19 Pandemic*, OECD Publishing, Paris, https://doi.org/10.1787/427d2616-en. [5]

OECD (2016), *Tax Policy Reforms in the OECD 2016*, OECD Publishing, Paris, https://doi.org/10.1787/9789264260399-en. [2]

Notes

[1] Country coverage varies across and within Chapters due to the different data sources used. As in previous editions of the Tax Policy Reforms Report, the Tax Revenues Chapter uses data for all OECD countries as well as Argentina, Brazil, China, Indonesia and South Africa. The Chapter largely draws on data from the *OECD Revenue Statistics* publication. Notably, 2020 revenue data were not available for individual tax categories for certain OECD countries at the time of writing – Australia, Greece, Japan, and New Zealand. The latest data for the Inclusive Framework jurisdictions of Argentina, Brazil, China (People's Republic of), Indonesia and South Africa were from 2019.

Where the text references an average across OECD and selected Inclusive Framework jurisdictions, this represents the unweighted average for all OECD countries, as well as Argentina, Brazil, China, Indonesia, and South Africa, unless otherwise specified.

[2] See Box 1.2 in OECD (2021[1]) for details on the methodology used to calculate the tax-to-GDP ratio.

[3] Argentina, China and Türkiye have also not been included in Figure 2.5 and Figure 2.4, as the data used in the figures are in nominal amounts, high levels of inflation can have a significant impact on the change in nominal tax revenues and nominal GDP. Türkiye, for example, recorded 12.3% inflation in 2020 as compared to 1.4% in the OECD on average, pushing both the change in nominal GDP and tax revenues by a notably larger amount than other OECD and partner countries. Similarly, Argentina recorded 54.4% annual inflation in 2019. China began providing social security contributions data to the OECD from 2019 and thus there is an anomalous increase in the country's tax-to-GDP ratio for the years covered by Figures 2.4 and 2.5.

[4] Chile has a dividend imputation system (either total or partial), therefore part of its revenues from personal income taxes are computed as corporate income tax revenues.

3 Tax Policy Reforms

This chapter provides an overview of the tax reforms adopted by 71 member jurisdictions of the OECD/G20 Inclusive Framework on Base Erosion and Profit Shifting, including all OECD countries. It looks at the reforms that were announced and implemented in 2021, examining trends in each category of tax including personal income taxes and social security contributions, corporate income taxes and other corporate taxes, taxes on goods and services (including value added taxes, sales taxes, and excise duties), environmentally related taxes and property taxes.

This chapter provides an overview of the tax reforms adopted in the 71 Inclusive Framework jurisdictions that responded to the OECD's annual tax policy reform questionnaire.[1] It looks at the reforms that were introduced or announced in 2021. It examines trends in each category of tax including personal income taxes and social security contributions(Section 3.1), corporate income taxes and other corporate taxes (Section 3.2), taxes on goods and services, including value added taxes, sales taxes and excise duties (Section 3.3), environmentally related taxes (Section 3.4) and property taxes (Section 3.5).

The discussion in this chapter is primarily based on countries' responses to the 2022 Annual Tax Policy Reform Questionnaire, which was completed by countries between January and February 2022. This annual questionnaire asks responding countries to describe their tax reforms as well as to provide details on their expected revenue effects and other relevant information; including the rationale for the tax measures (see Box 3.1).

Country coverage varies across this Chapter. Differences in country coverage may be the result of variances between the categories of the reforms that countries reported on as well as the different data sources used.

Each Section of Chapter 3 starts with a short discussion of tax revenue trends within the five aforementioned tax categories, followed by descriptions of the tax reforms introduced or announced by countries. As in previous editions of the *Tax Policy Reforms* report, tax revenue data covers 43 countries – all 38 OECD countries as well as the five non-OECD Inclusive Framework jurisdictions of Argentina, Brazil, China, Indonesia and South Africa.[2] As with Chapter 2, preliminary 2020 data were not available for these five non-OECD countries nor for some OECD countries (Australia and New Zealand for the most part, but also Greece and Japan for some tax categories) at the time of writing the report.

The tax policy trends sub-sections that follow cover the 71 member jurisdictions of the OECD/G20 Inclusive Framework on Base Erosion and Profit Shifting that responded to the OECD questionnaire. Furthermore, the description of these tax reforms is often complemented by more detailed policy analysis using data from existing OECD publications. This may include effective tax rates on labour (Section 3.1), corporations (Section 3.2) or carbon (Section 3.4), for example, whose country coverage varies from the tax revenue and tax policy trends sub-Sections described above. All differences in country coverage are explained in the body of the report or in accompanying endnotes.

Box 3.1. The OECD Annual Tax Policy Reform Questionnaire

At the Working Party No.2 on Tax Policy Analysis and Tax Statistics (WP2) meeting in November 2009, delegates from OECD countries agreed to start collecting information on the main tax measures adopted in each country in a more systematic fashion. The motivation for this proposal was to provide consistent and comparative information on tax reforms to inform policy discussions in OECD and non-OECD countries.

At the November 2010 WP2 meeting, the following criteria were agreed for deciding whether a tax policy measure was sufficiently substantial to be reported in the questionnaire:

- A significant change in a tax rate;
- A change in the tax base that is expected to change revenue from that base by more than 5% of total tax revenue or 0.1% of GDP; and
- A politically important systemic reform.

Any central or sub-central tax policy measure that was implemented, legislated, or announced in the previous calendar year that meets at least one of the criteria listed above must be reported in the questionnaire.

For each reform, the questionnaire requests information on the type of tax; the dates of entry into force, legislation, or announcement; the direction of the rate and/or base change; and a detailed description of the reform. The questionnaire also asks for the rationale behind the reform and estimates of the revenue effects of the tax measures.

3.1. Personal income tax and social security contributions

Countries continued to lower the tax burden of personal income taxes (PIT) and social security contributions (SSCs) in 2021 to support low-income households amid the COVID-19 pandemic and promote economic recovery. Most of the countries that responded to the OECD tax policy reforms questionnaire introduced PIT and SSC reforms in the tax year 2021, mostly through lowering tax rates and reducing the size of tax bases. The most common rationale behind these reforms was to boost economic growth, while, at the same time, promoting equity in personal income taxation, particularly for those on low and middle incomes. While the latter rationale represents a broad continuation of PIT reforms in recent years, the focus on economic growth has gained renewed importance in response to the economic repercussions of the COVID-19 crisis. PIT rate changes have been less common than in previous years, and mostly involved rate reductions for low- and middle-income households. PIT base narrowing measures have been frequent and often sought to promote employment and provide in work-benefits, as well as supporting families with children and particularly those on lower incomes. More limited changes in the taxation of household capital income were introduced. Finally, reforms to SSCs largely came in the form of SSC reductions in 2021, several of which involved temporary rate cuts and base narrowing measures in response to the adverse economic effects of the COVID-19 pandemic.

3.1.1. PIT and SSCs are major sources of tax revenue

PIT and SSCs are significant sources of tax revenues in most countries. Together, they account for around half of total tax revenues, with PIT making up 23% and SSCs 26%, of total tax revenue on average across OECD countries and the five selected non-OECD Inclusive Framework jurisdictions (Argentina, Brazil, China, Indonesia, and South Africa). As shown in Figure 3.1, PIT, SSCs and payroll taxes accounted for over 60% of total tax revenue in Austria, Germany, Spain, Slovenia, Sweden, and the United States. In the Czech Republic, Japan, the Slovak Republic, and Slovenia, SSCs alone accounted for at least 40% of total tax revenues while PIT accounted for 40% or more of total tax revenues in Australia, Denmark, Iceland, and the United States. PIT, SSCs and payroll taxes represent a much smaller share of tax revenues in Argentina (27%), Chile (18%) and Indonesia (14%).

Figure 3.1. Tax revenue share of PIT, SSCs and payroll taxes by country, 2020

Share of total tax revenues

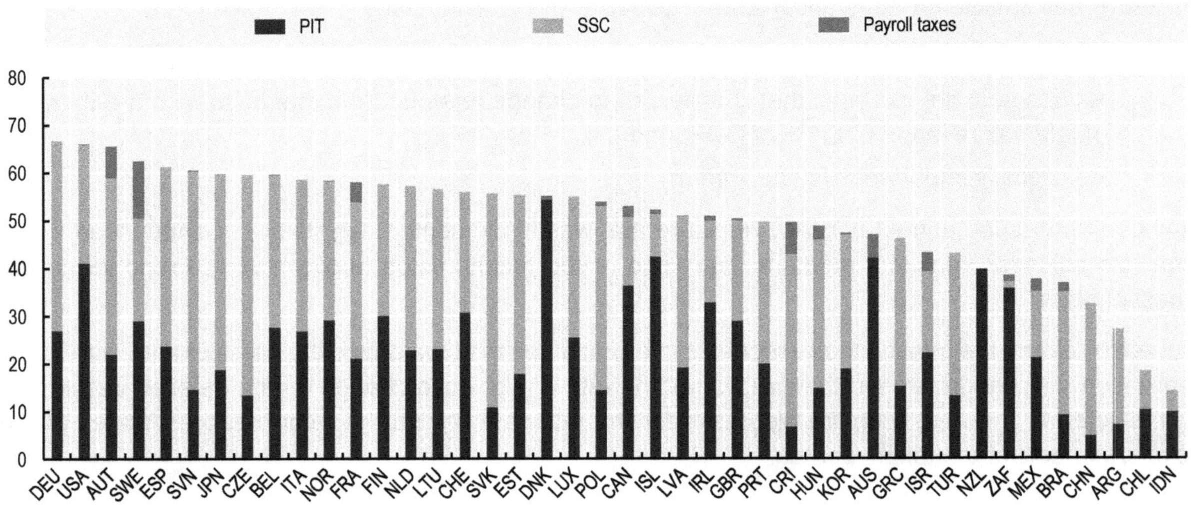

Note: 2019 data for Argentina, Australia, Brazil, China, Greece, Indonesia, Japan, New Zealand, and South Africa. The OECD average includes the latest data available for OECD. The five additional Inclusive Framework jurisdictions included are Argentina, Brazil, China, Indonesia and South Africa.
Source: OECD Global Revenue Statistics Database, OECD Revenue Statistics Database.

StatLink https://stat.link/q56sha

Over the past five decades, SSCs have gradually overtaken PIT as the most important source of tax revenue in OECD countries, while PIT and SSCs are more volatile and less significant as a share of total tax revenue in the selected non-OECD Inclusive Framework jurisdictions. In both OECD countries and non-OECD Inclusive Framework jurisdictions, the sum of PIT and SSCs has slightly increased over time, however, considerable differences remain in their respective tax mix (Figure 3.2). Across OECD countries, PIT has gradually declined as a share of total revenue while SSCs have increased. In 1965, SSCs comprised 17.6% of tax revenues on average while PIT accounted for 26.2% of total taxation. By 1995, they were about equal at approximately 25%. In 2020, SSCs represented 27.7% of total tax revenues on average, surpassing the PIT share of 23.5%. In the five non-OECD Inclusive Framework jurisdictions, PIT and SSCs accounted for a much smaller share of total tax revenues in 2019 (the latest year for which data is available for all countries covered), with 13.3% and 15.8%, respectively while their share in total tax revenues is also more volatile. The proportion of SSCs in the total tax mix increased significantly both in OECD countries and the non-OECD Inclusive Framework jurisdictions in the aftermath of the global financial crisis, with a similar increase observed in OECD countries in response to the COVID-19 pandemic.

Figure 3.2. Average tax revenue share of PIT, SSCs and payroll taxes in OECD and partner countries, 1990-2020

Share of total tax revenues (%)

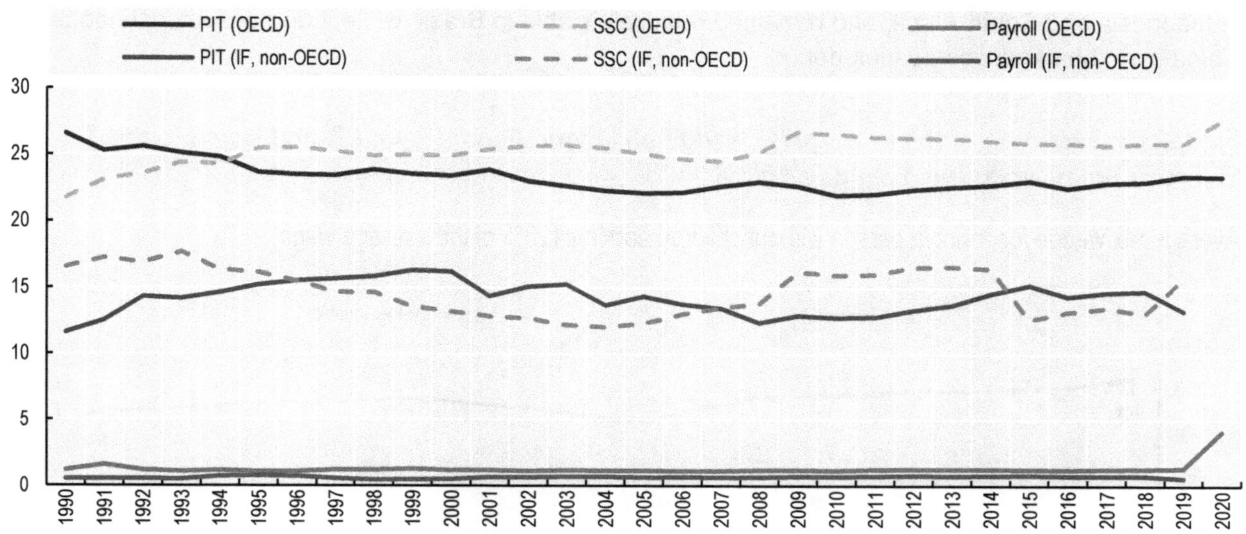

Note: The five additional Inclusive Framework jurisdictions included are Argentina, Brazil, China (People's Republic of), Indonesia and South Africa. For Indonesia, data are included from 2002-2019; for China, data are included for 2019; for other Inclusive Framework jurisdictions, 2019 data are the latest available.
Source: OECD Global Revenue Statistics Database, OECD Revenue Statistics Database.

StatLink https://stat.link/kszuvb

PIT and SSCs were increased in most OECD countries in 2020 following the COVID-19 pandemic, both in absolute terms and as a share of total tax revenue.[3] In the 34 OECD countries for which provisional data were available for 2020, 19 countries recorded an increase and 15 countries a decrease in both nominal PIT and SSC revenues. As a share of total tax revenue, 27 countries saw their PIT revenue increase while seven countries recorded a fall. The share of SSCs in total tax revenues increased in 28 countries while it fell in six countries. In several countries, the relative PIT and SSC tax revenue decline was therefore smaller compared to the decrease in total tax revenues. On average across the 34 OECD countries for which data are available, the share of SSCs in total tax revenues increased by 1.8 p.p. in 2020 (from 25.9%) while the PIT revenue share remained stable at 23.5% compared to the previous year. These trends highlight the efforts of governments to promote job and income security in the face of the economic repercussions of the COVID-19 crisis.

3.1.2. Taxes on labour income continued to decline on average in 2020

The average tax burden on labour income has declined in recent years in OECD countries while it has increased in the five selected non-OECD Inclusive Framework jurisdictions over the same time period (Figure 3.3). The average tax wedge – the total tax payments on labour income as a percentage of total labour costs – for single workers earning the average wage was 13 p.p. higher in OECD countries compared to partner countries in 2019, however, with considerable cross-country variation among the five non-OECD Inclusive Framework jurisdictions. In Brazil and China, the average tax wedge in 2019 was 32.5% and 30.7% respectively, close to the OECD average of 35.0%, while it was estimated at 16.9% in South Africa and 7.8% in Indonesia. Over time, the average tax wedge has declined from 36.4% in 2000 to 34.6% in 2020 in OECD countries while it increased marginally from 21.4% in 2010 to 22.0% in 2019 in the five non-OECD Inclusive Framework jurisdictions. The increase in the tax wedge between 2009 and 2013 in OECD economies largely reflects fiscal consolidation measures taken in response to the global financial crisis. Since then, the average tax wedge has declined consistently, with a particularly marked reduction of 0.39 p.p. between 2019 and 2020 in response to the COVID-19 pandemic. Between 2010 and 2019, the average tax wedge in the non-OECD Inclusive Framework jurisdictions increased consistently in Indonesia and South Africa, and remained relatively stable in Brazil, while it decreased continuously in China over the same observation period.

Figure 3.3. Evolution of the average tax wedge on labour income in OECD and selected non-OECD Inclusive Framework jurisdictions, 2000-2020

Average tax wedge for a single person without children earning 100% of the average wage

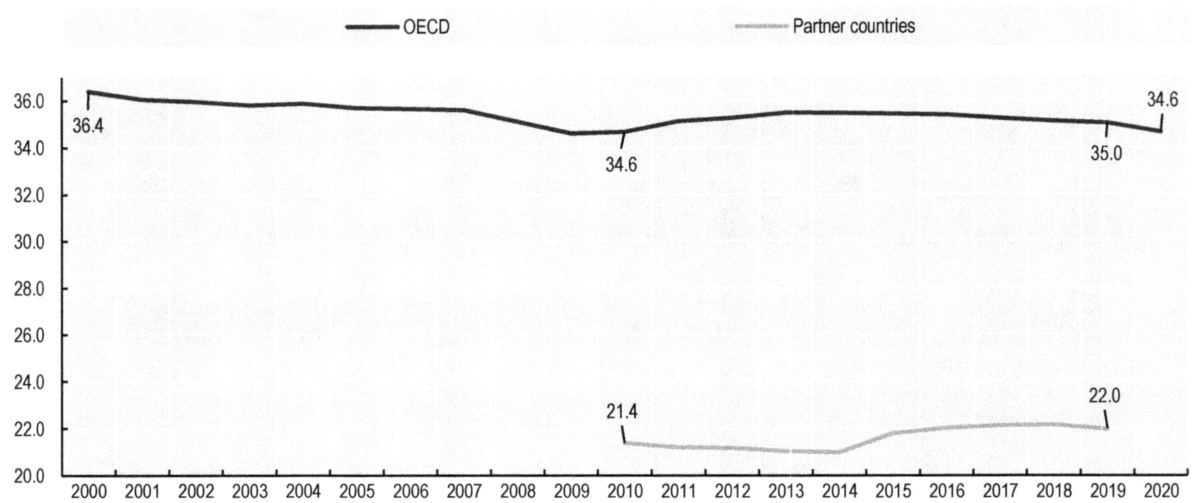

Note: Comparable data were not available for Argentina, Brazil, China, Indonesia, and South Africa. The non-OECD IF jurisdiction average includes data for Brazil, China, Indonesia, and South Africa from 2010-2019; for China, the model assumes that the worker is based in Shanghai.
Source: OECD Taxing Wages Database, OECD (2021[1]).

StatLink https://stat.link/kezfoh

The decrease in the tax burden for single earners without children earning the average wage has mainly been driven by lower income taxes. Between 2019 and 2020, the tax wedge fell in 29 out of 37 OECD member countries.[4] For 21 out of the 29 OECD countries, the decrease in the average tax burden was predominantly driven by lower income taxes, linked to policy changes, including measures related to the COVID-19 pandemic, but also partially due to lower nominal average wages. In five OECD countries, the decrease in the average labour tax burden was mainly linked to lower SSCs (Finland, Greece, Hungary, the Netherlands, and the United Kingdom) while increases in Canada and the United States reflected the temporary cash transfers paid to single-worker households during the COVID-19 crisis who would not typically receive these types of benefits. In Iceland, the decline was driven equally by a reduction in income taxes and employer SSCs as a share of labour costs. In seven countries, the increase in the average tax burden has mainly been associated with growth in wages, which has seen workers on the average wage move into higher tax brackets (OECD, 2021[2]).

There are significant differences between the taxation of workers and families with and without children across Inclusive Framework jurisdictions (Figure 3.4). In OECD countries, the average tax wedge for a one-earner married couple with two children was 9.5 p.p. lower compared to a single person with no children in 2019. Across different family types, policy-related factors were the predominant driver of lower average tax burdens. Governments across the OECD relied mainly on enhanced or one-off cash benefits instead of support programmes granted within the labour tax system. A particular focus has been on families with children, which is reflected in the notable decline in their average tax burden.

Figure 3.4. Evolution of the average tax wedge in OECD and selected non-OECD Inclusive Framework jurisdictions, by family type, 2000-2020

Average tax wedge

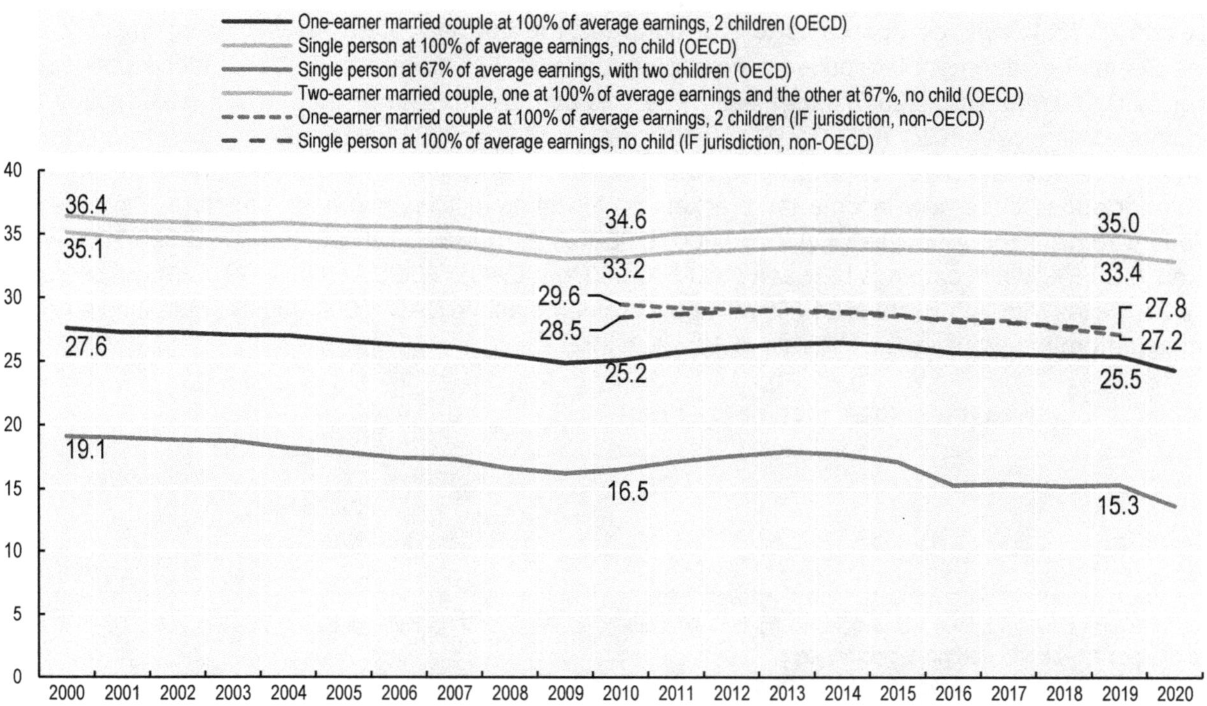

Note: Comparable data were not available for Argentina, Brazil, China, Indonesia, and South Africa. The partner country average includes data for Brazil, China, Indonesia, and South Africa from 2010-2019; for China, the model assumes that the worker is based in Shanghai.
Source: OECD Taxing Wages Database; OECD (2021[1]).

StatLink https://stat.link/mzna7d

3.1.3. Top PIT rate increases and PIT rate reductions for low- and middle-income households have raised the progressivity of tax systems

PIT reforms are important tools for governments to achieve different policy objectives, including raising tax revenues, stimulating economic growth, and enhancing the redistributive impact of the tax system. These reforms can involve the upward or downward adjustment of PIT rates and the broadening or narrowing of PIT bases but may require a trade-off between equity and efficiency. For instance, while PIT rate increases on those in the upper income brackets strengthen progressivity and fairness, in some cases they may also reduce economic incentives to work, save and invest. This section looks at the PIT reforms that were recently introduced in the 71 member jurisdictions of the OECD/G20 Inclusive Framework on Base Erosion and Profit Shifting that responded to the OECD questionnaire, beginning with PIT rate reforms followed by PIT base changes.

Very few countries increased their top PIT rates in 2021 to raise the progressivity of their tax systems

Three countries undertook top PIT rate reforms, which involved rate increases (Table 3.1). Canada, New Zealand and Norway raised their top PIT rate through the introduction of new income tax brackets at the top of the PIT rate schedule. Norway introduced a fifth band for income over NOK 2 million (USD 232 829)[5] effective from January 2022, which is taxed at a rate of 17.4%, and is paid in addition to the 22% general income tax rate (and the 8% SSC for employees). This reform represents a 1 p.p. net increase in the top PIT rate from 2020 and 2021 (employee SSCs were reduced by 0.2 p.p.). A tax rate of 16.4% will be applicable to the fourth income tax band from the beginning of 2022.[6] The New Zealand government introduced a new top tax rate of 39% from April 2021 for individuals earning over NZD 180 000 (USD 128 570) per year. The previous top tax rate of 33%, which was applied to all income earned over NZD 70 000 (USD 50 000) up to March 2021, was subsequently applicable to earnings between NZD 70 000 and up to NZD 180 000. The Canadian province of Newfoundland and Labrador added three new income tax brackets on top of its existing five band structure. Effective from January 2022, income between CAD 250 000 (USD 199 380) and CAD 500 000 (USD 398 760) will be taxed at 20.8%, while earnings between CAD 500 000 and CAD 1 000 000 (USD 797 520) will be subject to a 21.3% tax rate. A tax rate of 21.8% will apply to income above CAD 1 000 000, representing a notable increase from the previous top PIT rate of 18.3% in 2021.[7]

Table 3.1. Changes to personal income tax rates

	Rate increase	Rate decrease
	2021 or later	
Top PIT rate	CAN [1], NOR, NZL	
Non-top PIT rate		ARM, AUT, ITA, LUX [2], MLT [2], POL

Note : 1. Signifies that tax reform was implemented at the sub-central level (Province of Newfoundland and Labrador). 2. Signifies that PIT tax rate changes apply to income from temporary work.
Source: OECD Annual Tax Policy Reform Questionnaire.

Countries continue to cut PIT rates for low and middle-income earners

More countries introduced non-top PIT rate reforms compared to top rate measures, many of which were comprised of rate cuts to support low and middle-income earners. Italy introduced a significant PIT reform (see Box 3.2), which included a reduction in the number of tax brackets from five to four as well as a reduction in PIT rates for the second- and third-income band. The rate for the second income band was cut from 27% to 25% while the rate for the third band was reduced from 38% to 35%. The fourth tax bracket was eliminated, which was previously composed of a tax rate of 41% applicable to taxable income between EUR 55 000 (USD 65 051) and EUR 75 000 (USD 88 706). The top PIT rate remained unchanged at 43% but applies now to taxable income above EUR 50 000 (USD 59 137) (IBFD, 2022[3]). Armenia reduced its flat PIT rate from 23% to 22% in January 2021. Austria will reduce the PIT rates that apply to the second and third tax bracket from 35% to 30% and 42% to 40%, respectively, with effect from July 2023.

Several countries introduced PIT rate reforms for part-time employment and other professional groups. Poland reformed the lump-sum tax rates for certain businesses on the registered revenues that apply to specific business activities. A flat rate of 14% is applied to income earned, for instance, by doctors and engineers, while the revenue of IT specialists will be taxed at a rate of 12% from 2022 onwards. Malta reduced the tax rate it applies for the first EUR 10 000 (USD 11 827) of income earned from part-time work from 15% to 10% – by decreasing the labour tax burden, the government hopes to partially address labour shortages in certain sectors. Luxembourg also introduced a reform to the taxation of income received by temporary workers. From 2022, income paid by temporary work agencies is taxed at a flat rate of 10% (tax applies on the gross wage after the deduction of social security contributions) if the hourly gross wage does not exceed EUR 25 (USD 30).

Box 3.2. Personal income tax reform in Italy

Italy announced several significant tax reforms in 2021, which aim at simplifying the tax system and promoting economic growth. These reforms are expected to reduce tax revenues by EUR 4.8 billion (USD 5.68 billion) in 2022 and around EUR 7 billion (USD 8.28 billion) in 2023 and 2024. The child benefit tax credit (ANF) and other benefits supporting children have been replaced by a universal child benefit (AUF). The main beneficiaries of the PIT reform are expected to be middle-income households.

Reform of the income tax schedule

The reforms included a reduction in income tax brackets from five to four as well as a reduction in the marginal tax rates for the second and third bracket (Table 3.2). The reform also redefined the third income tax band, lowering its upper threshold to EUR 50 000 (USD 59 137). The fourth income band was eliminated while the top income rate applies to all taxable income above EUR 50 000.

Table 3.2. Changes in tax bands and marginal PIT rates

2021			2022		
Lower bound	Upper bound	Tax rate	Lower bound	Upper bound	Tax rate
0	15 000	23%	0	15 000	23%
15 001	28 000	27%	15 001	28 000	25%
28 001	55 000	38%	28 001	50 000	35%
55 001	75 000	41%	50 001		43%
>75 000		43%			

Note: Amounts in EUR.
Source: OECD Annual Tax Policy Reform Questionnaire.

Changes to allowances and tax credits

Italy also revised the structure of its tax credit system for employment, self-employment, and pension income. Tax credits were generally increased for lower- and middle-income earners while tax credits for higher income earners were reduced. The upper income threshold (i.e., income for which tax credits are reduced to zero) was lowered from EUR 55 000 (USD 65 050) to EUR 50 000.

Reform of the child tax credit

The PIT reform also replaced the child benefit tax credit and other benefits (e.g., child allowance) with a single, universal allowance ("*assegno unico e universale*"), which will become effective as of March 2022. The allowance includes a monthly cash-transfer, the amount of which is based on the economic situation of the household and calculated with the help of the Equivalent Economic Situation Indicator ("*Indicatore della Situazione Economica Equivalente*"). Parents with children under the age of 21 are eligible to receive the benefit. The universal allowance is generally more generous compared to previous arrangements, though it depends on the individual economic situation of the household. Notably, it also benefits households on low incomes who are not liable to PIT (which were previously excluded).

Source: OECD Annual Tax Policy Reform Questionnaire; IBFD (2022[3]); Panteghini and Pellegrino (2022[4]).'

3.1.4. Reforms narrowing PIT bases have continued in 2021

Many countries have continued to narrow their PIT bases. Overall, these measures are expected to reduce tax revenues. Of the countries undertaking PIT base reforms, 57 were base narrowing and nine were base broadening measures (Table 3.3), which generally follows trends observed in recent years. Most PIT base reforms introduced in 2021 or later were aimed at supporting individuals and families on low incomes who were often particularly hard hit by the economic impact of the pandemic. Several reforms also sought to reduce the tax burden on middle-income households with the intention of increasing household consumption and promoting economic recovery. Thirteen reforms involved increases in personal tax allowances, tax credits and tax brackets to support low-income earners and employment, while nine reforms were aimed at supporting children and other dependents. PIT base reforms also aimed at supporting the elderly, particularly those on low incomes. Five countries expanded the scope of their earned income tax credit (EITC) and other in-work benefits. Promoting economic recovery while alleviating the tax burden on low-and medium-income households was the predominant rationale behind many base narrowing tax provisions.

Table 3.3. Changes to personal income tax bases

	Base broadening	Base narrowing
	2021 or later	
Personal allowances, credits, tax brackets	ITA, NOR, GBR [2], URY [1,2]	ALB, BRA, CAN, CZE, FIN, IRL, ITA, LTU, LVA, NOR, POL, SWE, ZAF
Provisions targeted at low-income earners, EITCs and other in-work benefits		CAN, FIN, ITA, SWE [1], USA
Self-employed and unincorporated business		AUT, DEU, POL, MEX, TUR
Children and other dependents		AUT, BEL, BGR [1], CAN, CHE, CZE, FIN [1], ITA, POL
Elderly & disabled		CAN, MLT, POL, SWE
Employment	BEL, NLD, SWE	AUS, AUT, BEL, CAN, DEU, HUN, IRL, NLD, NOR
Environmental sustainability		ITA, BEL [1], CAN, FIN [1], MYS, SWE
Miscellaneous expenses, deductions, and credits	ESP, NOR	AUS, CAN, DEU, HUN, KOR LVA, SWE

Note: Temporary COVID-19 response measures are not included in the table.
1. Denotes a temporary PIT reform.
2. Denotes a new tax.
Source: OECD Annual Tax Policy Reform Questionnaire.

Many countries increased the generosity of their general PIT allowances and credits

In nine countries the basic tax allowance was increased to reduce the PIT burden and support the progressivity of the tax system. Increases were introduced in seven OECD and two non-OECD Inclusive Framework jurisdictions. In Poland, the basic allowance will be raised almost four-fold from PLN 8 000 (USD 2 072) to PLN 30 000 (USD 7 768), from 2022 onwards. Lithuania has indicated that it will increase its basic allowance from EUR 4 800 (USD 5677) to EUR 5 520 (USD 6529) from 2022 for people earning below the national average wage. For taxpayers whose income exceeds the national average wage the tax-free threshold of EUR 4 800 (USD 5677) continues to apply (IBFD, 2021[5]). Latvia increased its monthly basic allowance from EUR 300 (USD 355) to EUR 350 (USD 414) as from January 2022 onwards, while a further increase to EUR 500 (USD 591) will apply from July 2022 onwards. Norway increased its basic allowance from NOK 52 450 (USD 6 106) to NOK 58 250 (USD 6 781), ensuring that the allowance increased more than average growth in wages (KPMG, 2021[6]). In Finland, the basic allowance for municipal tax purposes was raised to EUR 3 740 (USD 4 423) from EUR 3 630

(USD 4 293). Brazil raised its monthly income tax-exempt threshold from BRL 1 904 (USD 35) to BRL 2 500 (USD 463) (IBFD, 2021[7]). In Albania, the basic allowance was increased from ALL 30 000 (USD 290) to ALL 40 000 (USD 386) as from 2022 onwards. In Prince Edward Island, Canada, the personal income tax exemption level was raised from CAD 10 500 (USD 8 374) to CAD 11 250 (USD 8 972) with effect in 2022.

In Canada, the Czech Republic and Ireland, general tax credits were expanded. Ireland announced that it will increase its Personal Tax Credit from EUR 1 650 (USD 1 952) to EUR 1 700 (USD 2 011) from 2022. The Canadian province of Prince Edward Island increased its low-income tax credit threshold from CAD 19 000 (USD 15 153) to CAD 20 000 (USD 15 951), for a tax credit of up to CAD 350 (USD 279) per person (with additional claims possible for those with a spouse and children), effective from 2022.

Tax brackets were shifted upwards in several countries in 2021. Ireland increased standard rate bands for all earners by EUR 1 500 (USD 1 774) from 35 300 (USD 41 750) to EUR 36 800 (USD 43 525) for single individuals and from EUR 44 300 (USD 52 395) to EUR 45 800 (USD 54 170) for married couples and civil partners with one earner. A tax rate of 20% applies below the threshold while a rate of 40% is levied above the threshold. Iceland introduced an annual adjustment factor applied to the tax-free threshold and tax brackets, which is determined by the yearly change in the Consumer Price Index plus a one percentage point increase to account for annual rises in productivity. Poland revised its band threshold upwards from PLN 85 528 (USD 22 147) to PLN 120 000 (USD 31 073) and from January 2022, income above PLN 120 000 will be taxed at a rate of 32% while income below is taxed at a rate of 12%. Albania increased the base of its second tax bracket, with the top PIT rate applying from ALL 200 000 (USD 1 930), up from ALL 150 000 (USD 1 450). Finland raised the thresholds for all its income tax brackets by EUR 1 100 (USD 1 300). The adjustments account for the general increase in the earnings level and is aimed at supporting sustained household purchasing power. Tax bands in South Africa were also adjusted upwards to account for inflation.

Several countries introduced PIT measures aimed at supporting particularly lower income households with children as well as promoting the compatibility of work and family life.

Several countries introduced PIT measures aimed at supporting families and children. In Austria, the child tax credit will be raised from EUR 1 500 (USD 1 774) to EUR 2 000 (USD 2 365) per child under the age of 18 from July 2022. Moreover, the child tax refund for single-earner and single-parent households was raised to EUR 350 (USD 414) (EUR 450 (532 USD) from 2023 onwards) and extended to people in partnerships. The Czech Republic increased the child tax credit from CZK 19 404 (USD 895) to CZK 22 320 (USD 1 030) for the second child and from CZK 24 204 (USD 1 117) to CZK 27 840 (USD 1 284) from the third child, taking effect retrospectively from January 2021. Poland introduced an additional tax relief for families with four or more children, which exempts income from certain sources (i.e., labour) from personal income tax up to PLN 85 528 (USD 22 146). In Canada, several measures were introduced throughout 2021 to support families and children. The province of Quebec enhanced the refundable tax credit for childcare expenses to align the costs of non-subsidised childcare services with the cost of subsidised services. The province of Newfoundland and Labrador introduced a Physical Activity Tax Credit, which provides a tax credit of up to CAD 2 000 (USD 1 595) per family for expenses related to physical activities, including for instance sport club registration or membership fees.

Several PIT measures were also aimed at reducing disincentives for second earners to participate in the labour market and at reconciling work and family life. Tax policies can play an important role in promoting gender equity and reducing income and wealth inequalities more broadly (Box 3.3). Italy introduced a major reform unifying its former child benefit tax credit and other minor benefits into one single, universal allowance (Box 3.2), with the explicit aim to strengthen second earner labour market participation. In Switzerland, deductions for external childcare for federal income tax purposes were increased from CHF 10 100 (USD 11 052) to CHF 25 000 (USD 27 357) in 2022. Finland raised the maximum tax credit for household expenses on domestic and care work in a two-year trial to assess the potential employment effects.

Box 3.3. Gender and taxation

Promoting gender equality, as reflected in the Universal Declaration of Human Rights and the Sustainable Development Goals, is a human rights objective for many governments, including in G20 and OECD countries (OECD, 2022[8]). Improving gender equality is not only an issue of fairness but can also produce a significant economic dividend. Working towards more inclusive economies in which women participate fully is important for economic growth and, in the context of the COVID-19 pandemic, will be crucial in ensuring an inclusive and robust recovery. Research shows that improving gender equality and reducing gender-based discrimination can generate substantial economic benefits, by increasing the stock of human capital, making labour and product markets more competitive, and increasing productivity.

Tax policy can contribute to gender equality and to governments' efforts to reduce inequalities. A growing body of research shows that even in tax systems that do not include explicit gender biases, other implicit biases exist due to the interaction of the tax system with differences in the nature and level of income earned by men and women, consumption decisions, the ownership of property and wealth, and the impact of different social expectations on male and female taxpayers.

Against this background, governments can act to improve the gender outcomes of taxation; removing overt biases and reconsidering tax settings that currently result in implicit gender biases; and evaluating avenues within the tax system to design and implement tax policy that promotes gender equality.

The first analysis of its kind

The report *Tax Policy and Gender Equality: A Stocktake of Country Approaches* (OECD, 2022[8]) is the first cross-country report to analyse national approaches to tax policy and gender outcomes, including assessments of explicit and implicit biases, tax policy reforms to improve gender equity, and policy processes and priorities. Covering 43 countries from the G20, the OECD and beyond, the report was prepared as part of the OECD's efforts to mainstream gender equality under the Indonesian G20 Presidency.

The report focuses on various aspects of tax policy design and implementation, on a cross-country basis. It explores the extent to which countries consider gender equality in tax policy development and tax administration, how they address explicit and implicit gender biases in their tax systems, and the availability and use of gender-disaggregated data. It analyses country perspectives on how and to what extent gender should be considered in the tax policy development process (including via gender budgeting). It also takes stock of the impact of the COVID-19 pandemic on gender equality in the tax system and highlights how countries consider gender outcomes in their tax responses to the pandemic.

Key findings and country priorities

The report finds that gender equality is an important consideration in tax policy design for most countries, and that about half of them have already implemented specific tax reforms to improve gender equity, most commonly in the taxation of personal income.

Although few countries noted examples of explicit bias in their tax system, more than half of the countries indicated that there was a risk of implicit bias. As with explicit biases, these implicit biases can either exacerbate or reduce gender inequalities already present in society and the examples noted by countries suggest a more nuanced policy response to gender bias in taxation is needed.

Most countries have access to gender-differentiated data for policy analysis, but access to data is concentrated on male and female incomes and labour market participation. Detailed data on consumption and on property and wealth ownership is less commonly available and was identified by several countries as a key data gap.

Finally, countries indicated that aspects of labour taxation were the key priority for future work to improve tax systems to increase gender equality. Identified policy areas include the impact of tax credits and allowances on gender equality, the taxation of second earners, the relationship between the progressivity of the tax system and gender equality, and the impact of social security contributions. A secondary priority is work on identifying the policy rationales and an assessment framework for considering the use of explicit biases to reduce gender inequality. Another common priority is exploring gender bias in the taxation of capital income and capital gains, notably in wealth and inheritance taxes.

Source: OECD (2022[8]).

Several countries significantly increased the generosity of their Earned Income Tax Credits and other in-work tax benefits

More countries introduced reforms to Earned Income Tax Credits (EITCs) and other in-work benefits compared to previous years. In-work benefit programmes typically involve tax reductions or cash transfers, which are conditional on labour market participation. The value of EITCs commonly depends on the recipient's earned income. Typically, the value of the credit increases gradually with income (phase-in) until it reaches the maximum credit amount (plateau). Beyond a certain earned income threshold (the phase-out threshold), the value of the credit is gradually reduced to zero. Programmes are typically means-tested and may be targeted at specific groups. When designed correctly, such measures have the potential to improve labour market participation and reduce poverty.

Canada, Finland, Italy, and the United States increased in-work tax credits to promote work incentives and provide financial support for low-income households. The United States raised the maximum credit amount for workers without qualifying children from USD 538 to USD 1 502. Moreover, certain eligibility criteria have been relaxed, including for instance limits on investment income, the allowance that applies to separated spouses claiming EITCs and for taxpayers with qualifying children who fail to meet certain identification requirements (IRS, 2022[9]). In Canada, the federal government increased its in-work tax credit by raising phase-in rates and phase-out thresholds, while also increasing phase-out rates. Finland increased its maximum earned income tax credit to EUR 1 930 (USD 2 283) from EUR 1 840 (USD 2 176) and raised its phase-in and phase-out rates. Italy reformed the structure of its earned income tax credit, generally increasing tax credits for low-income and medium-income taxpayers (Box 3.2).

A few countries introduced PIT base reforms for the self-employed and unincorporated businesses.

Austria, Poland and Türkiye reported PIT base reforms for the self-employed and unincorporated businesses, which generally reduced their tax burdens. In Austria, the percentage of profits that partnerships and the self-employed can claim as tax exempt was raised from 13% to 15% with effect from 2023 – this basic tax-free allowance can be claimed only on profits up to a value of EUR 30 000 (USD 35 482), i.e., a maximum EUR 3 900 (USD 4 615). Austria also introduced several new tax credits for investments. Poland enhanced PIT reliefs to support research and development (in parallel with changes to its CIT), including for instance an increase (of up to 200%) in the deduction of qualified costs for R&D centres and an increase (of up to 200%) in the deduction of qualified costs related to employing staff conducting R&D for all taxpayers. Poland also introduced a robotisation relief that allows for an additional deduction of up to 50% of eligible costs related to robotisation. Türkiye introduced a provision whereby social content creators (e.g. influencers) and app developers are subject to a 15% withholding tax (and not the personal income tax) if their earnings do not exceed the amount specified in the fourth income segment of the personal income tax return (IBFD, 2021[10]). Taxpayers previously liable to small business taxation were also exempt from income tax.

Several countries provided support for the elderly through their PIT regime

Malta, Poland, and Sweden introduced PIT measures to support the elderly, some of which also incentivise pensioners to stay active in the labour market. Supporting low-income older people continues to be an important policy rationale for age-related tax concessions. Latvia increased the monthly basic allowance for pensioners from EUR 300 (USD 355) to EUR 330 (USD 390) in January 2021, with a further raise to EUR 500 (USD 591) taking effect from July 2022 onwards. Similarly, Sweden increased the basic allowance for elderly people in 2022. In Estonia, the basic allowance for pensioners will be raised to the same level as the average-old age pension in 2023, making average old age pensions tax exempt. In Malta, pension income will no longer be counted as part of the PIT base between 2022 and 2026. This measure is intended to encourage pensioners to remain active in the labour market after reaching the age at which they can receive their pension. Poland also introduced a personal income tax exemption (up to PLN 85 528 (USD 22 146)) for people who continue working after reaching the statutory retirement age and do not take their retirement pension.

In Canada, PIT measures introduced for the elderly involved tax credits for care services and home improvements. The Canadian province of Quebec enhanced the refundable senior assistance tax credit targeting low-income seniors starting in 2021 and increased the generosity of the refundable tax credit for home-support services for seniors, effective from 2022. Ontario extended the temporary seniors' Home Safety Tax Credit for the tax year 2022, for renovations that improve safety and accessibility or help elderly people to be more functional or mobile at home.

Several countries have sought to facilitate employment in a changing work environment through employment-related tax provisions

Countries are supporting employers and employees to manage changing work environments and the transition to increased working-from-home. Ireland started allowing for the deduction of heat, electricity, and broadband expenses for home office days from 2022 onwards. In the Netherlands, employers may pay a tax-free "working from home" allowance of EUR 2 per day (USD 2.37). To simplify the regulation of temporary employment, Sweden reformed its rules governing the place of employment and temporary work, with expenses for temporary work and assignments in a different location now being tax deductible if the assignment lasts less than one month and the distance between the workplace and home is more than 50 kilometres. Germany allows taxpayers to fully depreciate computer hardware and standard business software in the year of acquisition instead of over a three-year period, taking effect from January 2021, retroactively. Austria introduced a non-taxable expense compensation for working from home of up to EUR 3 (USD 4) per day for a maximum of 100 days within a tax year, which will be in place until December 2023. Similarly, Canada simplified the rules for deducting home office expenses and increased the temporary flat rate to CAD 500 (USD 399) for the tax years 2021 and 2022 tax year.

Several countries reformed the tax provisions of employee share schemes. For employee share schemes in Australia, the termination of employment is no longer considered a taxable point, which aims at increasing the attractiveness of employee share plans. Germany clarified the tax rules that apply to shares and options that workers receive as part of their remuneration as employees of start-ups and SMEs. Germany also increased the income tax exemption threshold for employee share plans from EUR 360 (USD 426) to EUR 1 440 (USD 1 703) from July 2021. Norway, on the other hand, abolished the tax-free benefit for employees buying shares at a discount in the company they work in. Thereby, the benefit from the purchase of the shares (at a discount) is included in the tax base. At the same time, Norway also introduced a more favourable scheme for the taxation of options in start-ups, which is aimed at attracting talent and promoting entrepreneurship. Sweden reformed the eligibility criteria for the beneficial tax treatment of employee stock options (qualified employee stock options), which includes for instance a deferral of personal income taxes for the employee and social security contributions for the employer until the point of sale of the shares. From January 2022, these rules also apply to larger companies and board members (Baker McKenzie, 2022[11]).

Hungary introduced favourable tax provisions for young workers. From January 2022, Hungary exempts taxpayers below the age of 25 from PIT if their income falls below the average gross wage for a full-time employee in July of the preceding year. The reform is intended to increase employment of younger people and promote their financial independence (European Social Policy Network, 2021[12]).

Sweden introduced tax relief measures related to pensions, unemployment insurance and other work-related benefits. From July 2022, Sweden will increase the tax reduction for pension and social insurance benefits, including, for instance, sickness compensation. The tax reduction is greater for low incomes and falls as income increases up to a maximum of SEK 1 500 (USD 175). Sweden also introduced tax relief for unemployment insurance contributions, aimed at increasing insurance coverage.

PIT provisions encouraging environmental sustainability have become more common

Several countries have granted or expanded tax incentives for home renovations to support the environmental transition towards net zero greenhouse gas (GHG) emissions. Italy introduced and extended multiple tax credits for sustainable building renovations aimed at, for instance, increasing buildings' energy efficiency and seismic resilience. Finland temporarily increased the tax credit for household expenses to a maximum of EUR 3 500 (USD 4 140) (from EUR 2 250 (USD 2 661) for households moving from oil heating to more sustainable energy sources between 2022 and 2027.

PIT measures related to environmental sustainability also involved tax incentives for carbon-efficient transportation. Between 2021 and 2025, Belgium will grant a tax deduction of up to EUR 675 (USD 798) (this amount is reduced over the five-year period) for taxpayers installing an electric charging station in their homes. Malaysia announced that it will introduce a relief for expenses related to the purchase, rental, and related installation costs of electric vehicles of up to MYR 2 500 (USD 604) per tax year in 2022 and 2023. Finland granted tax provisions for hybrid vehicles and Sweden for low-emission vehicles and bicycles provided as an in-kind benefit by employers.

Several temporary PIT measures were introduced or extended in response to the COVID-19 pandemic

Some countries continued to provide temporary PIT tax relief to encourage employment. Sweden introduced a temporary in-work tax credit for 2021 and 2022, which intends to support middle-income households. For incomes between SEK 60 000 (USD 6 996) and SEK 240 000 (USD 27 983), the tax credit increases to a maximum amount of SEK 2 250 (USD 262). The credit is then phased out for incomes between SEK 300 000 (USD 34 979) and SEK 500 000 (USD 58 298) (Sveriges Riksdag, 2021[13]).

Countries also introduced a wide range of other measures aimed at supporting households and businesses. Germany introduced an exemption for bonuses of up to EUR 1 500 (USD 1 774) paid to employees during the COVID-19 pandemic (between March 2020 and March 2022). The government also prolonged tax deferrals and simplified procedures to reduce pre-payments for the self-employed. In Greece, private sector employees will be exempt from special solidarity surcharge for the tax year 2022. Latvia extended the deferral of personal income tax advance payments for the self-employed. Viet Nam exempted individuals and households located in areas affected by the COVID-19 pandemic from personal income tax and other taxes on income for the second and fourth quarter of 2021 (IBFD, 2021[14]). Australia exempted individual assistance support payments from the PIT base. Chile and Cabo Verde extended the deadlines for income tax return filing in 2022. Malaysia extended and increased several tax credits, including for instance for fees of self-study courses, medical expenses, and costs for childcare services. The province of Ontario, Canada, introduced a temporary Staycation Tax Credit for the 2022 tax year, for eligible accommodation expenses paid for by Ontario residents, which would also help the tourism and hospitality sectors. Quebec introduced a one-time cost of living allowance of CAD 200 (USD 160) per adult for eligible households. Korea introduced a temporary five percentage point rise in tax credits for donations made during 2021 to promote charitable giving.

Several countries continue to provide PIT relief to support families, particularly for those on low incomes. Hungary refunded PIT payments for families with children for the tax year 2021, capped at tax payments for income at the average annual wage. Ontario introduced a one-off 20% increase in the refundable income-tested tax credit that provides families with childcare support. Bulgaria introduced a temporary child tax relief granting a deduction of BGN 4 500 (USD 2 721) per child (up from BGN 200 (USD 121)) for the tax years 2021 and 2022 to support the income of families.

3.1.5. A few countries introduced measures which broadened PIT bases

Both Italy and Norway decreased their tax band thresholds for higher income earners while the Netherlands will abolish the possibility to average taxable income. Norway reduced the lower thresholds for its third and fourth bracket and adjusted the first and second tax brackets in line with average wage growth. A new top tax band was also added for income above NOK 2 000 000 (USD 232 828). Italy also reduced the tax band threshold for the fourth tax bracket from EUR 55 000 (USD 65 051) to EUR 50 000 (USD 59 137). With effect in 2023, the Netherlands will abolish the averaging scheme, which allowed taxpayers with significant income fluctuations to average their income over three consecutive years. The reform aims at simplifying the tax system and increasing tax compliance.

Spain and Norway amended the tax treatment of pension and welfare contributions while the Netherlands reformed PIT tax support for families. Spain lowered the maximum amount of annual contributions to qualifying pension plans that taxpayers can deduct from their net taxable income from EUR 2 000 (USD 2 365) to EUR 1 500 (USD 1 774), taking effect in 2022. Similarly, Norway amended the tax treatment of pension accounts, reducing the maximum tax-favoured amount of savings in individual pension accounts from NOK 40 000 (USD 4 657) to NOK 15 000 (USD 1 746). The reform will come into effect in January 2022 and is aimed at raising revenue and efficiency in the tax system. The Netherlands reduced the maximum income dependent combination tax credit by EUR 395 (USD 467), with the aim to partially fund free childcare. The tax credit, which is provided at a rate of 11.45% of taxable income, is aimed at supporting working single parents or the partner in a family with the lower income, conditional on children being below the age of 12 and the taxable income from employment exceeding EUR 4 993 (USD 6 240) (OECD, 2020[15]).

Other tax base broadening measures affected the highly skilled labour force in Belgium and the self-employed in the Netherlands. Belgium reformed its legal framework on the tax treatment of foreign (non-Belgian national or citizen) executives and researchers working for Belgian companies or entities with the intention of providing more legal certainty to expatriates and limiting the maximum duration of the special tax treatment regime to five years (this was previously indefinite). The regime allows taxpayers, subject to several eligibility criteria, to be considered as non-resident for income tax purposes and therefore to only be taxed on Belgian income sources, while living in Belgium and maintaining the centre of economic and personal activities (e.g., contribution to pension plans, real estate ownership) in another country. In the Netherlands, the tax deduction for the unincorporated self-employed will be gradually phased-out until 2030, by EUR 650 (USD 769) per year, from EUR 6 310 (USD 7 463) in 2022.

The United Kingdom and Uruguay introduced temporary PIT measures, which broadened the tax base and sought to address the increased funding needs following the COVID-19 pandemic. The

United Kingdom has frozen the Income Tax Personal Allowance and the Basic Rate Limit (i.e., income tax band liable to a 20% tax rate) for a four-year period at 2021-22 levels. Uruguay introduced a temporary income tax to fund measures mitigating the economic impact of the COVID-19 pandemic (IBFD, 2021[16]). Between May and June 2020, a temporary income tax was implemented, similar to a measure passed in 2020 to finance an emergency COVID-19 solidarity fund, which applied a progressive tax to income derived from employment in the public sector (exempting employees working in the healthcare sector), and from pension income. The applicable tax rate was determined by a five-band income tax rate schedule, with rates between 0% (for income below UYU 120 000 (USD 2 755)) and 20% (for income over UYU 180 000 (USD 4 133)).

3.1.6. Changes to personal capital income taxation have been limited

There were two countries reporting changes to their capital income tax rates, while eight countries introduced changes to their capital income tax bases. Changes in tax rates involved rate increases, both of which were aimed at strengthening the neutrality between different economic and investment activities. Tax base broadening measures were predominantly introduced in the area of capital gains taxes while some countries also introduced changes to the taxation of interest income, pensions, and other types of capital income.

The Netherlands announced a reform of the capital income tax system. Following a ruling by the Dutch Supreme Court ("*Hoge Raad der Nederlanden*") in December 2021, which deemed the taxation of income from savings and investments based on presumptive returns incompatible with the European Convention on Human Rights, the government announced that it would revise the current tax method (IBFD, 2022[17]). In the Netherlands, income-producing assets are assigned an assumed yield, which increases with the size of the asset base, regardless of the actual gain or loss of the respective asset. The capital income is then taxed at a rate of 31%. With the implementation of the tax reform, capital income taxation will be based on actual returns from 2025, abolishing the current system. During the transition period, the exemption threshold (applied to the asset base) will be raised from EUR 50 650 (USD 59 906) in 2022 to EUR 80 000 (USD 94 619) in 2023. As part of the reform, the method to estimate the economic value of rental property will also be revised to broaden the tax base.

Brazil and Norway increased the tax rates on certain capital income, to promote neutrality in the tax system. As part of a comprehensive income tax reform, Brazil revised the taxation of income earned in financial markets – for example, gains from stock exchange transactions and income from investment funds – to simplify the tax system and strengthen the neutrality between different types of investments. A key component of the reform was the introduction of a 15% withholding tax on dividend distribution (which previously went untaxed) (IBFD, 2021[7]). Norway also increased the tax rate on dividends to reduce the difference in marginal tax rates between shareholder income and wages, and thereby reduce the incentives for income shifting. In Norway, the ordinary yield of dividends is taxed at the company level while gains above the ordinary yield are taxed at the shareholder level at a flat rate of 22% multiplied by the adjustment factor. The reform raised the adjustment factor from 1.44 to 1.6, increasing the effective dividend tax rate from 31.68% (100 x 22% x 1.44) to 35.2% (100 x 22% x 1.6) (IBFD, 2021[18]).

Table 3.4. Changes to tax rates on personal capital income

	Rate increase	Rate decrease
	2021 or later	2021 or later
Dividend or interest income/equity or bond investment	BRA, NOR	

Note: No tax rate changes were implemented in the area of capital gains, rental income, employee share acquisition deductions and the tax treatment of pensions and savings account.
Source: OECD Annual Tax Policy Reform Questionnaire.

Capital tax base broadening measures were introduced in Nigeria, New Zealand, and the United Kingdom. New Zealand introduced several base broadening reforms with the aim of reducing investors' demand for existing residential property and thereby improving housing market accessibility. The deductibility of mortgage interest on debt to purchase rental residential property will be phased out between October 2021 and March 2025. The government also extended the bright-line test, by which realised gains from the sale of residential property within ten years of its acquisition are subject to income tax. While New Zealand does not apply a tax on capital gains, the bright-line test effectively allows the taxation of gains on residential property (with certain exemptions for newly constructed buildings). Nigeria broadened its capital income tax base by removing certain tax exemptions on sales of shares. From January 2022, a 10% capital gains tax is applied to gains from the sale of shares above a threshold of NGN 100 million (USD 278 700)[8] generated in any 12 consecutive months. The capital gains tax does not apply if the proceeds of the sale are reinvested in shares in the same or another Nigerian company within the same tax year. In the United Kingdom, the maximum lifetime allowance for pension contributions (the limit at which the tax benefits of pensions can be maintained) will be kept at its nominal level of GBP 1 073 100 (USD 1 475 934) (its 2021-22 level) until the tax year 2025-2026. Given inflation expectations, an unchanged nominal limit amounts to a decline in real terms and hence a broadening of the capital tax base of pension income.

Austria and Hungary also broadened their tax bases by introducing taxes on income from crypto currencies. The taxation of income derived from crypto has become a growing area of policy focus (see Box 3.12), with current capital income tax reforms aiming predominantly at promoting neutrality between crypto and other asset classes while also raising tax revenue. Hungary introduced a 15% flat tax on income generated from some crypto currency transactions (equivalent to the 15% capital gains tax). A taxable event is triggered if the asset leaves the digital space when realised or if crypto assets are exchanged in a standard currency or for any other good. The costs related to the crypto transaction and acquisition are deductible from the tax base, while income from crypto mining or exchanges of crypto assets are not included in the tax base (IBFD, 2021[19]). Austria also introduced a tax on income from crypto transactions by which income derived from crypto currency sales is subject to a flat rate of 27.5% (equivalent to the capital gains tax rates). Income from crypto currencies includes the current income generated from crypto currencies as well as income derived from increases in realised values (IBFD, 2021[20]).The tax applies from March 2022 onwards for all sales of crypto currency after February 2021. Given the growing importance of crypto currency taxation, the OECD is also developing a global tax transparency framework, to facilitate the automatic exchange of tax information on transactions in crypto-assets in a standardised manner (see OECD (2022[21])).

Belgium, Bulgaria, and Malta introduced measures in 2021 that have narrowed their capital tax bases. Bulgaria abolished the taxation of interest income on bank deposits (and their branches), where banks are established in an EU Member State or in another State that is party to the Agreement within the European Economic Area. The reform responded to the continuing decline in interest rates on bank deposits in recent years, with corresponding declines in tax revenue. In this context, the administrative burden on banks and taxpayers was deemed disproportionate to the revenue potential of the tax. To promote the growth of start-ups, Belgium doubled the share capital eligible to the tax shelter regulation from EUR 250 000 (USD 295 685) to EUR 500 000 (USD 591 370) and from EUR 500 000 to EUR 1 million (USD 1.25 million) for companies carrying out activities in markets with growth potential. The tax shelter regulation for start-ups provides a tax reduction for private investors on a share of their investment in a start-up (between 25% and 45% of the invested amount). Malta introduced a capital gains tax exemption for the first EUR 750 000 (USD 937 500) of the property transfer value for certain properties subject to eligibility criteria.

Table 3.5. Changes to personal capital income tax bases

	Base broadening	Base narrowing
	2021 or later	2021 or later
Dividend or interest income/equity or bond investment	NZL	BGR, BEL
Capital gains	AUT, HUN, NGA, NZL	MLT
Rental income		
Tax treatment of pensions and savings account	GBR	
Employee share acquisition deductions		

Source: OECD Annual Tax Policy Reform Questionnaire.

3.1.7. SSC reforms introduced by countries continued to reduce contributions

Several countries have introduced SCC reforms, several of which involved temporary SCC reductions in response to the COVID-19 pandemic. To provide financial relief to households and companies, and to promote the economic recovery, several countries have reduced the SSCs paid by workers and employers for a discrete period, both through SCC rate reductions and base narrowing measures. Several countries have increased SSCs permanently to respond to demographic and fiscal challenges.

Permanent changes to SSC rates have been limited while several countries introduced temporary cuts in response to the COVID-19 pandemic

Three countries introduced permanent SSC rate reforms in 2021, including two rate increases and two rate reductions. Germany increased the additional contribution rate to statutory long-term care insurance by 0.1 p.p. to 0.35% for both employees and the self-employed without children, starting from January 2022. This increase reflects the continuation of a trend of rising contribution rates in response to an ageing population and a higher expected dependency ratio. Hungary's SSC measures moved in the opposite direction, as employer SSCs were reduced from 15.5% to 13% in January 2022, having already been cut by 2 p.p. in July 2020. The 1.5% training fund contribution levied on employers was also phased out in 2022. In Norway, SSCs for employees were reduced from 8.2% to 8.0% and for the self-employed from 11.4% to 11.2%.

Italy and Sweden introduced temporary SSC rate cuts to alleviate financial pressure on companies and private households and promote economic recovery amid the COVID-19 pandemic. Italy has temporarily reduced SSCs for incomes below EUR 35 000 (USD 41 396) from 9.19% to 8.39% for the tax year 2022, with the aim of promoting economic recovery and supporting lower-income households. Sweden further decreased SSCs paid by employers for employees aged between 19 and 23 years old. The temporary reduction was first introduced in January 2021 and the augmented reductions will apply between June 2022 and August 2022. The reform intends to promote the employment of young workers as well as to support companies in the sectors that were significantly affected by the pandemic.

Table 3.6. Changes to social security contribution rates

	Rate increase	Rate decrease
	2021 or later	2021 or later
Employers SSCs	JPN	HUN, SWE[1]
Employees SSCs	DEU, JPN	ITA[1], NOR
Self-employed	DEU	
Payroll taxes		

Note: 1. Denotes a temporary SSC reform.
Source: OECD Annual Tax Policy Reform Questionnaire.

Most countries have continued to narrow their SSC bases, often in response to the economic repercussions of the COVID-19 pandemic

Bulgaria and Norway increased the minimum threshold for SSCs, reducing their countries' SSC bases. Bulgaria increased its minimum income threshold for SSCs from BGN 7 800 (USD 4 716) to BGN 8 520 (USD 5 152). The new threshold also applies to self-employed workers and registered farmers and tobacco producers (previously minimum threshold of BGN 5 040 (USD 3 048)). Similarly, in Norway, the minimum income limit was raised from NOK 59 650 (USD 6 944) to NOK 64 650 (USD 7 526) for the tax year 2022.

Some countries introduced SSC measures to promote education and employment, which also narrowed SSC bases. Argentina introduced an employer SSC deduction for new hires participating in vocational training in knowledge-intensive sectors (IBFD, 2021[22]), to promote skills development in these areas. In Australia, to encourage employers to help workers transition to new employment opportunities, employers are exempted from the fringe benefits tax, if benefits are provided for retraining and reskilling to redundant, or soon to be redundant, employees. In Manitoba, Canada the exemption threshold for the Health and Post-Secondary Education Tax Levy on employers was raised from CAD 1.5 million (USD 1.2 million) to CAD 1.75 million (USD 1.4 million) of total annual remuneration paid to employees. The threshold below which employers pay a reduced rate was also increased from CAD 3 million (USD 2.4 million) to CAD 3.5 million (USD 2.8 million), effective from January 2022.

Several base narrowing measures were extended or introduced in response to the COVID-19 pandemic. Sweden continued the tax-exempt status of certain benefits-in-kind offered by employers for their employees, such as free parking and certain gifts to encourage consumption. Argentina extended the 95% reduction in SCCs for employers providing health care services, first introduced in March 2020 until June 2022 (IBFD, 2022[23]). Uruguay introduced a temporary exemption from SSCs for employers in the catering and hospitality sector between July 2021 and October 2021.

Three countries broadened their SSC bases. In Bulgaria, the maximum social security income base was increased from BGN 36 000 (USD 21 768) to BGN 40 800 (USD 24 671), applicable to both employer and employee contributions from April 2022. Latvia raised its SSCs income ceiling from EUR 62 800 (USD 74 276) to EUR 78 100 (USD 92 372), effective from January 2022. Romania introduced a health contribution for pensioners with pension income above RON 04 000 (USD 961).

Table 3.7. Changes to social security contribution and payroll tax bases

	Base broadening	Base narrowing
	2021 or later	2021 or later
Employers SSCs	BGR	ARG, AUS, CAN
Employees SSCs	BGR, LVA	BGR, NOR, SWE[1], URY[1]
Self-employed		BGR, BEL

Note: 1. Denotes a temporary reform. The narrowing of the payroll tax base in the United States was the result of changes to the employee retention credit and the deferral of social security taxes originally introduced as part of the CARES Act.
Source: OECD Annual Tax Policy Reform Questionnaire.

3.2. Corporate income taxes and other corporate taxes

The declining trend in statutory corporate income tax (CIT) rates is widespread and continuing, leading to further convergence in CIT rates across countries. In addition, many countries have continued to increase the generosity of their corporate tax incentives to stimulate investment and innovation, particularly in the field of environmental sustainability. Regarding international taxation, efforts to protect CIT bases against corporate tax avoidance have continued with the adoption of measures in line with the OECD/G20 Base Erosion and Profit Shifting (BEPS) project. A major break-through has been reached with more than 135 jurisdictions worldwide having joined a new two-pillar plan to reform the international taxation rules and ensure that multinational enterprises (MNEs) pay a fair share of tax wherever they operate and generate their profits.

3.2.1. Trends in CIT revenues have varied across countries

The ratios of CIT to GDP and CIT revenues as a share of total tax revenues continue to vary substantially across Inclusive Framework jurisdictions. CIT revenues ranged from 0.7% of GDP in Latvia to 4.7% of GDP in Australia in 2020 (Figure 3.5). As a share of total tax revenues, CIT ranged from 2.3% of total taxation in Latvia to 32.3% of total tax revenues in Indonesia (Figure 3.6). Multiple factors can explain differences in revenues from CIT including statutory CIT rates, the breadth of the CIT base, the degree to which firms are incorporated, the phase in the economic cycle and the degree of cyclicality of the corporate tax system, as well as countries' reliance on other taxes. These factors likely contributed to the large variations in revenues observed between 2000 and 2020 in several countries, including Norway, Finland, and Luxembourg. Figure 3.6 shows that CIT tends to represent a larger share of revenue in countries with significant natural resources and in emerging economies. In the case of emerging economies, total tax revenues are generally lower as a percentage of GDP and personal income tax revenues tend to play a smaller role than the CIT.

Figure 3.5. Corporate income tax revenues as a share of GDP, 2000 and 2020

Share of GDP (%)

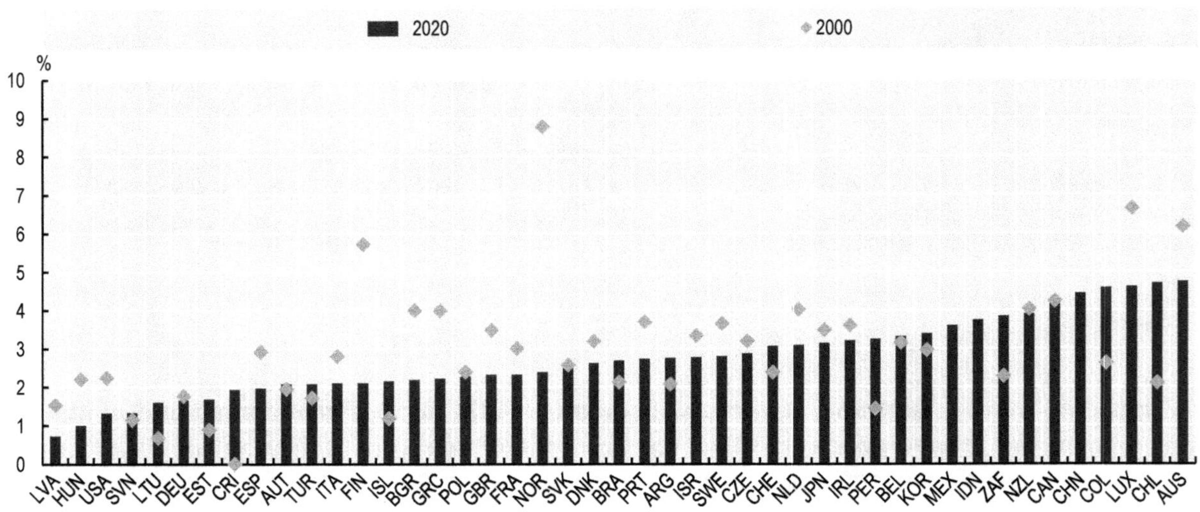

Note: Data for CIT revenues in 2000 were not available for China (People's Republic of), Indonesia and Mexico. 2019 data were used for Australia, China (People's Republic of), Greece, Indonesia, New Zealand, and South Africa where 2020 were not yet available.
Source: OECD Global Revenue Statistics Database.

StatLink https://stat.link/vsog69

Figure 3.6. Corporate income tax revenues as a share of total tax revenues, 2000 and 2020

Share of total tax revenues (%)

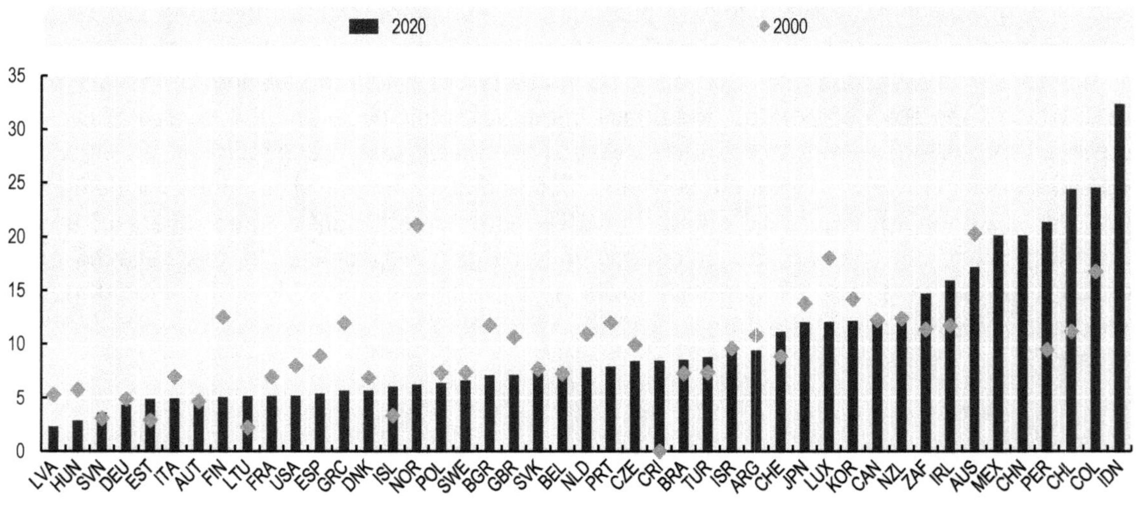

Note: Data for CIT revenues in 2000 were not available for China (People's Republic of), Indonesia and Mexico. 2019 data were used for Australia, China (People's Republic of), Greece, Indonesia, New Zealand, and South Africa where 2020 were not yet available.
Source: OECD Global Revenue Statistics Database.

StatLink https://stat.link/p52jn4

CIT revenues as a share of GDP and as a share of total tax revenues have fallen between 2019 and 2020 as a result of the COVID-19 pandemic. For the 35 OECD countries for which 2020 data are available,[9] the average value of corporate income tax revenues as a share of GDP fell from 3.0% in 2019 to 2.6% in 2020 (Figure 3.7). Similarly, the average value of corporate income tax revenues as a share of total tax revenues fell from 9.4% to 8.5%. This is the most significant reduction seen since the global financial crisis of 2008 and the average corporate income tax revenues as a share of GDP are now lower than the previous lows seen in 2009 and 2010 in the aftermath of that crisis.

Figure 3.7. Evolution of the average combined statutory CIT rate and average CIT revenues in OECD countries, 2000-2020

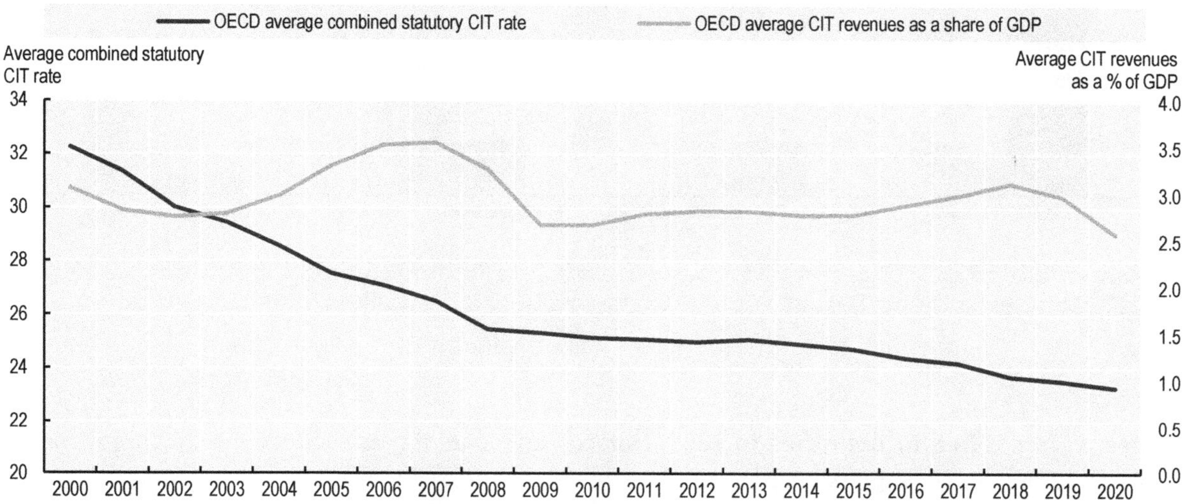

Note: Combined statutory CIT rates refer to central and sub-central statutory CIT rates.
Source: OECD Revenue Statistics Database and OECD Tax Database.

StatLink https://stat.link/ckqion

3.2.2. *There has been a steady and widespread decline in corporate income tax rates*

Standard corporate income tax rates

The decline in CIT rates has been a steady and widespread trend. Figure 3.8 shows the changes in the distribution of CIT rates between 2000 and 2021 across the 51 countries for which data are available[10] and highlights major shifts in the CIT landscape. In 2021, there were only three countries with CIT rates above 30%, compared to 28 in 2000. Meanwhile, the number of countries with CIT rates below 20% increased from three in 2000 to 20 in 2021. Overall, in the OECD, the average combined (central and sub-central) CIT rate has declined from 32.2% in 2000 to 23.3% in 2021.

Figure 3.8. The distribution of combined statutory CIT rates, 2000 and 2021

Number of countries

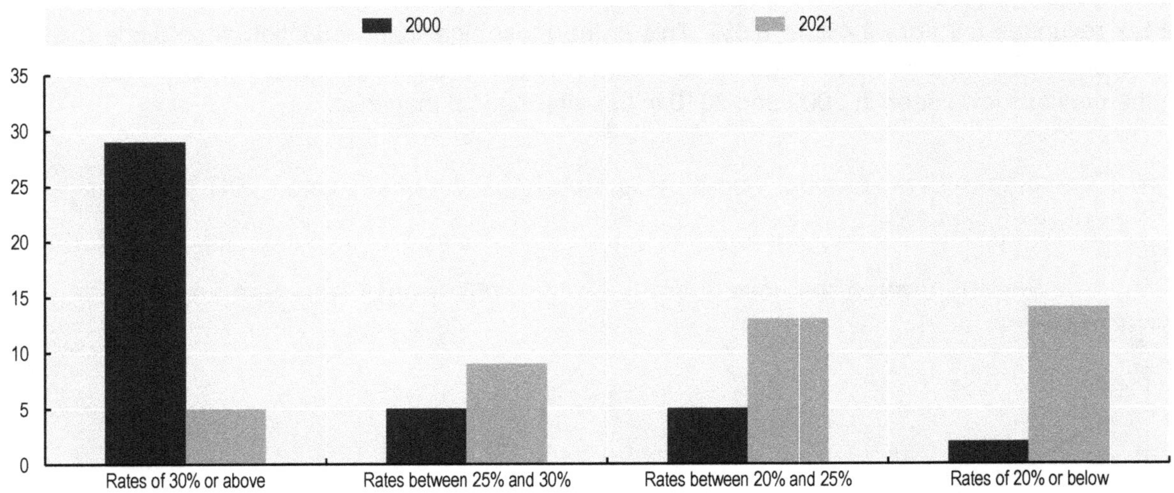

Note: Countries covered include OECD member jurisdictions plus Argentina, China (People's Republic of), Indonesia, and South Africa.
Source: OECD Corporate Tax Statistics Database, OECD Tax Database and OECD Annual Tax Policy Reform Questionnaire.

StatLink https://stat.link/1cpsed

CIT rates were cut in four countries in 2021. Notably, only one of these reductions was in response to the COVID-19 pandemic, suggesting that countries have in general identified other approaches to support recovery from the COVID-19 pandemic. Reductions in combined CIT rates were introduced in Colombia, France, Sweden, and Switzerland. In Colombia, the standard CIT rate was lowered to 31% as part of the government's 2019 legislation to progressively reduce CIT rates (from 33% in 2019 to 30% by 2022). France also lowered its standard CIT rate, to 27.5% for companies with an annual turnover exceeding EUR 250 million (USD 296 million) and to 26.5% for companies with an annual turnover lower than EUR 250 million. These cuts were part of a previously legislated CIT rate reduction, which is expected to progressively bring the CIT rate down to 25% by 2022. Sweden implemented a permanent cut in its standard CIT rate from 21.4% to 20.6% as a part of the government's response to the COVID-19 pandemic. In Switzerland, 11 of 26 cantons made small reductions to their corporate tax rates. The largest were made by those cantons with the highest rates, namely the Cantons of Valais (-1.6%), Zurich (-1.5%) and Bern (-0.6%). These cuts reduced the combined corporate income tax rate in Switzerland from 21.15% in 2020 to 19.7% in 2021.[11]

However, three countries – Colombia, Türkiye and the United Arab Emirates – announced increases in their headline CIT rates. At the end of Q3 of 2021, Colombia enacted a Law under its Social Investment Act to increase the corporate income tax rate to 35% from 1 January 2022 – a notable change of direction from the planned decreases described above. In addition, this Law imposed a 3% surtax on the taxable income of financial institutions earning more than 120 000 tax units (approximately USD 1.1 million) from 2022 to 2025 (their total income tax rate will therefore rise to 38% for these institutions). Following an increase to 22% for the fiscal years 2018-2020, Türkiye further raised its corporate tax rate to 25% in 2021.[12, 13]

The United Arab Emirates announced an historic change to their tax system, with the introduction of a generalised Corporate Income Tax from mid-2023. The tax will operate as a federal corporate tax on business profits and will enter into force from Q3 2023. The proposed CIT rate of 9% on taxable income above AED 375 000 (USD 100 000) is expected to apply to all business activities in the UAE, while a different rate (yet to be confirmed) is envisaged to apply to large multinationals that generate consolidated global revenues above EUR 750 million (USD 887 million). Exceptions to this new CIT are planned for the extraction of natural resources, which is already subject to taxation at an Emirate-level.

Table 3.8. Changes in corporate income tax rates

	Rate increase		Rate decrease	
	2020	2021 or later	2020	2021 or later
Standard CIT rate		(ARE), (COL), TUR	BEL, CAN, FRA, GRC, IDN	CAN[1], CHE, COL, FRA, SWE, (TUR)
SME CIT rate			CAN, HUN, NLD, SVK	BRN, CAN[1], CPV, HUN
Patent box/IP regime rate			CHE	ITA

Note: Countries in brackets have only announced reforms.
1. The CIT rate decrease in Canada for 2021 applies to zero-emission technology manufacturing profits. The CIT rate decrease will reduce the general corporate income tax rate and small business income tax rate on eligible profits to 7.5% (from 15%) and to 4.5% (from 9%), respectively, for taxation years beginning after 2021 and before 2029.
Source: OECD Annual Tax Policy Reform Questionnaire.

CIT rates for Small and Medium-Sized Enterprises

Reduced CIT rates for small and medium-sized enterprises (SMEs) are common across the Inclusive Framework jurisdictions that responded to the Tax Policy Reforms questionnaire. Several countries provide reduced CIT rates for SMEs, although the design of these reduced tax rates varies significantly. Some countries apply lower tax rates on the first tranche(s) of profits, regardless of total income levels; some have reduced CIT rates for corporations with income below a certain level; and others determine eligibility for small business tax rates based on non-income criteria (e.g., turnover or assets) instead of, or in addition to, income criteria.

Several countries changed the CIT rates for SMEs between 2020 and 2021 (and beyond). To reduce the tax burden for SMEs, Hungary decreased its small business tax from 12% to 11% in 2021 and by another percentage point to 10% in January 2022. In addition, the maximum local business tax for SMEs with income of less than HUF 4 billion (USD 12.99 million) has been set to 1% for 2021 and 2022. Canada introduced a 50% reduction to business income taxes for companies that manufacture zero-emission technologies from the start of 2022. This reduction in the general corporate income tax rate and small business income tax rate on eligible profits to 7.5% (from 15%) and to 4.5% (from 9%), respectively, will be gradually phased out from 2029 with elimination envisaged by 2032. Moreover, reductions to SME CIT rates at the provincial and territorial level (Northwest Territories, Prince Edward Island, Quebec, Yukon) took effect in early 2021.

A small number of developing countries also temporarily reduced the effective SME CIT rate that businesses need to pay due to the COVID-19 impact on economic activity. Brunei Darussalam, for instance, will provide a 50% CIT discount for the tax year 2022, targeting sectors that were particularly affected by the pandemic such as tourism, hospitality (including hotels and lodging houses), restaurants and cafes, and air and water transportation. In Cabo Verde, SMEs whose sales were particularly impacted by the pandemic were exempt from paying the islands' Unified Special Tax of 4% in 2021.

Other business taxes

Germany and Mexico reformed their tax frameworks for some individuals and unincorporated businesses. Germany modernised its corporate income tax law affecting unincorporated businesses. With the introduction of the reform in January 2022, partnerships have the option to be treated as corporate entities for tax purposes, in which case their income is liable to corporate income tax (15.825%) and local trade tax (7% to 17% varying by municipality) instead of being taxed under the federal personal income tax regime (up to 45% plus solidarity surcharge, church tax and SSCs) as a pass-through entity. The tax reform, thereby, reduces the discrepancy in tax treatments and aims to improve the tax framework especially for small and medium-sized partnerships and family businesses. In introducing the comprehensive 2022 tax reform (Box 3.4), Mexico established a new tax regime ("Simplified Reliance Regime") which aims to facilitate the tax payment process and simplify the taxation of small and medium-sized companies and individuals carrying out business activities with an income below MNX 35 million (USD 1.7 million). The new regime applies a progressive rate structure taxing gross income (without allowing for any deduction) below MNX 300 000 (USD 14 798) at a tax rate of 1% and income exceeding this threshold at a rate 2.5%, with effect in 2022.

Box 3.4. The 2022 Mexican Tax Reform

Both chambers of the Mexican Congress approved the 2022 Tax Bill in November 2021. Its provisions entered into effect on 1 January 2022. The comprehensive reform aims to promote competitiveness and economic growth, facilitate voluntary compliance, broaden the tax base, and prevent tax base eroding activities. It concentrates on measures adopted within the OECD/G20 BEPS Project and on activities in relation to the digital economy.

Changes to the Federal tax code

Implemented changes to the federal tax code attempt to address tax evasion and avoidance behaviour and improve compliance by individuals and corporates. For instance, a change in tax residency to a low tax jurisdiction will no longer result in the automatic loss of Mexican tax residency. Voluntary compliance will be strengthened by implementing specific voluntary disclosure programmes following international best practices. Assessments by the tax authority of the effective control of entities and the transfer of business assets have been reinforced. Tax inspectors will also be allowed to question business reasons in relation to the tax-free treatment of mergers and spin-offs within five years prior and subsequent to the transaction. Additional measures combat criminal tax offences such as tax fraud or activities related to hydrocarbon black markets.

Income tax law changes

To support economic recovery and encourage investment, a preferential tax regime has been established for individuals and companies. Apart from eliminating formalities, annual incomes of individuals below USD 173 000 are subject to a maximum tax rate of 2.5%, which is levied on gross income without allowing for any deduction. Companies incorporated by individuals with incomes below USD 1.7 million profit from preferential depreciation rates. Other amendments include new reporting requirements for the transfer of shares among residents abroad, the limitation of corporate restructurings at tax cost for companies residing in Mexico, and alternative range-adjustment methodologies in transfer pricing.

Mexico City tax reform

Digital events whose transmissions are made live in the territory of Mexico City and require payments to access the event broadcasts are charged with an 8% tax on public shows. Moreover, individuals or legal entities that facilitate activities related to the delivery or reception of food, grocery, or other types of merchandise through online platforms (e.g., promotion, intermediation, administration) are subject to a 2% exploitation tax ("*aprovechamiento*") on gross commissions or fees charged. The Mexico City Tax Code has also been amended to now include a 5% tax on lodging services.

Taxation of the digital economy and technology-driven tax audits

Mexico joined the OECD Two-Pillar framework in July 2021 together with more than 120 other jurisdictions and together with more 135 other jurisdictions agreed to the *Statement on a Two-Pillar Solution to Address the Tax Challenges Arising from the Digitalisation of the Economy* in October 2021. Further work is ongoing in line with the international agreements reached regarding the global tax reform around Pillars One and Two, which comprise the reallocation of taxing rights with respect to business profits and the establishment of a minimum global income tax for MNEs.

Source: OECD Tax Policy Reforms Questionnaire; Baker McKenzie (2022[24]).

Taxes on the financial sector

A relatively small number of countries that responded to the tax policy reforms questionnaire impose taxes on their financial sector. Financial sector taxes gained attention in the aftermath of the global financial crisis – they are generally collected on top of ordinary corporate taxes and can be applied on different bases including bank deposits, capital assets and risk-weighted assets. As described earlier in this section, Colombia will introduce a 3% surcharge on the taxable income of financial institutions that earn more than 120 000 tax units (approximately USD 1.1 million) for the period of 2022-2025. The Swedish government also announced an additional tax on the financial sector, which is scheduled to take effect in 2023.

Intellectual property regimes

Intellectual property (IP) regimes allow income that results from the exploitation of IP to be taxed at a lower rate than income that is derived from other sources. IP regimes have been introduced in an increasing number of countries, and these usually involve a significant reduction in the tax rate applicable to IP-related income compared to the tax rate that would otherwise apply (Figure 3.9). While reduced tax rates provide an indication of the generosity of the tax instrument, they do not allow a direct comparison of the generosity of IP regimes, as they do not incorporate differences in the tax base.

There were a limited number of changes to IP regimes in 2021. In its 2021-2022 budget, the Australian government announced that it would introduce a patent box that would tax corporate income derived from eligible Australian patents in the medical and biotechnology sectors, at a concessional rate of 17%, effective from 1 July 2022. Australia generally taxes profits generated by patents at the headline corporate rate – 30% for large businesses and 25% for SMEs. As of 2022, Italy will change its IP regime into an expenditure-based tax provision whereby research and development (R&D) expenditures related to qualifying IP assets will benefit from a 110% increase in their deductible value. Qualifying IP assets will include software protected by copyright; patents, business and technical industrial know how; and other legally protected IP, such as designs and models. This new tax incentive can be used alongside Italy's existing R&D tax credit. The province of Quebec in Canada introduced an IP regime that allows corporations commercialising a qualified intellectual property asset developed in Quebec to benefit from an effective tax rate of 2% on the qualified portion of its taxable income attributable to that qualified intellectual property asset – the general provincial corporate income tax rate being 11.5%. This regime has replaced the previously established deduction for Innovative Manufacturing firms.

Figure 3.9. Reduced CIT rates under selected non-harmful intellectual property regimes, 2020

Tax rate

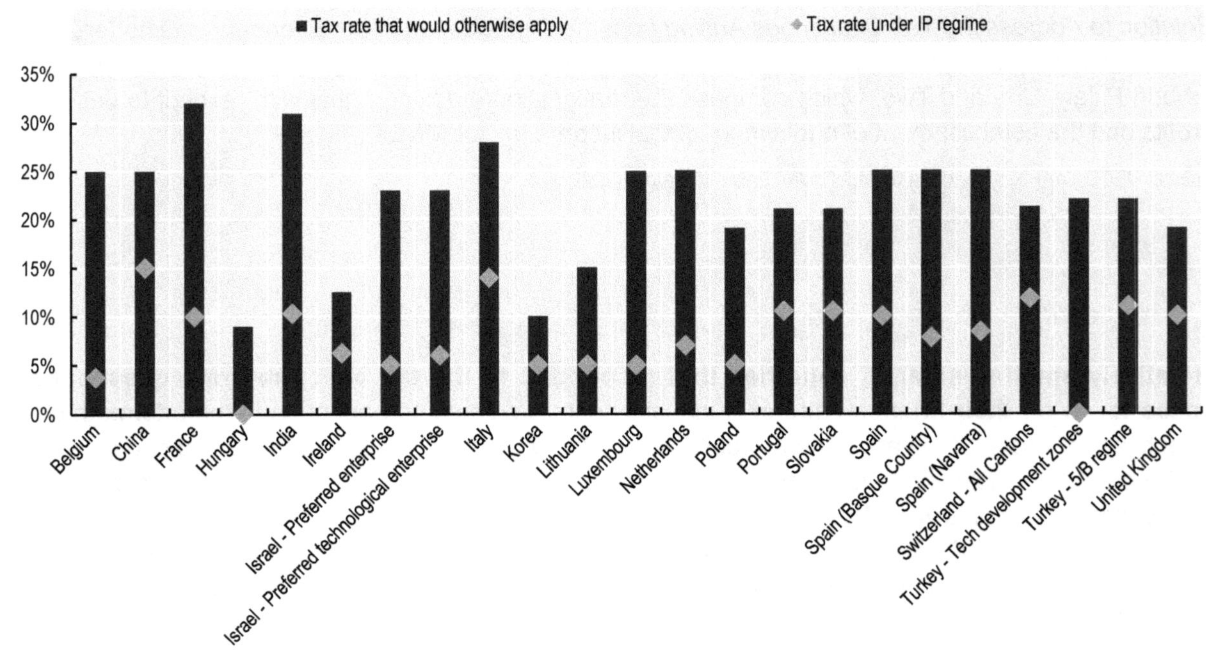

Note: This chart refers to reduced tax rates applicable in 2020. The status of the regimes covered refer to the results of the Forum of Harmful Tax Practices peer review as of November 2020. For Switzerland, the rates displayed represent the combined effective tax rate applicable in case of maximum relief at the cantonal level accounting for all tax liabilities for an investment in the city of Zurich in 2020 and include the effect of the patent box and the general limitation rules of tax relief that cap the amount of relief firms can obtain from the use of tax instruments at the cantonal level. Depending on the canton, the applicable rates under the schemes in 2020 vary between 9.1% and 13.9% while the rates that would otherwise apply vary between 11.9% and 21.6%.
Source: Corporate Tax Statistics Database.

StatLink https://stat.link/i8zd50

Several IP regimes were reviewed in 2021 as part of the BEPS Action 5 peer review processes. BEPS Action 5 of the OECD/G20 BEPS project aims to address harmful tax practices, including IP regimes where certain substance requirements are not met. In the past, IP regimes could be designed in a way that allowed taxpayers to access preferential tax treatment by strategically locating the IP asset. The modified nexus approach under Action 5 requires that substantial economic activity be undertaken by the taxpayer to benefit from relief. Substantial activity is proxied through the nexus ratio that makes the amount of income eligible for benefits under the IP regime proportional to the amount of expenditures undertaken by the taxpayer to develop the IP. Since Action 5 is a minimum standard, all members of the Inclusive Framework are committed to its implementation and are subject to the peer review process. This has led to countries aligning their regimes to be compliant with the minimum standard (OECD, 2015[25]). The Forum on Harmful Tax Practices (FHTP) conducts peer reviews of preferential tax regimes (IP and non-IP regimes). Among the nine regimes reviewed in November 2021, five were found to be non-harmful or non-harmful in their amended version, one is in the process of being amended, two have been abolished and one is still under review.

Marginal effective tax rates

Most countries have CIT base narrowing provisions that lower companies' effective tax burdens. Corporate tax systems differ across jurisdictions regarding the provisions that affect their tax base. Forward looking effective tax rates (ETRs), as calculated by the OECD (OECD, 2021[26]) capture information on corporate tax rates and bases as well as other relevant provisions within a single framework, providing a basis to compare corporate tax systems across jurisdictions. In particular, effective marginal tax rates (EMTRs) measure the extent to which taxation increases the pre-tax rate of return required by investors to break even. This indicator is used to analyse how taxes affect the incentive to expand existing investments given a fixed location.

EMTRs can diverge considerably from statutory tax rates. EMTRs will be lower than the statutory corporate income tax rate when fiscal depreciation is generous compared with the true cost of economic depreciation or if there are other significant base narrowing provisions. On the other hand, if tax depreciation does not cover the full cost of economic depreciation, effective taxation will be higher. The EMTRs reported in Figure 3.10 show the effects of fiscal depreciation and other allowances and deductions, such as allowances for corporate equity, half-year conventions and inventory valuation methods. These CIT base narrowing provisions lower corporate EMTRs compared to statutory CIT rates in most countries, reflecting their positive effects on businesses' incentives to expand investment. Certain CIT base narrowing provisions, in particular accelerated depreciation rules (e.g., Austria, Chile, Germany, New Zealand, United Kingdom) can reduce EMTRs considerably, which may mean that EMTRs end up reaching negative values. In addition to the impacts of these changes in the tax base, in 2020, EMTRs also fell in Colombia, India and Indonesia, among others, due to decreases in the statutory CIT rate.

Figure 3.10. Composite marginal effective tax rates, 2020

Tax rate

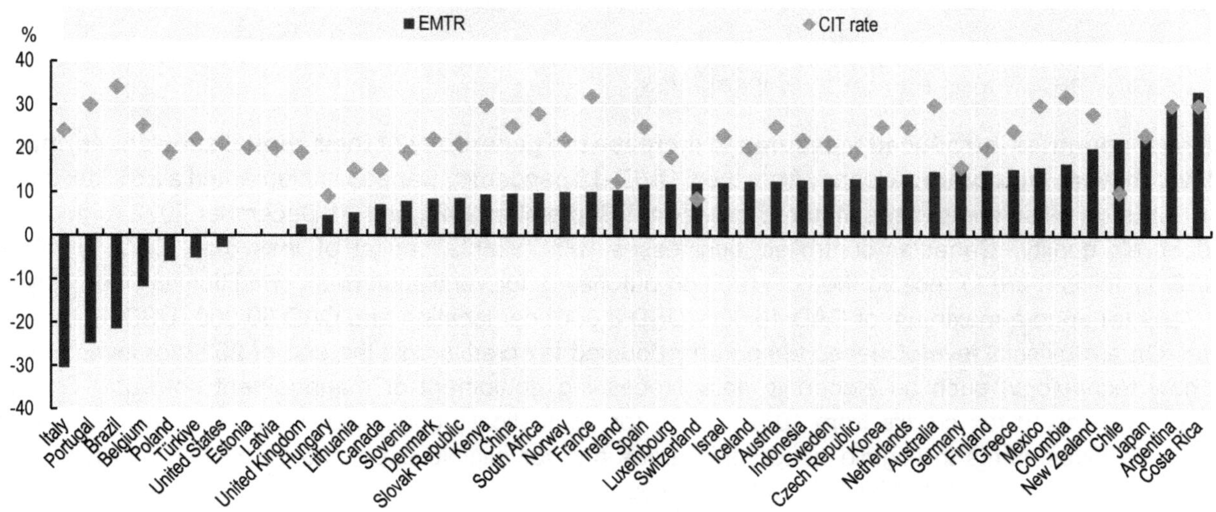

Note: The results are based on the macroeconomic scenario with constant 3% interest and 1% inflation rates. The composite Effective Marginal Tax Rate (EMTR) is constructed as a weighted average across finance- and asset-specific EMTRs. It is a synthetic tax policy indicator measuring the extent to which taxation increases the pre-tax rate of return required by investors to break even on their investment. This indicator is used to analyse how taxes affect the incentive to expand existing investments given a fixed location (along the intensive margin).
Source: OECD Corporate Tax Statistics Database.

StatLink https://stat.link/1xnucv

Countries have generally increased the generosity of their tax incentives through tax reforms affecting CIT bases. Several countries have increased the generosity of their CIT incentives to stimulate investment, innovation, and environmental sustainability (Table 3.9). These measures will contribute to further reducing corporate EMTRs. Tax incentives to stimulate investments are a widely used instrument and show notable differences across OECD countries as shown in Box 3.5.

Table 3.9. Changes to corporate tax bases

	Base broadening		Base narrowing	
	2020	2021 or later	2020	2021 or later
Capital allowances and general incentives		NGA	AUS, CHL, DEU, FIN, ITA	CAN, GBR, MUS, POL
Environmentally related tax incentives	ITA		CAN, ISL, ITA, SVK, USA	CAN, IRL, MYS
R&D tax incentives and patent box regimes			IRL, ITA, SVK	AUS, ESP, FIN, ISL, ITA, JPN, MUS, NLD, NZL, POL, SWE
SME-related tax base changes			HUN, POL, SVK	CAN, DEU, JPN
Other business tax incentives				
Loss carryforward and carryback provisions			FRA, SVK	FRA, HUN
Notional interest deductions			ITA	ITA

Note: Countries in brackets have only announced reforms. Italy appears in both the base narrowing and broadening categories for the impact of environmentally related tax incentives for 2020 as a result of measures such as its tax on plastics (broadening) and incentives implemented to encourage the green transition (narrowing). See Chapter 2 of OECD (2021[27]) for more detail.
Source: OECD Annual Tax Policy Reform Questionnaire.

Capital allowances and general incentives

Several countries introduced measures to increase the generosity of their capital allowances, many of which were temporary. A legacy from the COVID-19 pandemic, Canada implemented a 25% tax credit for SMEs on eligible expenses incurred between 1 September 2021 and 31 December 2022 to improve indoor air quality. Canadian-controlled businesses with taxable capital of less than CAD 15 million (USD 12 million) are to receive the tax credit on purchases for ventilation or air conditioning (if employed in Canada) up to a maximum of CAD 10 000 (USD 8 000) per location and CAD 50 000 (USD 40 000) in total. On a provincial level, Quebec temporarily doubled tax credits until the end of 2022 for investments in new technology, such as electronic data processing equipment or management software. Ontario temporarily raised tax credits from 10% to 20% for domestically controlled private businesses making qualifying investments in eligible geographic areas and for eligible expenditures between CAD 50 000 (USD 40 000) and CAD 500 000 (USD 400 000) during the period from 24 March 2021 to 1 January 2023.[14] Poland aims to enhance its industrial transformation by introducing a supplementary tax deduction of up to 50% for businesses investing in robotics. Tax relief is available to all businesses and related to costs incurred from purchasing, for example, robots, peripheral devices, remote management devices and training services. To support investment, the United Kingdom implemented an upfront super-deduction of 130% for investments in plant and machinery that are taxed at the standard rate and a 50% first-year allowance for investments that qualify for a special tax rate, running for two years as of Q2 of 2021.

A limited number of jurisdictions introduced more generous capital allowance schemes to foster investments in green technology and the digital transition. To promote environmental sustainability and energy efficiency, Ireland extended the existing Accelerated Capital Allowance Scheme for Gas Vehicles and Refuelling Equipment to 31 December 2024, which allows taxpayers to deduct the full cost of expenditure from taxable profits in the year of purchase and to include hydrogen-powered vehicles and refuelling equipment. At the same time, fossil fuel equipment was disqualified for eligibility to the Accelerated Capital Allowances Scheme for Energy Efficient Equipment. In 2020 and 2021, Canada expanded its immediate expensing measures to include more types of clean energy equipment and zero-emission vehicles. Effective in 2021, Quebec introduced a synergy capital tax credit, which provides a 30% tax credit for investments by SMEs in green technology, information technology, life sciences, innovation manufacturing, and artificial intelligence. In October 2021, Malaysia introduced an investment tax allowance of up to 100% for a maximum period of 10 years on qualifying capital expenditures that promote environmental sustainability or support R&D investments. Malaysia also expanded its green investment and income tax exemption schemes to include rainwater-harvesting projects. In July 2021, Mauritius introduced the possibility of deducting from corporate income twice the expenses incurred for specialised software and operating systems during the respective income year. As of 2022, in contrast, Nigeria started to limit capital allowances that can be claimed by companies on qualifying expenditure used in generating tax-exempt income with the aim to make the tax system more equitable.

R&D and innovation tax incentives

Many countries incentivise business investment in R&D through tax incentives. The number of OECD countries offering tax relief for R&D expenditures increased from 20 OECD countries in 2000 to 34 of 38 OECD countries in 2021. As shown in Figure 3.11, the average implied marginal rate of R&D tax subsidy has markedly increased across OECD countries since the year 2000, with implied subsidies being typically larger on average for SMEs due to targeted preferential tax treatment towards these smaller businesses. Rising R&D tax subsidy rates reflect the introduction of new R&D tax incentives and the increasing generosity of existing R&D tax relief provisions over time. Since 2013, the level of implied subsidies has tended to stabilise, but it increased in 2020 through the expansion or enhancement of tax relief measures in certain cases in response to the COVID-19 pandemic (see below).

Figure 3.11. Aggregate trends of implied marginal tax subsidy rates on R&D expenditure, 2000-2021

Unweighted averages, 1-B-Index, OECD countries, all firms

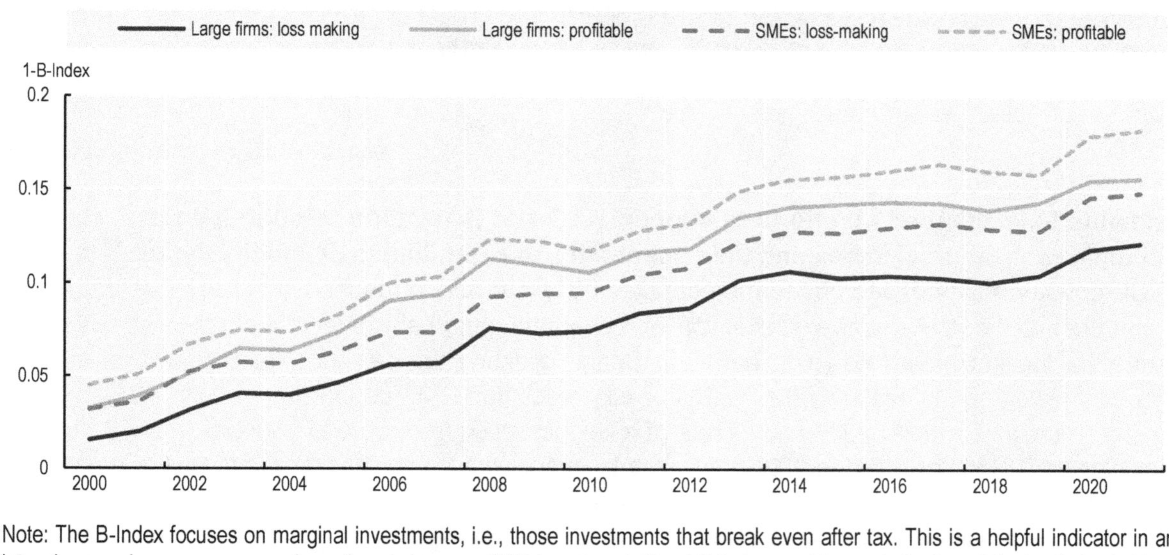

Note: The B-Index focuses on marginal investments, i.e., those investments that break even after tax. This is a helpful indicator in analysing intensive margin responses, e.g., incentives to increase R&D investment. The 1-B-Index provides an indication of the implied subsidy on a one unit of additional investment. More information on the B-Index methodology can be found at http://www.oecd.org/sti/b-index.pdf.
Source: OECD R&D Tax Incentive Database.

StatLink https://stat.link/1w4nyh

There are notable differences in the implied tax subsidy rates on R&D expenditures for large, profitable firms across countries and years (Figure 3.12). In 2021, R&D tax incentives for marginal investments were particularly generous for large, profitable firms in Chile, France, and the Slovak Republic, with the largest increases in generosity compared to 2010 (among countries offering tax support) observed in Chile, Colombia, and Greece. The ranking changes for other firm types, e.g., for SMEs, whereby Colombia, Iceland and the Slovak Republic offered the greatest support to profitable SMEs in 2021.

Figure 3.12. Implied marginal tax subsidy rates on R&D expenditures, 2010, 2020 and 2021

1-B-Index, large profitable firms, OECD countries

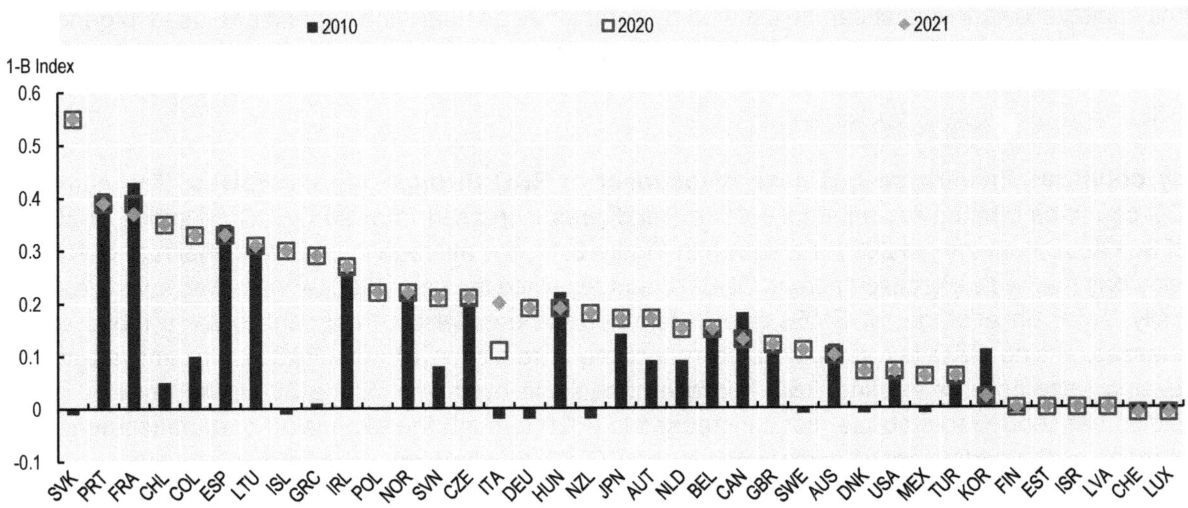

Note: The B-Index focuses on marginal investments, i.e., those investments that break even after tax and is a helpful indicator in analysing intensive margin responses, e.g., incentives to increase R&D investment. 1-B-Index provides an indication of the implied subsidy on a one unit of additional investment. To analyse discrete choices, e.g., where to locate R&D investment, effective average tax rates for R&D can be accessed in OECD Corporate Tax Statistics (González Cabral, Appelt and Hanappi, 2021). Tax incentives captured in this chart only refer to national R&D tax incentives on expenditure and therefore does not include R&D tax incentives provided by sub-national jurisdictions.
Source: OECD R&D Tax Incentive Database.

StatLink https://stat.link/saz836

Governments have stepped up efforts to support R&D and innovation through the tax system by introducing new measures, increasing their generosity, or extending their validity period.[15] In 2021, one OECD country (Finland) and one IF member country (Mauritius) introduced new tax provisions. Eight OECD countries and one IF member jurisdiction increased the generosity of their tax incentives, either via an increase in the incentive rate (e.g., Italy and Spain) or lifting the cap that limits tax benefits (e.g., Australia and Sweden). In Finland, the R&D tax allowance for R&D cooperation costs with research organisations was extended to 2027 and its rate of relief increased from 50% to 150% as of 2022. In Italy, the tax credit for R&D introduced in 2020 that aims to encourage the green transition and investment in innovative technology was extended to 2022. The credit rates and ceiling that bounded the amount of qualifying R&D expenditure for activities related to R&D, green transition, or industry 4.0 have also been increased. Mauritius has introduced a 100% tax allowance for the R&D expenditures of manufacturing firms related to market research and product development for the African market.

Poland introduced a tax reform that significantly expanded tax relief for R&D and innovation. This reform includes a number of different measures aimed at encouraging greater investment in R&D. One of these measures is an increase in the R&D tax allowance for R&D centres to 200% of qualifying costs (except for patent-related costs), and an increase in the allowance on labour costs of employees conducting R&D to 200% for all companies eligible for the R&D tax relief. Provisions also include the possibility to simultaneously use the patent box and the R&D tax allowance. Another relief measure, dedicated to taxpayers who incur losses or whose income in a tax year is lower than the qualified R&D costs, reduces the advance payment of personal income taxes for innovative employees.

Some countries have taken steps to expand support to SMEs and young firms, and to foster collaboration amongst different-sized firms. Germany has introduced a provision that defers taxation of employee stock options until their sale, the termination of contract or 12 years after assignment to boost their attractiveness and retain and incentivise a skilled workforce. To incentivise collaboration between large enterprises and start-ups, Japan has extended its Open Innovation Tax Incentive that provides a tax deduction equal to 25% of the amount invested in start-up companies for two additional years and eased the criteria to benefit for relief. The minimum period firms are required to hold shares in a start-up to claim relief was reduced from five to three years, while the length of time start-ups need to have been established has been extended from 10 to 15 years.

Beyond R&D, some countries have sought to promote the acquisition or commercialisation of intellectual property. As discussed, beforehand, Italy has changed its intellectual property regime into an expenditure-based tax provision linked to the expenses of qualifying IP assets. Poland has also introduced tax relief for prototypes for expenditures connected with the trial production or placing of products in the market as a way of promoting commercialisation in innovative sectors. Mauritius has implemented a 100% tax allowance for expenditures incurred from the acquisition of patents for firms in the biotechnology, medical, and pharmaceutical sector.

Loss carryforward and carryback provisions

Loss carryforward and carryback tax provisions were introduced in a few countries to support businesses throughout the COVID-19 pandemic and in the recovery. France allowed loss carrybacks up to a limit equal to first-time deficits incurred from the start of Q3 of 2020 to the end of Q2 of 2021. If eligible, these losses could be applied to profits from the previous three tax years. Hungary introduced a loss carryforward scheme on the income tax of energy suppliers, with 2021 as the first year of eligibility.

Notional interest deductions

The Italian allowance for corporate equity (ACE) was extended and increased in 2021 to support investment and increase firm resilience following the COVID-19 pandemic. The allowance had previously been reintroduced in 2019. The Italian ACE, which allows for a notional interest deduction to be applied to the CIT base up to EUR 5 million (USD 5.9 million), was exceptionally set at 15% (formerly at 1.3%) where it is related to capital injections introduced during 2021. The available tax deductions can also be granted as a tax credit.

Box 3.5. Investment Tax Incentives

Building an Investment Tax Incentives Database

The OECD has constructed an Investment Tax Incentives database, which compiles granular details on CIT incentives for investment. The database, which currently covers 36 developing and emerging economies, presents quantitative and qualitative information collected on investment tax incentives is classified according to three dimensions: design features, eligibility conditions and their legal basis.

Preliminary results

The data reveal that tax exemptions are the most widely used CIT instrument across the 36 countries and identifies notable differences between the incentives used within and outside of Special Economic Zones (SEZs). In 80% of countries covered, at least one tax incentive supports an area related to the Sustainable Development Goals.

Around two-thirds of the countries studied have at least one incentive allowing investors to fully exempt their income from corporate tax temporarily, while one-quarter of countries grant at least one permanent tax exemption on some types of income. In these countries, most full tax exemptions are clustered in SEZs, where their median application length is ten years, versus the six-year median application period outside the zones.

Another common type of investment tax incentive that countries offer is tax allowance schemes, which usually target capital expenditures like machinery and equipment but may also relate to current expenditures. Around two thirds of the countries in the database have at least one tax allowance scheme for investors, and those schemes tend to operate outside SEZs.

Although sector and eligibility conditions vary widely among countries, nearly any sector can benefit from tax incentives. Few countries specify sector conditions narrowly, i.e., limiting tax relief to a small set of sub-sectors. In these cases, they often target sub-sectors of high economic importance to the country as measured in terms of their exposure to exports.

Countries also use tax incentives to target sustainable development goal objectives laid out by the United Nations, such as boosting exports and employment creation. Over half the countries in the database use tax incentives designed to increase exports, and over one-third use incentives to create employment and improve job quality.

Typically, investment tax incentives are introduced by many different laws and governed by several departments. They might be found in income tax laws, investment laws, or SEZ laws and be administered and monitored through the ministries of finance and economy, the investment promotion agency, and SEZ authorities.

The paper cautioned that "such complexities and overlapping responsibilities can result in limited transparency and accountability [and] may reduce the effectiveness of investment tax incentives and can increase discretionary and profit-shifting behaviours."

Source: Celani, Dressler and Wermelinger (2022[28]).

3.2.3. Historic multilateral agreement reached to address the tax challenges arising from the digitalisation of the economy

Efforts to address the tax challenges arising from digitalisation reached an historical moment in 2021 after 137 Inclusive Framework members agreed to a two-pillar solution to address the tax challenges of the digitalisation of the economy. Digitalisation has led to the emergence of new business models and these changes have put pressure on some of the key principles underlying the international tax system. The OECD/G20 Inclusive Framework, which has more than 140 members, all participating on an equal footing, was mandated to provide a solution to these challenges. The Two Pillar solution, which has been agreed by 137 jurisdictions representing more than 95% of global GDP, is the outcome of negotiations co-ordinated by the OECD over the last decade. Under the agreement, more than USD 125 billion of profits from around 100 of the world's largest and most profitable MNEs will be reallocated to countries worldwide, and will introduce a global minimum tax set at an effective rate of 15%.

Pillar One would offer market jurisdictions new taxing rights over MNEs, whether or not they have a physical presence in their jurisdiction. Pillar One will ensure a fairer distribution of profits and taxing rights among countries with respect to the largest and most profitable multinational enterprises. It will re-allocate some taxing rights over MNEs from their home countries to the markets where they have business activities and earn profits, regardless of whether firms have a physical presence there. Specifically, multinational enterprises with global sales above EUR 20 billion and profitability above 10% – that can be considered as the winners of globalisation - will be covered by the new rules, with 25% of profit above the 10% threshold to be reallocated to market jurisdictions. The agreement to re-allocate profit under Pillar One includes a commitment to the removal and standstill of unilateral measures, including Digital Services Taxes (DSTs). Pillar One also includes features to ensure dispute prevention and dispute resolution to address any risk of double taxation, but with an elective mechanism for some low-capacity countries.

Pillar Two provides a minimum 15% tax on corporate profits, and puts multilaterally agreed limits on tax competition. Pillar Two introduces a global minimum corporate tax rate set at an effective rate of 15%. The new minimum tax rate will apply to companies with revenue above EUR 750 million and is estimated to generate around USD 150 billion in additional global tax revenues annually. Tax incentives provided to spur substantial economic activity will be accommodated through a carve-out. Pillar Two also protects the right of developing countries to tax certain base-eroding payments (like interest and royalties) when they are not taxed up to the minimum rate of 9%, through a "Subject to tax rule" (STTR).

Since the agreement in October 2021, further progress has been made towards implementing the Two Pillar solution. In December 2021, the Pillar Two Model GloBE rules were released and detailed technical guidelines on the application and operation of the rules was agreed and released in March 2022. Ongoing public consultations are also taking place on the Pillar One building blocks.

In addition, progress has been made on the issue of the repeal and standstill of unilateral measures. Following the Agreement on the two-pillar solution in October 2021, a joint statement from the United States and Austria, France, Italy, Spain, and the United Kingdom, laid out a plan for the roll back of DSTs in those countries and threatened retaliatory tariff once the Pillar One rules are implemented. On 22 November 2021, a joint statement by the US Treasury and Türkiye announced that Türkiye had agreed to the same terms.

3.2.4. The challenge of reducing tax avoidance continues through the wider OECD/G20 BEPS programme

Further progress on the implementation of the OECD/G20 BEPS package was made in 2021. The OECD/G20 BEPS package, which includes 15 Actions aimed at addressing tax planning strategies that artificially shift profits to low or no-tax jurisdictions, was delivered in October 2015. The BEPS package sets out a variety of measures, including four minimum standards (Actions 5, 6, 13 and 14), common approaches that will facilitate the convergence of national practices, and guidance drawing on best practices. Countries are carrying out the implementation of the BEPS package through the Inclusive Framework (IF) on BEPS, which currently brings together 141 jurisdictions.

As of March 2022, the provisions of the Multilateral Instrument to Implement Tax Treaty Related Measures to Prevent BEPS (MLI) had taken effect for approximately 880 tax agreements. The MLI, concluded by over 100 jurisdictions in November 2016, allows jurisdictions to implement measures to strengthen existing tax treaties and protect governments against tax avoidance strategies that inappropriately use tax treaties to artificially shift profits to low or no-tax jurisdictions. The MLI includes measures against hybrid mismatch arrangements (Action 2), treaty abuse (Action 6), a strengthened definition of permanent establishment (Action 7) and measures to make mutual agreement procedures (MAP) more effective (Action 14). The MLI entered into force on 1 July 2018 and its provisions started to take effect from 1 January 2019. As of March 2022, the MLI covered 99 jurisdictions and 71 jurisdictions had deposited their instrument of ratification, acceptance, or approval. Overall, it covers more than 1 800 bilateral tax agreements, which will be modified by the MLI once its provisions take effect for each of these agreements. More jurisdictions are expected to deposit their instrument of ratification, acceptance, or approval of the MLI in the remainder of 2022.

As one of the four minimum standards, BEPS Action 6 identified treaty abuse, and in particular treaty shopping, as one of the principal sources of BEPS concerns. Treaty shopping typically involves the attempt by a person to access indirectly the benefits of a tax agreement between two jurisdictions without being a resident of one of those jurisdictions. To address this issue, all members of the IF have committed to implementing the BEPS Action 6 minimum standard and participate in annual peer reviews to monitor its accurate implementation. The fourth peer review report, which was released in March 2022, shows that members of the Inclusive Framework are respecting their commitment to implement the minimum standard on treaty shopping. It further demonstrates that the MLI has been the tool used by most jurisdictions that have begun implementing the BEPS Action 6 minimum standard, and that the MLI has continued to significantly expand the implementation of the minimum standard for the jurisdictions that have ratified it. The impact and coverage of the MLI are expected to rapidly increase as jurisdictions continue their ratifications and as other jurisdictions with large tax treaty networks consider joining it.

In line with Action 13, automatic exchanges of country-by-country (CbC) reports have increased notably. Action 13 requires the ultimate parent entity of an MNE group to file a CbC report in its jurisdiction, providing information (on turnover, profits, employees, taxes paid, etc.) for each of the jurisdictions in which it operates. The tax administration of the country where the ultimate parent entity is a tax resident will then exchange this data with the tax authorities of other countries. As of March 2022, there were over 3 000 bilateral exchange relationships activated with respect to jurisdictions committed to exchanging CbC reports (for more information see Box 3.6).

Action 14, which deals with mutual agreement procedures (MAP), has also seen significant progress. Action 14 aims to improve mechanisms to resolve tax treaty-related disputes to make them more effective. The MAP peer review process is conducted in two stages. Under Stage 1, the implementation of the Action 14 minimum standard is evaluated by Inclusive Framework members. Stage 2 monitors the implementation of any recommendations resulting from the Stage 1 peer reviews. The Stage 2 peer review monitoring reports of the BEPS Action 14 minimum standard evaluate the progress made by Brunei Darussalam, Curaçao, Guernsey, Isle of Man, Jersey, Monaco, San Marino, and Serbia in implementing recommendations resulting from their Stage 1 peer review. They consider any developments in the period 1 April 2019 – 31 December 2020 and build on the MAP statistics for 2016-2020. The Multilateral Instrument was signed by Curaçao, Guernsey, Isle of Man, Jersey, Monaco, San Marino, and Serbia. It has already been ratified by all these countries, which brings a substantial number of their treaties in line with the Action 14 minimum standard. Brunei Darussalam, Curaçao, Guernsey, Isle of Man, Jersey, Monaco, and San Marino now have a documented bilateral notification/consultation process that they apply in cases where an objection is considered as being not justified by their competent authority. Curaçao, Guernsey, Isle of Man, Jersey, and Serbia closed MAP cases within the pursued average time of 24 months, whereas the remaining jurisdictions had no MAP experience. Brunei Darussalam, Curaçao, Guernsey, Isle of Man, Monaco, and San Marino ensure that MAP agreements can always be implemented notwithstanding domestic time limits. All the concerned jurisdictions have issued or updated their MAP guidance. The OECD will continue to publish Stage 2 peer review reports in batches in accordance with the Action 14 peer review assessment schedule. To date, 82 Stage 1 peer review reports and 69 follow-up Stage 2 peer monitoring reports have been published.

Box 3.6. BEPS Action 13: Automatic exchanges of country-by-country (CbC) reporting

The lack of high-quality data on MNEs' global activities has been a significant weakness in assessing BEPS risks, making it difficult for tax administrations, for instance, to carry out audits and assess transfer pricing activities within company groups. Action 13 of the OECD/G20 BEPS package, one of the four BEPS minimum standards, addresses this limitation by providing for an annual automatic exchange of CbC reports, which contain information of MNEs in scope (>EUR 750 million of consolidated group revenue) on their allocation of income, taxes and business activities on a jurisdiction level (OECD, 2015[29]).

CbC Mechanism

The automatic exchange of CbC reporting between jurisdictions is based on the multilateral Convention on Mutual Administrative Assistance in Tax Matters, which requires Competent Authorities to mutually agree on the scope of the exchange and the procedures to comply with. Subsequently, separate competent authority agreements set forth procedures necessary for exchanging CbC reports. These reports are prepared by the reporting entity of an MNE group in scope and exchanged annually between the tax authorities of the jurisdiction of tax residence of that entity and the tax authorities of all jurisdictions in which the MNE group operates. To facilitate the exchange of CbC reports between jurisdictions, the OECD provides a standardised electronic format, the CbCR XML Schema.

Outcomes

The first automatic exchanges of CbC reports took place in June 2018. As of March 2022, over 3 000 bilateral exchange relationships have been activated. These include exchanges between 92 signatories to the CbC Multilateral Competent Authority Agreement, between EU member states under EU Council Directive 2016/881/EU and between signatories to bilateral competent authority agreements under Double Tax Conventions or Tax Information Exchange Agreements, including 41 bilateral agreements with the United States. Anonymised statistics, which are aggregated at the level of the tax jurisdictions where MNEs operate, are shared by tax authorities with the OECD and regularly published within OECD Corporate Tax Statistics (OECD, 2021[26]). The publications support the analysis of corporate income tax policy in general, and of BEPS. The CbC reports also assist tax administrations in assessing their exposure to tax avoidance risks.

Next steps

The implementation of the standard continues across the world and regular guidance has been issued to aid that process. Since 2017, CbC implementation by jurisdictions has also been subject to annual peer reviews by the OECD. Including more jurisdictions every year, the peer review process assesses the domestic legal framework, the exchange of information framework, and confidentiality and appropriate use of CbC reports. This will help to further increase the usefulness of CbC reporting for tax authorities.

Beyond BEPS minimum standards

Beyond the BEPS minimum standards, BEPS Actions 2, 3 and 4 have been adopted by a growing number of countries. These actions include common approaches to neutralising hybrid mismatches (Action 2) and to limiting excessive interest deductions (Action 4) as well as best practices in the design of effective controlled foreign company (CFC) rules (Action 3).

Following the EU Council's adoption of BEPS Actions 2, 3, and 4, several EU countries completed the implementation of the Anti-Tax-Avoidance Directive (ATAD) in national legislation. Germany implemented and adjusted the rules on exit taxation and hybrid mismatch prevention retroactively as of 1 January 2020. Both tax provisions together with a reform of CFC rules in compliance with ATAD Articles 7 and 8 entered into force on 1 January 2022. In a separate Act, Germany also enacted stricter rules related to the deduction of work-related expenses connected to low-tax jurisdictions, tighter withholding tax measures and restricting measures in relation to profit distributions and sales of shares.[16] Effective as of 1 January 2022, Ireland completed the transposition of the ATAD by introducing anti-reverse hybrid rules and an interest limitation rule in its Finance Act 2021. Poland introduced additional measures to counteract aggressive tax planning in relation to CFC rules by extending the definition of a controlled foreign entity. Changes to Poland's CFC rules also cover the modification of current CFC premises (i.e., value of assets such as shares, real estate, intangible assets) by extending the catalogue of passive revenues or by adding new premises to prove the existence of a CFC.

Further progress has also been made outside the EU. Ukraine implemented Action 3 of the OECD/G20 BEPS Action Plan by levying corporate income tax on the adjusted profit of a CFC owned by a controlling legal entity who is a tax resident in the Ukraine, with the tax due to come into effect on 1 January 2022.

Actions 8 to 10 contain transfer pricing guidance to ensure that transfer pricing outcomes are in line with value creation in relation to intangibles and other high-risk transactions. Through this work, the OECD Transfer Pricing Guidelines (Guidelines) have been modernised, and a new edition was published in July 2017. In June 2018, guidance on the application of the transactional profit split method and additional guidance addressed to tax administrations on the application of the approach on hard-to-value intangibles were approved and incorporated into the Guidelines. The recently published 2022 edition builds on the revised guidance from 2018 and includes the new transfer pricing guidance on financial transactions approved in 2020.

As recommended by BEPS Action 11, significant progress continues to be made in improving the quality of available corporate tax statistics, which is a critical step towards strengthening the Inclusive Framework's ongoing efforts to measure and monitor BEPS and the impact of the BEPS package. The third edition of Corporate Tax Statistics, released in July 2021, expanded the number of jurisdictions that provided aggregated and anonymised CbCR statistics to the OECD from 26 to 38, covering around 6 000 CbC reports from the 2017 fiscal year. The third edition of Corporate Tax Statistics also continued to cover corporate tax revenues and rates and includes new indicators on R&D tax incentives related to innovation. The fourth edition of Corporate Tax Statistics, planned for release in the second half of 2022, will build on the previous edition with an expansion in the coverage of existing data series.

Finally, a growing number of countries have announced plans to introduce or have already introduced or expanded their mandatory disclosure rules, in line with BEPS Action 12. BEPS Action 12 contains recommendations regarding the design of mandatory disclosure rules for aggressive tax planning schemes, taking into consideration the need to avoid disproportionate administrative and compliance costs and drawing on the experiences of the increasing number of countries that have such rules. With the adoption of the EU Directive on mandatory disclosure rules by EU Member States, there has been a significant increase in jurisdictions that now have mandatory disclosure rules. Non-EU countries that have recently adopted mandatory disclosure rules include Canada, Israel, Mexico, Norway, South Africa, the United Kingdom, and the United States.

3.3. Taxes on goods and services

This Section shows that the base of Value Added Taxes (VAT) was subject to a large number of changes in 2021, while standard and reduced VAT rates were largely maintained. The stabilisation of standard VAT rates observed across countries is a continuation of the trend observed over the last six years, with both countries who reduced standard rates in 2020 (Germany and Ireland) returning these to pre-pandemic levels.

The vast majority of temporary VAT changes made in 2020 were reversed in 2021. As pandemic-related restrictions were eased in 2021 relative to the previous year, reduced VAT rates that had temporarily been applied to hard-hit sectors to encourage consumption and reduce costs were largely returned to the standard rate. However, most countries prolonged VAT exemptions on COVID-19-related medical supplies to reduce their cost and a small number of countries extended the time-period applicable for reduced VAT rates on sectors that continued to require short-term support, such as tourism.

Some countries applied reduced VAT rates to a wider range of goods and services on a permanent basis in 2021, while several countries also temporarily applied reduced VAT rates to electricity and natural gas during Q4 of 2021. Both types of measures narrowed these countries' VAT base. Examples of permanent changes to the VAT base included the adoption of reduced VAT rates on certain basic items to address perceived inequalities in the tax system. Reduced VAT rates were applied to electricity and natural gas in several countries as energy prices rose substantially from the end of Q3 of 2021. Excise duties were once again increased in many the countries surveyed. Increased excise duty rates were applied to tobacco and tobacco-substitute products (in some countries to harmonise their taxation), as well as on alcohol and sugar-sweetened beverages.

3.3.1. Consumption taxes, in particular VAT, remain a major source of revenue in most countries

Taxes on goods and services remain a major source of revenue for most countries covered in the report. On average, taxes on goods and services, which includes VAT, sales taxes and excise duties (also referred to in this Section as 'consumption taxes') account for 33.3% of the total tax mix in the OECD and non-OECD Inclusive Framework jurisdictions for which data were selected.[17] They ranged from 54.9% and 52.2% of total tax revenues in Chile and Argentina, respectively, to 18.7% and 16.9% of total tax revenues in Switzerland and the United States[18] in 2020 (Figure 3.13). As illustrated in Chapter 2 and discussed in previous editions of this report (OECD, 2020[30]), revenues from taxes on goods and services tend to account for higher shares of total tax revenues in emerging economies relative to developed countries. OECD statistics show that in Africa, Asia and the Pacific, and Latin America and the Caribbean, consumption taxes were by far the largest source of revenue as a share of total taxation, accounting for between 49.8% and 51.9% of total tax revenues, respectively, on average (OECD/AUC/ATAF, 2021[31]; OECD et al., 2022[32]; OECD, 2021[33]).

Figure 3.13. Tax revenues from taxes on goods and services, 2020

Share of total tax revenues (%)

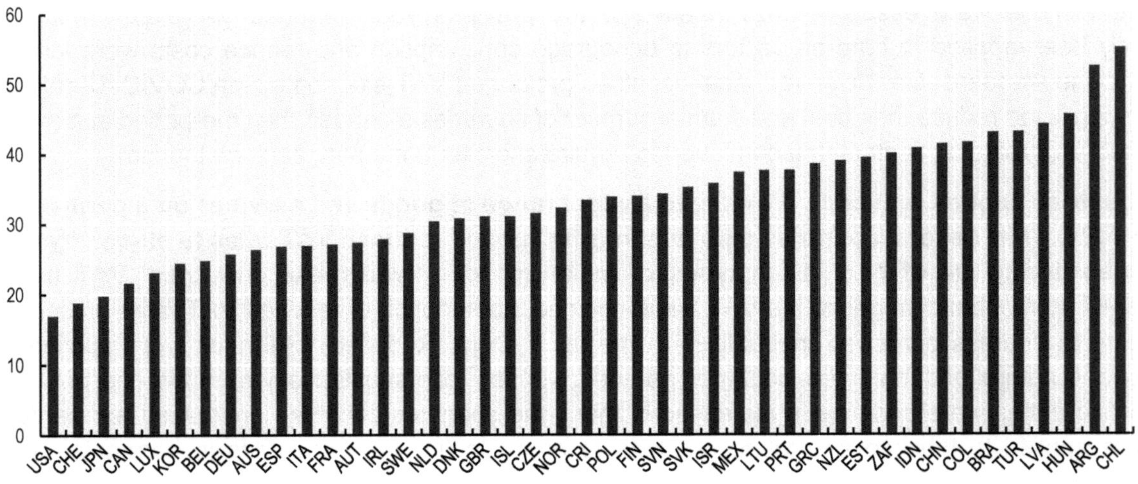

Note: Taxes on goods and services refer to Tax Revenue Statistics category 5000. Data for Argentina, Australia, Brazil, China, Indonesia, Japan, and South Africa are from 2019 as data from 2020 were not available at the time of writing.
Source: OECD Revenue Statistics Comparative Tables and OECD Global Revenue Statistics Database.

StatLink https://stat.link/qykxwu

VAT is the largest source of revenues from taxes on goods and services. VAT accounted for more than 60% of total tax revenues from goods and services taxes in 28 of the 43 OECD countries and selected non-OECD Inclusive Framework jurisdictions (see endnote 17). The share of consumption tax revenues within total taxation has remained stable over the last 30 years, varying between 32.5% and 35.6%, but as illustrated by Figure 3.14 the composition of these revenues has changed. Excise duties and other specific consumption taxes, which made up 14% of total tax revenues in 1990 across OECD countries and selected non-OECD Inclusive Framework jurisdictions, accounted for just 9.7% in 2019 - this figure is notably lower for OECD countries (at 9.5% of total taxation on average) than for the non-OECD countries for which data has been selected (11.3%). One of the explanations behind this overall decrease is that import duties were reduced across countries over the period covered, reflecting the continuation of global trends towards removing trade barriers, as well as the replacement of other general consumption taxes with VAT in several countries. Over the same period, the share of VAT in total tax revenues has grown, from 19.4%% in 1990 to 21.4% in 2019 on average for OECD countries and selected non-OECD Inclusive Framework jurisdictions.

Figure 3.14. Revenues from general and specific taxes on goods and services (left and right panel, respectively), 1990-2019

Share of total tax revenues (%)

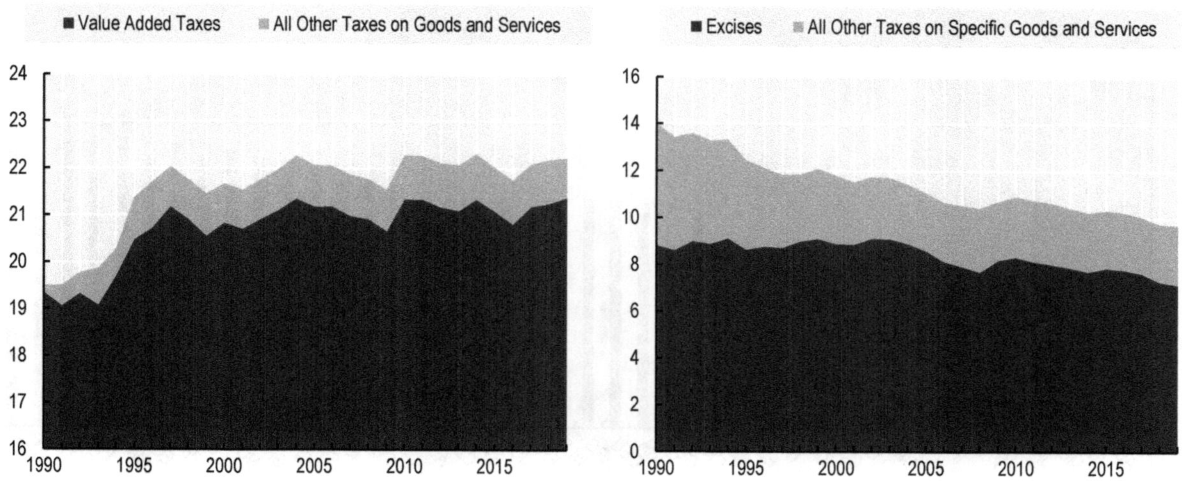

Note: The above categories of taxes on goods and services refer to the following Tax Revenue Statistics categories: Value Added Taxes – 5111; All Other Taxes on Goods and Services – General Taxes on Goods and Services (5110) minus Value Added Taxes (5111); Excises – 5121; All Other Taxes on Specific Goods and Services – Taxes on specific goods and services (5120) minus Excises (5121). The unweighted average for each year includes all OECD countries, as well as Argentina, Brazil, China (People's Republic of), Indonesia, and South Africa. The averages for 2016 include the one-off revenues from stability contributions in Iceland.
Source: Authors calculations based on OECD Revenue Statistics Comparative Tables and OECD Global Revenue Statistics Database.

StatLink https://stat.link/sixrum

Nevertheless, the amount and evolution of revenues collected from VAT have varied across countries. Across the OECD countries and non-OECD Inclusive Framework jurisdictions for which data were selected (see endnote 17), VAT revenues ranged from 9.8% of GDP in Hungary to 2.9% of GDP in Switzerland in 2020 (Figure 3.15). Over two-thirds of the countries covered experienced increases in their VAT revenues as a share of GDP between 2000 and 2019, with the most significant increases recorded in Canada, Colombia, and Japan. However, there were some notable exceptions to this general trend. For example, Ireland (-39%) experienced the largest decrease in VAT revenues as a share of GDP between 2000 and 2019 – this was not due to a fall in nominal or real VAT revenues, but rather was because Ireland's GDP grew at a significantly faster rate than its VAT revenues and other taxes took on a more prominent role in the country's overall tax structure. Indeed, all 42 Inclusive Framework jurisdictions for which data were selected recorded an increase in nominal revenues from VAT between 2000 and 2019.[19]

Figure 3.15. VAT revenues by country, 2000, 2019 and 2020

Share of GDP (%)

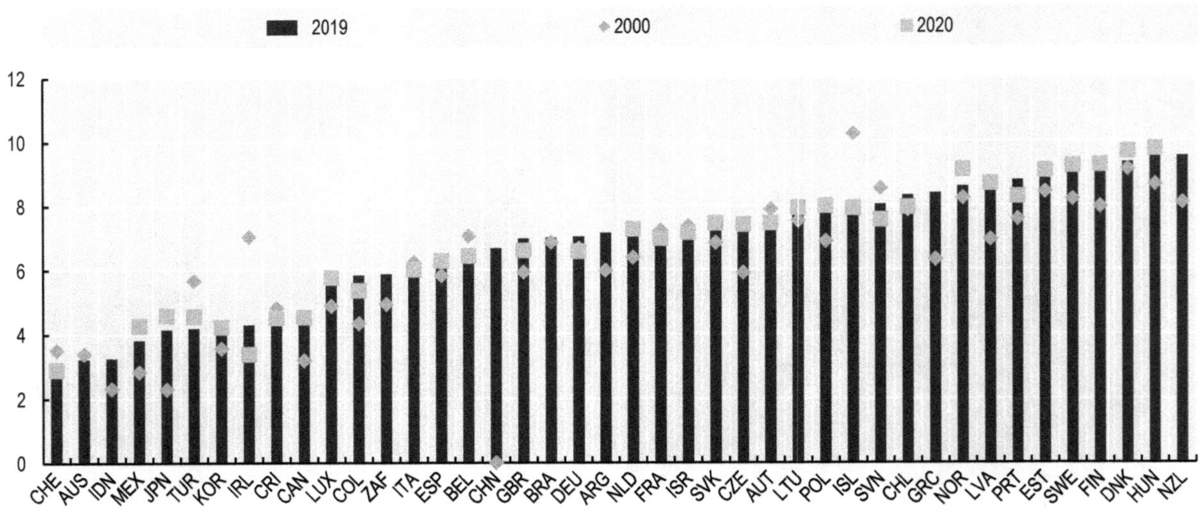

Note: Value Added Taxes refer to category 5111 within Tax Revenue Statistics. The United States is not included, as it does not operate a federal VAT. Instead, State governments have their own sales or use taxes.
Source: OECD Global Revenue Statistics Database.

StatLink https://stat.link/4gnoul

Nominal revenues from VAT decreased slightly on average across OECD countries between 2019 and 2020. Of the 34 OECD countries where data were available[20], reductions in nominal VAT revenues were recorded in 18 countries (falling by -0.27 p.p. on average), whereas increases were recorded in 16 (increasing by 0.22 p.p. on average). In most of the OECD countries covered, VAT revenues were relatively closely correlated to changes in GDP, which is reflected in their relative stability as a share of GDP on average. As such, no significant change was observed in the average share of VAT to GDP in 2020 – a very small decrease of -0.04 p.p. was recorded by countries overall. VAT revenues decreased as a share of GDP in 18 countries and increased in the other 16 countries that apply VAT, with half of these changes situated between -0.2 p.p. and +0.1 p.p. of GDP. The largest fall was seen in Ireland (-0.9 p.p.) due to the temporary VAT rate cut during the COVID-19 pandemic (from 23% to 21% from September 2021 to February 2022, inclusive) as well as the decrease in economic activity. Germany also temporarily cut its standard VAT rate (from 19% to 16% for the second half of 2020) and experienced a -0.45 p.p. decrease in VAT revenues as a share of GDP – the fifth largest decrease. Of the 34 OECD countries for which data were available, the largest increase was seen in Norway, at 0.5 p.p.

3.3.2. Standard VAT rates continue to stabilise

Standard VAT rates remained at the same level in 2020 and 2021 in all but three countries for which data were selected.[21] The average standard VAT rate across OECD countries rose marginally, from 19.2% in 2020 to 19.3% in 2021 (Figure 3.16), as Germany and Ireland returned their standard rates to 19% and 23%, respectively, following six-month temporary decreases (up from 16% and 21%). Outside of the OECD, Saudi Arabia tripled its standard VAT rate from 5% in 2019 to 15% in 2020, having first introduced the tax in 2018. Among OECD countries, 12 had a standard VAT rate equal to or above 22% in 2021 and 24 below 22% (Figure 3.17); this ratio has remained the same since 2014. The limited changes recorded in OECD countries are an indication that VAT rates may have stabilised. In some of these OECD countries, high standard VAT rates reflect, in part, changes made in the aftermath of the global financial crisis when a common strategy for governments seeking to undertake fiscal consolidation was to raise VAT rates to provide immediate revenues without directly affecting competitiveness.

Figure 3.16. Evolution of the OECD average standard VAT rate, 1990-2021

Tax rate (%)

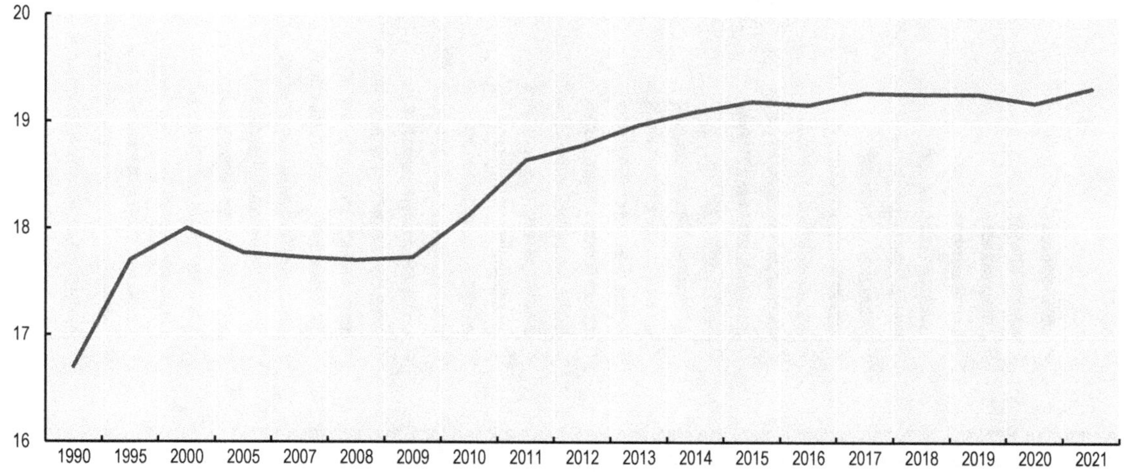

Note: The average standard VAT rate reflects the unweighted average of 36 OECD countries, not including Costa Rica or the USA. Comparable data was not available for Costa Rica or for the Inclusive Framework jurisdictions of Argentina, Brazil, China, Indonesia, and South Africa at the time of writing. The USA does not operate a federal VAT. In Germany, the standard VAT rate was reduced from 19% to 16% between 1 July 2020 and 31 December 2020. In Ireland, the standard VAT rate was cut from 23% to 21% for the period of 1 September 2020 until 28 February 2021. The lower rates for Germany and Ireland were included as their respective rates for the full year in 2020.
Source: OECD Tax Database 2021.

StatLink https://stat.link/89bigv

Substantial differences in the rates imposed by individual countries remain. As Figure 3.17 shows, five OECD countries had VAT rates of 10% or below in 2021 while a further seven had rates of 24% or higher. Excluding the temporary cuts in the standard VAT rate implemented in Germany and Ireland, Iceland is the only country to have recorded a small reduction in its standard rate, from 24.5% in 2008 to 24% in 2021. Standard VAT rates remained at the same level in ten OECD countries between 2008 and 2021 and rose in all others.

Figure 3.17. Standard VAT rates by country, 2008, 2020 and 2021

Tax rate (%)

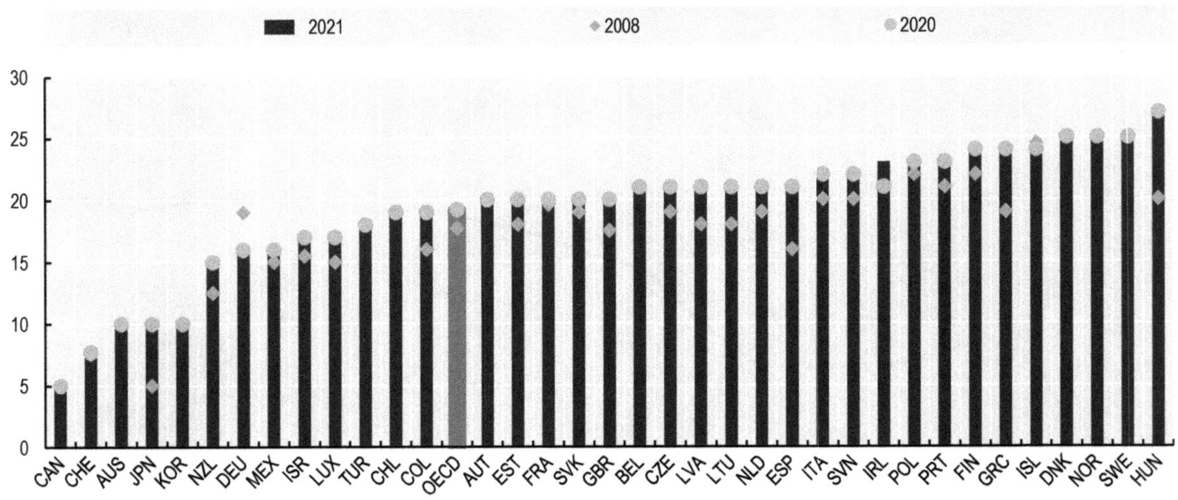

Note: See note for Figure 3.16 for an explanation of the standard VAT rates applied for Germany and Ireland in 2020. Comparable data were not available for Costa Rica or for the selected non-OECD Inclusive Framework jurisdictions (Argentina, Brazil, China, Indonesia, and South Africa) at the time of writing.
Source: OECD Tax Database 2021.

StatLink https://stat.link/hnidfb

3.3.3. Several countries reversed the temporary expansions in the scope of reduced VAT rates that were introduced in 2020

Many countries apply reduced VAT rates to a wide range of goods and services. Many of these reduced rates – such as those for basic goods – are intended to enhance equity. In some countries, other reduced VAT rates are in place to achieve non-distributional goals, such as supporting labour-intensive industries or promoting access to cultural activities. However, empirical evidence has shown that reduced VAT rates may not be the most effective way of attaining equity goals (OECD, 2020[34]). For example, reduced rates for necessities that aim to lower the tax burden on low-income households have been shown to provide greater benefits, in absolute terms, to richer households, even if they might benefit low-income households more in relative terms. Where reduced VAT rates apply to non-essential items such as hotel, restaurant services and cultural activities, the overall distributional effect tends to be regressive, benefiting the rich more both in aggregate terms and as a proportion of expenditure (Thomas, 2020[35]).

Almost all countries covered in *Tax Policy Reforms 2021* temporarily expanded the scope of their reduced VAT rates in 2020 (i.e., bringing more goods and services within the reach of the reduced VAT rates that are in place) and added exemptions or zero rates for certain goods and services. Meanwhile, just three countries (China, Germany, and Ireland) temporarily cut their standard or reduced VAT rate. Measures taken to reduce the cost of VAT or provide relief from import duties were central to countries' efforts to ease access to essential medical supplies and services in response to the global pandemic. After the early waves of the pandemic, several countries extended the scope of reduced VAT rates, opening these up to specific sectors in severely affected areas of the economy to encourage demand and support businesses. In most instances, the duration of these measures was initially three to six months, but the measures were subsequently extended in many cases while restrictions on mobility and closures of public places, including restaurants, bars, shopping malls, remained in place.

There was only one substantial change to reduced VAT rates in 2021. Germany reinstalled its reduced VAT rate of 7%, having temporarily cut the rate to 5% in 2020 to encourage consumption during the COVID-19 pandemic.

Countries across the world made a large number of changes to VAT bases in 2021. As pandemic-related restrictions were eased in 2021 relative to the previous year, sectors that had temporarily been subject to reduced VAT rates to encourage consumption were largely returned to the standard rate. Of the 46 temporary VAT rate reduction measures that were recorded by countries in their responses to the previous year's questionnaire (not including those related to medical products), 43 of these were removed by 2021. However, most countries prolonged VAT exemptions on COVID-19-related medical supplies to reduce their cost.

A small number of countries extended temporary expansions in the scope of their reduced VAT rates from 2020 into 2021 to encourage greater consumption in struggling sectors. For example, Colombia made three changes to the sectors to whom reduced VAT rates apply in the calendar year 2021. It added hotels, restaurants, and tourism services to the zero-rate VAT and added airline tickets and related services to the goods and services to which its lower 5% reduced rate is applied.[22] In the United Kingdom, the 5% reduced VAT rate that had been applied to hospitality, holiday accommodation and admission to certain attractions in 2020 was extended for a further eight months until the end of September 2021. The UK government also announced in advance a gradual return to the standard VAT rate of 20% by the start of Q2 of 2022, with an interim 12.5% rate applying from October 2021 until the end of March 2022.

Some other countries also introduced new temporary VAT reduction measures in 2021 that were targeted at certain hard-hit sectors. Lithuania temporarily added catering services (for the second half of 2021), and artistic and cultural services (from Q3 to 2021 to the end of 2022) to its 9% reduced VAT rate. In Uruguay, tourism services were subject to the 9% reduced VAT rate from October 2021 until the end of April 2022 when paid for through electronic payment methods. In Viet Nam, businesses, and self-employed workers in the accommodation, cultural, hospitality and tourism sectors were able to benefit from 30% discounts on VAT rates for the last two months of 2021, where they were able to prove a year-on-year decline in activity caused by the pandemic. To support the domestic construction and housing market, Iceland announced an expansion and prolonging of its measures to reimburse the VAT costs related to the labour share of certain services involved in the construction and maintenance of residential housing. Reimbursement was increased from 60% to 100%, the scope of the companies covered was expanded and the measures were prolonged by a further six months to the end of August 2022.

Several countries also temporarily expanded the scope of their reduced VAT rates and VAT-exempt items in the second half of 2021 to support households and businesses facing rising prices. A more detailed description of countries' tax responses to the rise in energy and food prices during 2021 and up to the end of May 2022 is provided in the Special Feature in Chapter 4, while this paragraph refers only to the VAT measures introduced in 2021. Costa Rica, the Czech Republic, Estonia, Italy, Poland, and Spain all made temporary changes to VAT bases subject to the standard rate in response to rising global energy prices in the second half of 2021, while in Senegal measures were taken to limit price rises of staple food items. Costa Rica exempted fuel transportation and distribution services from VAT from September 2021, while in the Czech Republic electricity and gas were subject to a 0% VAT for the last two months of 2021.[23] In Estonia, the VAT rate applicable to gas, electricity and heating was lowered from the 20% standard VAT rate to its 9% reduced rate from December 2021.[24] As part of its initial response to rising energy prices, Italy temporarily added natural gas supplies for "civil and industrial uses" to the scope of its super-reduced VAT rate of 5%, from the start of Q4 of 2021, while the VAT on gas bills for households was cut to the 10% reduced VAT rate.[25] Poland announced in November of 2021 that it would temporarily reduce the VAT rate applicable to natural gas and district heating from the 23% standard rate to the 8% reduced rate. The measure came into force as of January 2022.[26] In June 2021, Spain's government reduced the VAT rate it applied to energy bills from the standard 21% VAT rate to its 10% reduced rate for a period of six-months.[27] Senegal applied a 0% VAT rate to flour from September 2021 in response to the rise in global food prices.

A small number of countries have also made permanent additions to the scope of reduced rate VAT regimes, citing equity concerns. Both Kenya and Uruguay reduced the VAT rate on staple food items, but the most common change recorded by countries was for female sanitary products. Austria, Italy, and Slovenia changed the VAT rate applied to feminine hygiene items, adding these products to their 10% reduced rate category (9.5% in Slovenia); while Mexico and the United Kingdom lowered the VAT rate they apply to these products to zero. Lowering the VAT rate on female sanitary products has become increasingly widespread over the last decade, with the aforementioned countries following in the footsteps of Australia, Belgium, Canada, Germany, Iceland, Kenya, and South Africa who all made changes from as early as 2011. The equity implications of reducing the rates applied to female sanitary products is more complex than might first appear. Whilst reduced rates on female sanitary products can be seen as an example of how the tax system can be used to mitigate gender inequality, recent research suggests that the distributional consequences of reductions in VAT on these products can be regressive and more costly than other potential policy responses (de la Feria and Walpole, 2020[36]).

Following trends from previous years, common permanent additions to the scope of reduced VAT rates were recorded for goods and services related to the media. Latvia and Romania added books, press and other mass media issued in the form of printed or electronic publications to the goods to which they apply their 5% reduced VAT rate, in line with EU VAT Directives. Elsewhere, Austria and Sweden added repair services to the items that are taxed at a reduced VAT rate, Türkiye lowered the VAT rate on used mobile phones from 18% to 1%, and Albania reduced the VAT rates applied to both the supply of agricultural inputs and the compensation rate for agricultural producers to 0%.

Table 3.10. Changes to reduced VAT rates introduced in 2021

	General	Food and basic items	Hotels, restaurants, and tourism	Newspapers and e-books	Culture	Other
Rate increase or scope narrowing	DEU					PER
Rate decrease or scope broadening		AUT, COL $^{e\,t}$, GBR^{0}, ITA, KEN^{0}, MEX^{0}, ROU, SVN, URY	COL$^{0\,t}$, GBR ^{t}, LTU ^{t}	LVA, ROU	LTU ^{t}	ALB^{0} AUT, COL, ISL, ITA, MEX, POL ^{t}, ROU, SWE, TUR

Note: E = tax-exemption.;
T = temporary.
0 = zero-rate.
Chapter 4 discusses changes to VAT rates on energy supplies in detail and such measures have thus not been included in Table 3.10.
Source: OECD Annual Tax Policy Reform Questionnaire.

3.3.4. VAT registration thresholds have been increased in several countries

The OECD countries and Inclusive Framework jurisdictions that responded to the Tax Policy Reforms questionnaire have very different VAT registration thresholds (Figure 3.18). The level of the threshold is generally the result of a trade-off between, on the one hand, minimising compliance and administration costs for small businesses and tax administrations, and on the other hand, the need to protect revenue and avoid competitive distortions. In a large majority of countries, smaller businesses are not required to register for VAT and/or to collect the tax on their outputs while the VAT on their inputs is not deductible (exemption without credit) as it is deemed that: (i) the accompanying compliance costs for businesses may be disproportionately large relative to their turnover; and (ii) for tax administrations, the costs of having these businesses account for VAT may be disproportionately high relative to the potential

VAT revenues they could provide. An additional consideration for tax authorities is that VAT registration thresholds can introduce competitive distortions between small businesses under and above the threshold. Each jurisdiction should therefore decide the most appropriate balance of these factors when setting these thresholds.

A very small number of countries altered their VAT registration thresholds in 2021. Across the OECD, just two countries reported a change in their VAT registration threshold. Upward revisions to thresholds were more common in previous years – from 2016 to 2018, nine countries increased their VAT collection/registration thresholds, while between 2018 and 2020, seven countries increased thresholds. As of 1 January 2021, Portugal increased its VAT registration threshold by 25% from EUR 10 000 (USD 17 640) to EUR 12 500 (USD 21 800), which remains significantly below the OECD average VAT registration threshold (Figure 3.18). The only other change was made in Colombia, where the turnover value at which certain individuals must be registered for VAT rose from COL 122.8 million (USD 91 060) to COL 127.1 million (USD 94 000) to account for inflation adjustments.

Some countries announced changes or qualifications in the application of VAT thresholds to ease administrative burdens and improve compliance. In Saudi Arabia, for instance, guidelines were released that clarify that the domestic VAT registration threshold (ZAR 375 000; USD 98 680) also applies to all (i.e., both domestic and foreign) e-commerce sellers to boost VAT compliance.

Figure 3.18. General VAT registration and collection thresholds in OECD countries, 2021

Annual turnover thresholds expressed in USD purchasing power parity

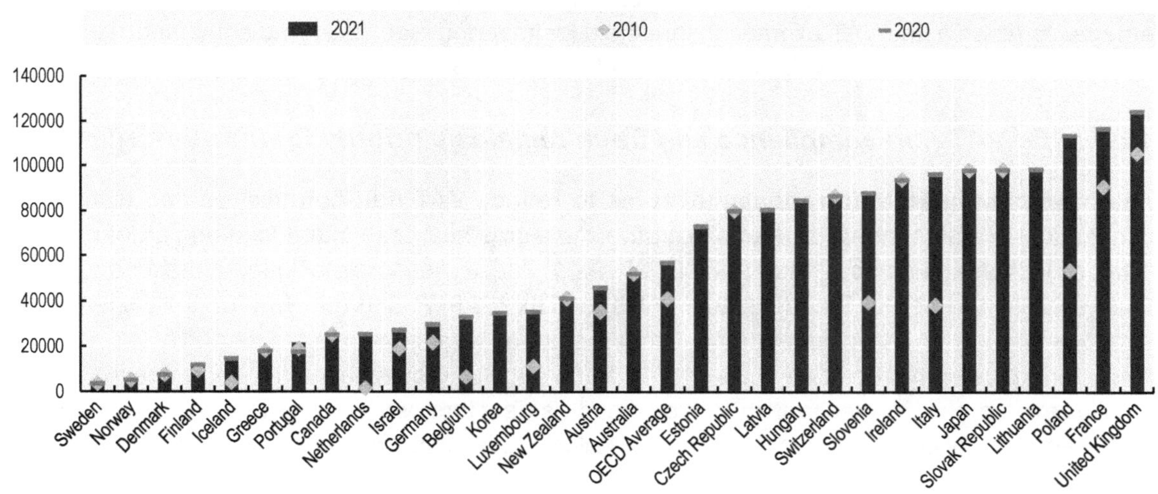

Note: Thresholds validated by delegates of OECD Working Party 9.
Source: OECD Tax Database 2021.

3.3.5. Governments continue to reduce VAT compliance burdens in the aftermath of the pandemic

Several countries have continued to modernise their input VAT refund procedures to enhance business cash flow and support investment, as well as to improve compliance. Many of these measures build upon those put in place during the pandemic, which highlighted the importance of flexible input VAT refund mechanisms in supporting businesses with liquidity challenges. Among the measures taken – and in some instances, continued from the pandemic – were reductions in the response times for tax administrations to treat refund requests, simplification of procedures and administrative requirements for obtaining refunds, and more flexibility in the late payment of VAT obligations for firms operating in sectors that had been particularly hard hit by the economic effects of COVID-19.

A small number of countries sought to modernise their VAT refund mechanisms. As part of Poland's wider reforms to the functioning of its VAT system, it has introduced a statutory guarantee that VAT refunds will automatically be made within 15 days. Alongside other specific qualifying criteria, access to this rapid refund system will only be available to retailers who use online or virtual cash registers. Georgia has also made a significant upgrade to its VAT refund system, where a fully automatic VAT refund system has been introduced, with excess VAT amounts being automatically credited to taxpayers' accounts without them needing to request payment. Slovenia has also sought to improve digitalisation of its VAT and excise systems, with beneficiaries able to receive refunds quicker when claims are made through upgraded electronic systems.

Some countries extended administrative measures implemented during the pandemic to support companies with continued liquidity challenges. In Germany, tax payment deferrals have been permitted until the end of Q2 of 2022, reduced pre-payments were enhanced, and enforcement rules have been eased until the end of Q3 of 2022. In Chile, VAT payments for companies whose sales in Q1 of 2021 were down by at least 20% relative to 2019 were able to be deferred to the start of Q4 of 2021 and paid in equal instalments over the following year. Saudi Arabia extended its relief from fines in case of late tax filing and payment for a period of six months until the end of June 2021. Viet Nam continued to extend repayment periods for VAT in 2021: allowing Q1 VAT payments to be delayed by five months, Q2 VAT payments by four months and Q3 VAT payments by three months. In Cabo Verde, the government prioritised accelerated tax refunds for companies to support firms facing liquidity difficulties, while the Finnish government sought to achieve the same objective by continuing the eased terms of repayment arrangements. In Albania, the VAT exemption threshold for imported machinery and equipment was raised ten-fold from ALL 50 million (USD 483 000) to ALL 500 million (USD 4.83 million).

3.3.6. Reducing VAT non-compliance and fraud remains a priority for tax authorities

Countries have continued to introduce measures to reduce VAT non-compliance and fraud. Prior to the pandemic, several technical and administrative measures had been introduced as part of efforts to improve tax collection and combat fraud (OECD, 2019[37]). These measures included enhanced reporting obligations, such as the use of Standard Audit Files for Tax (SAF-T) and real-time data transfers to tax administrations through VAT invoice reporting. Other measures were implemented to modify tax collection mechanisms and thus combat certain types of VAT fraud, including split payments and the expansion of the domestic reverse charge mechanism to high fraud-risk sectors, while some reforms also sought to extend VAT accountability to other entities in the value chain, such as online marketplaces (OECD, 2020[30]).

Previous editions of this report have emphasised the expanding use of the domestic reverse charge mechanism to address fraud. The domestic reverse charge mechanism can be used to combat missing trader fraud. A key feature of this type of fraud is that taxpayers charge and collect VAT from their customers and disappear without remitting the VAT to the tax authorities. The domestic reverse charge mechanism – which applies in principle to supplies of specific goods and/or services between VAT registered businesses established in the same country – aims at addressing this type of fraud by making the customer liable to collect the tax on supplies (instead of the supplier), thus preventing the supplier from collecting VAT and disappearing with it (OECD, 2017[38]). This mechanism has been increasingly applied by EU Member States to goods that are vulnerable to such fraud; often popular high-value goods that can easily be moved around such as mobile phones, laptops, and gold. Trade in certain intangibles, such as carbon credits, gas and electricity and green energy certificates, has also become particularly vulnerable to this type of fraud. Some developing countries have sought to introduce similar measures, including

Nigeria, where a reverse charge mechanism applies in circumstances where the supplier fails to collect the tax.

3.3.7. Reforms of VAT group rules were rare

Poland introduced significant reforms to its VAT system as part of a wide-ranging tax reform package. Among these changes was the introduction of VAT groups, whereby two or more VAT-eligible persons or businesses can be treated as a single taxable unit. This practice is commonplace in some OECD countries. The general purpose of the VAT grouping is to simplify VAT settlements between group members and increase the group's financial efficiency in dealings with third parties. In addition, VAT grouping can positively affect the financial liquidity of a group. It may also significantly limit the VAT compliance burden of a group's members. Poland has introduced the right for taxpayers to opt for the taxation of supplies of financial services (previously mandatorily exempt from VAT without credit) when such services are supplied to customers themselves subject to VAT (B2B supplies).

3.3.8. Countries are continuing to make progress in ensuring the effective taxation of online sales of goods, services, and intangibles

Countries continue to implement the rules and mechanisms recommended by the OECD's *International VAT/GST Guidelines* and its accompanying guidance to ensure the effective taxation of cross-border supplies of services and intangibles, in response to increasing digitalisation of the economy. The Guidelines provide specific recommendations to ensure the consistent allocation of taxing rights over internationally traded services and intangibles and to ensure the effective collection of VAT on these supplies (OECD, 2017[39]). For digital B2C supplies, the Guidelines recommend place of taxation rules mainly based on the customer's usual residence and a customer location rule for B2B supplies. The Guidelines also provide guidance on the VAT collection mechanisms for these supplies i.e., a "reverse charge" mechanism for B2B supplies (which imposes the VAT collection and remittance obligation upon the customer), and the implementation of a requirement for non-resident suppliers to register in the taxing jurisdiction to collect and remit the VAT on B2C supplies.

To support the implementation of these OECD standards and guidance for the application of VAT to digital trade in developing regions of the world, the OECD is producing several regional VAT Digital Toolkits in partnership with the World Bank Group (WBG) and with key regional organisations. As described in Box 3.7, the OECD has produced VAT Digital Toolkits for the Asia-Pacific region (with WBG and the Asian Development Bank) and for the Latin America and Caribbean region[28] (with WBG, Inter-American Center of Tax Administrations and the Inter-American Development Bank) to assist national tax authorities in the effective collection of VAT revenues by providing detailed guidance for the successful implementation of a comprehensive VAT strategy directed at e-commerce activities. The VAT Digital Toolkit for Africa will be released in 2022 (in partnership with WBG and African Tax Administration Forum).

Box 3.7. VAT Digital Toolkit for Latin America and the Caribbean

VAT is the largest source of tax revenue on average in the Latin America and Caribbean (LAC) region, at 27.7% of total tax revenues in 2019. Revenue from VAT as a percentage of GDP more than doubled for LAC countries on average between 1990 and 2019, from 2.2% of GDP in 1990 to 6.0% in 2019 (OECD et al., 2021[40]).

Safeguarding these crucially important VAT revenues in an economy that is being transformed by digitalisation and globalisation is a priority for many governments in the LAC region. Most jurisdictions that employ a VAT in other regions around the world confront similar challenges. The need for reform, however, may be more urgent in the LAC region, as it is one of the fastest growing e-commerce regions in the world and VAT reform in response to this new economic reality has remained relatively limited.

The LAC region is one of the fastest-growing regions for e-commerce worldwide. E-commerce has been estimated to reach 63% penetration of the total population in Latin America in 2022, compared to the 45% penetration rate observed at the beginning of 2020. Online trade in goods and in digital products and services are estimated to have grown in the LAC region at the respective rates of 21% and 20%-to-30% year-on-year in 2020 (OECD et al., 2021[40]).

The need for action to ensure that VAT is collected efficiently and effectively on the fast-growing volumes of e-commerce sales is therefore strong. Action is required not only to generate the revenues necessary to finance sustainable development and to strengthen the redistributive power of tax policy in the LAC region post-crisis, but also to avoid competitive distortions between online sellers and local "bricks-and-mortar" stores.

Figure 3.19. LAC region digital trade newcomers

Millions of consumers

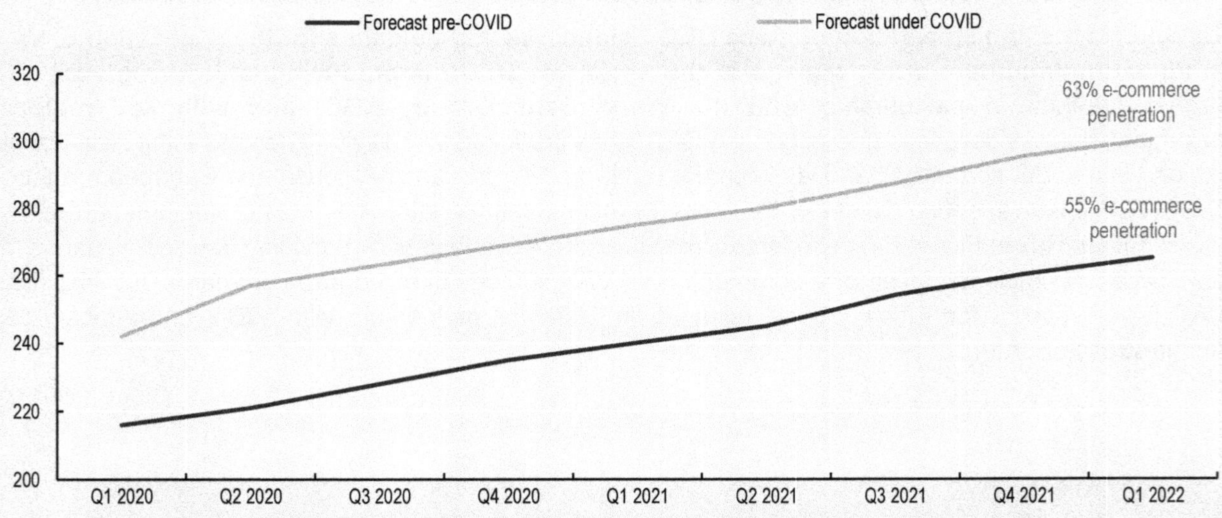

Notes: The original source does not provide specific data points. For illustrative purposes, the OECD has reproduced the graph with approximate estimates.
Source: EBANX/AMI data from EBANX (2021[41]).

StatLink https://stat.link/u9wvnx

In response, the OECD has delivered a comprehensive internationally agreed policy framework for addressing the VAT challenges of the digital economy, reflecting broad consensus on effective and efficient solutions among tax authorities worldwide. It results from an intense and inclusive policy dialogue among tax authorities from OECD member countries and non-member economies and key international and regional organisations over the course of several years. The core standards and principles are included in the *International VAT/GST Guidelines* and in the 2015 *Final Report on BEPS Action 1 Addressing the Tax Challenges of the Digital Economy* (OECD, 2015[42]). These standards have been complemented with detailed technical guidance on the design and implementation of mechanisms for the collection of VAT from non-resident online vendors; the VAT treatment of online marketplaces and other digital platforms; the collection of VAT on imports of low-value goods from online sales; and the VAT treatment of the sharing and gig economy.

The OECD policy framework for addressing the VAT challenges of digital trade has four main pillars:

1. Creating the legal basis for jurisdictions to assert the right to impose VAT on international digital trade. This includes internationally agreed standards for determining the "place of taxation" of online sales of services and digital products by reference to the location of the customer.
2. Ensuring the efficient collection of VAT on online sales of goods, services, and digital products from foreign vendors through simplified VAT registration and collection.
3. Boosting the efficiency of VAT collection by requiring digital platform operators, which dominate global digital trade, to collect and remit the VAT on sales carried out through their platform(s).
4. Enhancing VAT compliance by foreign online vendors through a modern risk-based compliance strategy and robust administrative co-operation.

The *VAT Digital Toolkit for Latin America and the Caribbean* provides comprehensive and detailed guidance for the policy design, implementation and operation of a comprehensive VAT strategy targeted at digital trade in the LAC region (OECD et al., 2021[43]). It is based on the internationally agreed OECD policy framework and draws on expertise and best practices from jurisdictions that have already successfully implemented these standards:

- ***Section 3*** of the Toolkit provides detailed analysis of the various components of the recommended policy framework for the application of VAT to digital trade and the available options for implementing them into a jurisdiction's VAT system, taking account of the specific LAC context. It focuses respectively on internationally traded services and intangibles (including digital services and products); on imports of low-value goods from online sales; and on the sharing and gig economy.
- ***Section 4*** presents detailed guidance on the key issues associated with the administrative and operational implementation of the OECD policy framework for the collection of VAT on digital trade. This includes the implementation of a simplified compliance regime for foreign online suppliers, the development of an online portal for registration and payment of the VAT and their integration into a tax authority's existing administrative and IT framework.
- ***Section 5*** of the Toolkit advises policymakers and administrators on the development of audit and risk management strategies for the application of VAT to digital trade.

To support policy makers and tax administrators with the application of the toolkit, the OECD and partner organisations have developed VAT e-learning modules that can be accessed through the *Knowledge Sharing Platform for Tax Administrations.*

Nine countries reported the adoption or announced the forthcoming adoption of the OECD standards for the collection of VAT on digital supplies by non-resident vendors in 2021. These countries included Cambodia, Canada, Kazakhstan, Kenya, Nigeria, Tajikistan, Thailand, the Ukraine and

Viet Nam. The scope of transactions covered by these new rules and the applicable VAT rate varies across these countries, but all now apply the same rate for wholly domestic and non-digital supplies. Egypt and Peru are continuing to adjust their VAT systems to collect VAT on inbound digital supplies.

A growing number of countries have now removed or are considering the elimination of VAT relief regimes for imports of low-value goods, as volumes of low-value imported goods from online sales grow. The imports of low-value goods were often exempt from VAT due to collection challenges for tax administrations and customs officials that had to verify that VAT was paid on a large amount of low-value imports. Countries have removed or are considering the elimination of VAT relief for imports of low-value goods because of the increasing revenue cost to governments and the competitive distortions that domestic retailers face. In these countries, the VAT on imports of low-value goods is collected via a simplified registration and compliance regime for online vendors and digital platforms, which are similar to those implemented for the collection of VAT on inbound supplies of services and intangibles. Countries having implemented such a regime so far are Australia, New Zealand, Norway, the United Kingdom, and the Member States of the European Union. Singapore has also announced the introduction of a vendor collection regime for low value imported goods.

Box 3.8. The Impact of the Growth of the Sharing and Gig Economy on VAT Policy and Administration

The emergence and rapid expansion of the sharing/gig economy in recent years has been remarkable. Digital platforms, acting as intermediaries for millions of new economic actors and consumers worldwide, have powered the rise of the sharing/gig economy. Subsequently, a wide range of previously non-monetised human or physical resources and/or assets has been made accessible for temporary ("shared") use by consumers.

The value of the sharing/gig economy in eight major global economies is projected to rise to USD 455 billion by 2023 as digitalisation accelerates and consumers become more receptive to the idea of the sharing economy (Mastercard and Kaiser Associates, 2019[44]). This growth has already created new commercial opportunities in several industries, such as transportation (e.g., "ride-sourcing") and accommodation (e.g., short-term rentals), and is expanding to a wider array of sectors, including professional services and finance.

Figure 3.20. Sharing/gig economy volume by sector, 2018

Billions USD

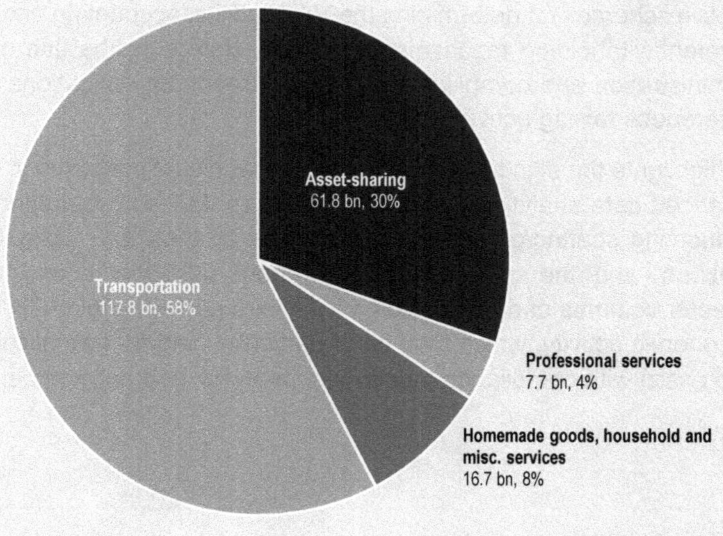

Note: The markets covered include Australia, Brazil, France, India, Indonesia, United Arab Emirates, United Kingdom, and the United States.
Source: Mastercard and Kaiser Associates (2019[44]).

StatLink https://stat.link/gemp8f

Given the huge economic volume and the unique characteristics of the gig/sharing economy, questions have been raised as to whether existing VAT frameworks are effective in protecting VAT revenues and minimising economic distortions. Concurrently, these "new ways of doing business", not least the role of sharing/gig economy platforms, may also create new opportunities to enhance tax compliance and administration. The OECD's report *The Impact of the Growth of the Sharing and Gig Economy on VAT/GST Policy and Administration* examines exactly these questions, building upon a series of previous OECD research on the design of VAT/GST policy to address the challenges of the digitalisation of the economy (OECD, 2021[45]).

The report sets out the core components of a comprehensive strategy for tax authorities to consider in designing and implementing their VAT policy and administration response to sharing/gig economy growth. Key considerations for these strategies include:

- **Jurisdictions' main objective may not necessarily be to bring all sharing/gig economy activities within the VAT net**. A jurisdiction may for instance wish to first monitor evolutions across sharing/gig economy sectors so as to allow fast and targeted policy action when needed;
- **Jurisdictions may opt for a sequenced strategy**, focusing their policy action first on the dominant sharing/gig economy sectors that may create the most immediate risks to VAT revenue and/or competitive neutrality;
- **The preferred policy response is one that is consistent with the general rules and principles of the jurisdiction's existing VAT system** and limits the introduction of new exceptions or special regimes. This notably reflects the desire of jurisdictions to ensuring an equal treatment of various distribution channels in a given market, whether traditional or digital;
- **Tax authorities will often face difficult trade-offs** between the need to protect revenue and minimise competitive distortion by bringing new actors within VAT systems, and the need to safeguard the efficiency of tax administration and to avoid undue compliance burden by limiting the entry of high numbers of new sharing/gig economy actors into the VAT/GST system;
- **A number of measures can be used to support a balanced response to this challenge**, including: considerations for the determination of a VAT registration and/or collection threshold; presumptive schemes for determining the VAT liability; accounting and reporting simplifications; split payment/withholding mechanisms for VAT collection; the use of technology to facilitate VAT administration and compliance; third-party reporting obligations; taxpayer education and other awareness raising activities

The report also highlights the significant opportunities that digital platforms in the sharing/gig economy – fuelled by advanced data analytics – offer for facilitating VAT administration and compliance. These could help in educating sharing/gig economy providers on their VAT obligations, implementing data reporting obligations, and the collection of VAT from participants in the sharing/gig economy. Furthermore, greater volumes of data, including from third parties, could help improve the visibility and traceability of economic activity, which may be of particular help for formalisation efforts in developing countries, and to assist with compliance monitoring, analysis, and enforcement.

Source: OECD (2021[45]).

3.3.9. Excise duties have continued to be raised

Excise taxes continue to offer a powerful tool in raising revenues and encouraging behavioural change. Excise taxes can cover a wide range of products, but those that are common in most countries and raise significant revenues for governments are excise duties on alcohol, tobacco, and hydrocarbon oils. In recent decades, governments have increasingly used these taxes not only to raise revenues, but also to influence behaviours and deter harmful consumption (see Box 3.9). This sub-Section covers non-energy excise duties (for environmentally related excise duties, see Section 3.4).

Taxes on tobacco products are particularly high. The relatively low-price elasticity of demand, the small number of producers and high consumption levels initially made tobacco products particularly attractive targets for excise taxation to raise revenue. Considering the negative health consequences of tobacco use and the effectiveness of tobacco taxation in reducing tobacco use, excise taxes on tobacco have increasingly been used as a tool to reduce tobacco use (World Health Organisation, 2017[46]). As a result, in 2018, the average share of total taxes in the price of cigarettes paid by consumers in OECD countries was 74.8% (OECD, 2020[34]).

Excise duty increases, especially on tobacco products, continued in 2021. Increases in excise duty rates on tobacco products were reported in Albania, Armenia, Belgium, Canada (both federally and in the provinces of British Columbia, Newfoundland and Labrador, and Saskatchewan), Germany, Lithuania, Kenya, the Netherlands, Poland, Slovenia, South Africa, and Sweden.[29] Armenia also noted that excise duties on tobacco products would be indexed to inflation from 2022 onwards. Tobacco products, such as vaping and associated materials have also been subject to increased taxation rates – in most countries to better align them with taxes on tobacco products. Denmark and Lithuania introduced a new tax on nicotine and on tobacco substitutes, respectively; while in Germany and Peru, plans were announced to tax tobacco substitutes from mid-2022, with further rate increases scheduled for the following three years. Contrary to this general trend, Togo reduced the excise duty on tobacco products in 2021 to better align its rates with other countries in the region, following several years of progressive increases. The lower price differentials should limit arbitrage opportunities and the potential for smuggling and contraband fabrication of cigarettes.

As in previous years, increases in tobacco excise duties have been more widespread than increases on excise duties on alcohol. Increases in excise duties on alcohol were reported in Armenia, Lithuania, South Africa, and Sweden. In the United Kingdom, reforms were announced in 2021 to harmonise and rationalise the structure of excise duties on alcohol from the beginning of 2023. Once the legislation has been implemented, excise duties on alcohol will be charged based on alcoholic strength (alcohol by volume) as opposed to the volume of the finished product, as is currently the case.

However, some countries reduced excise tax burdens on alcohol manufacturers, particularly of beer and wine products, to support industries that had struggled during the pandemic. In Australia, the Government increased the support available to brewers and distillers. From mid-2021, eligible brewers and distillers could receive a full remission (up from 60% previously) of any excise they pay, up to a limit of AUD 350 000 (USD 262 960) – this limit was also increased from the 2020 threshold of AUD 100 000 (USD 68 820). In Germany, the Government temporarily reintroduced reduced tax rates for small and medium-sized breweries, which had previously been in place until 2003. Elsewhere in Europe, Lithuania and Poland both introduced excise duty exemptions providing up to 50% relief for small and independent breweries (Lithuania) and alcoholic beverages (Poland).

Taxes on soft drinks continue to be an area of interest for countries, with new taxes being introduced and existing taxes being raised. The Canadian province of Newfoundland and Labrador implemented a new CAD 0.2 (USD 0.16) per litre sugar-sweetened beverage tax, which will become effective as of 1 April 2022. Israel also implemented a new tax on high-sugar drinks, to be charged at ILS 1 (USD 0.31) per litre, while diet soft drinks and those with less added sugar, such as flavoured waters, are to be taxed at a rate of ILS 0.7 per litre (USD 0.22). Nigeria also introduced excise duties of NGN 10 (USD 0.03) per litre on non-alcoholic, carbonated, and sweetened beverages, while the Netherlands increased its existing consumer tax on non-alcoholic beverages (excluding water).

Kenya changed excise taxes on several products and services in 2021. Kenya has introduced a significant reform of its excise duties; rates were increased for imported sugar confectionary, commission on loans, services related to betting and lotteries, furniture products and several food items; rates were decreased for telephone and internet data services; and a new excise duty was introduced for jewellery and plastic items. To encourage regional trade, excise duties are not imposed on most goods from countries belonging to the East African Community.

A small number of countries extended measures to ease the administrative requirements of paying excise taxes from the pandemic into 2021. Viet Nam temporarily extended the deadline for paying excise tax on domestically manufactured and assembled cars to support the struggling sector. Saudi Arabia allows importers to defer the payment of customs and import duties for a period of up to 21 days.

Box 3.9. Health Tax Design

Health taxes are imposed on products whose consumption is deemed harmful to health

Excise duties on tobacco and alcohol have a long history across the world, and taxes on sugar-sweetened beverages (SSBs) have become increasingly common in recent years. As of Q3 of 2021, 14 OECD countries and three non-OECD G20 countries had implemented such taxes (University of North Carolina, 2021[13]), and a growing number of countries are considering similar measures as evidence of the negative health effects of unhealthy diets has become more prevalent and recent evaluations highlight how their introduction can be a success (Saudi Arabia and South Africa, for example). Adoption of taxes on foods high in sugar, salt and fat has also increased in the past decade but remains very limited.

Across the OECD countries where data is available, health tax revenues accounted for 2.3% of total tax revenues and 0.8% of GDP on average in 2019. As indicated in Figure 3.21, revenue from health taxes has been relatively stable over the past two decades, declining somewhat since the global financial crisis. Notable differences in health tax revenues can be observed across countries, with the share of health tax revenues in total tax revenues relatively high in some Eastern and Northern European countries in particular, such as Latvia (5.3%), Estonia (4.9%) and Lithuania (4.5%), but very low in other countries such as Israel and the United States (below 1%). There is also divergence in the importance of health taxes within the overall tax composition of the three G20 non-OECD countries for whom publicly detailed breakdowns of information on health tax revenues are available – health tax revenues have been declining in Argentina (1.6% of total tax revenues) and Brazil (0.4%), while South Africa (3.3%) has experienced a growth in health tax revenue since 2017.

Figure 3.21. Revenues from health taxes

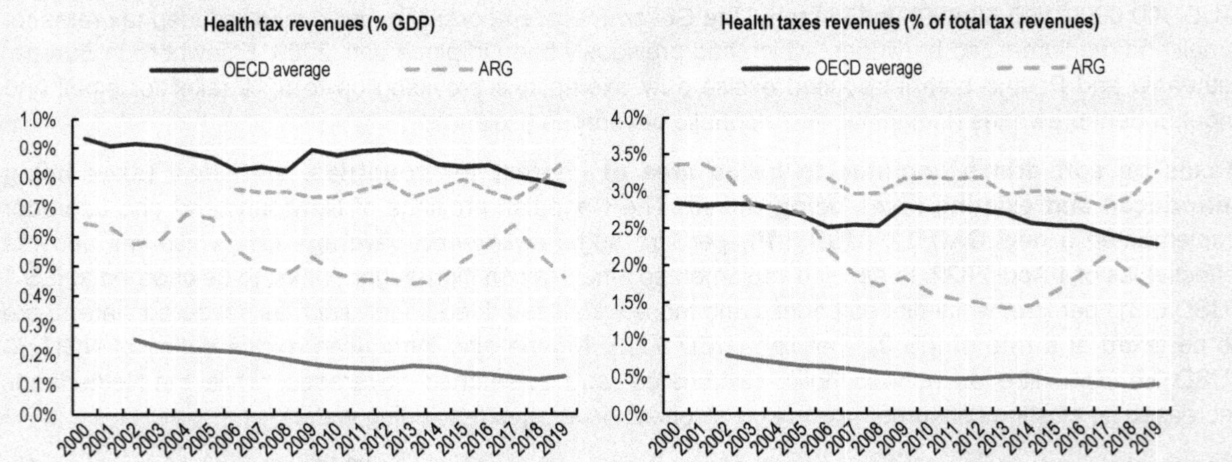

Note: Detailed information is not available for all countries, and for those countries who are able to provide complete information, it is likely that health tax revenues are underestimated due to insufficient decomposition of components. See Brys, Colin and De Melo (2022, forthcoming) for an in-depth discussion. There is no data available in OECD revenue statics for Australia, Iceland, Mexico, New Zealand and Türkiye.
Source: OECD Global Revenue Statistics Database.

StatLink https://stat.link/4z5i3y

Scope exists to strengthen the role of health taxes

Many countries could increase the rates and broaden the base of the health taxes they currently levy on unhealthy consumption. There is also scope to enlarge the base by taxing other goods that are unhealthy when consumed excessively (such as foods high in sugar, salt, and fat) and/or the inputs that are used in the production of these unhealthy consumption goods. Since the beginning of the COVID-19 crisis, several countries have (or are) considering increasing the role of health taxes to help restore public finances and/or finance healthcare systems. As described in the section on taxes on goods and services, the United Kingdom has simplified its excise duties on alcohol to discourage excessive consumption of high alcohol volume products, while India has increased alcohol taxation in some states, sometimes with a specific COVID-fee. Indonesia has also expressed interest in broadening the tax base for taxes on SSBs. Some countries have also bolstered VAT on certain products to discourage harmful consumption. Spain, for example, increased the VAT on SSBs from its reduced rate of 10% to the standard rate of 21% (with exceptions for baby milk and special dietary beverages) – national estimations suggest this measure will provide an additional EUR 340 million (USD 402 000) in 2021 and EUR 60 million (USD 71 000) in 2022.

Health taxes can also be part of countries' health protection and promotion policies

Some countries have a long history of earmarking a proportion of the revenues from health tax revenues to specific health programmes or general governmental health spending, such as Mexico and Indonesia. More recently, some countries decided to levy a COVID-specific fee on certain products deemed harmful to health and earmarked the spending of these revenues on goods and services related to the pandemic.

3.3.10. A small number of other taxes on specific goods and services have been introduced

Very few countries introduced or made changes to consumption taxes on specific products. In Canada, a new sales tax was introduced on the purchase of luxury cars and aircraft that have a retail sales price over CAD 100 000 (USD 79 740), and boats worth over CAD 250 000 (USD 199 360). The tax is calculated as the lesser of either 20% of the threshold values described above or 10% of the full value of the item. In Türkiye, the special consumption tax rates on certain vehicles were also revised upwards. Elsewhere, Sweden abolished its tax on advertising and decided not to introduce a tax on hazardous chemicals, which had previously been considered.

3.4. Environmentally related taxes

Promoting environmental sustainability has become increasingly central to the policy goals of taxing energy and vehicle use. Explicit carbon taxes on fuel were expanded in 2021. Several countries either adopted new legislation, increased the price of carbon (its rate per tonne of CO_2), or removed tax exemptions. Traditional motor vehicle taxes continued to evolve to better reflect greenhouse gas emissions and pollution profiles, and a range of existing incentives for alternative fuel or electric vehicles were extended in several countries. A selection of EU countries have introduced, or have announced plans to introduce, a tax on plastic in response to an EU initiative, the *new Own Resources Decision,* whereby member countries will pay a national contribution to the EU proportional to the quantity of plastic packaging waste that is not recycled (European Commission, 2021[47]).

However, countries differ in the degree to which they deploy environmentally related taxes. Environmentally related taxes are defined as any compulsory, unrequited payment to general government levied on tax bases deemed to be of particular environmental relevance. They encompass all taxes that are likely to have a strong environmental impact, regardless of the reason for their introduction, and cover a broad range of areas, including agrochemicals, energy, road use, vehicles, waste, water abstraction and water pollution. Among these, energy taxes, in particular fuel excise and carbon taxes, are particularly effective tools to reduce emissions of greenhouse gases. Austria and Indonesia are two countries that are stepping up the use of taxes in the context of their climate efforts (see Box 3.10).

Overall, effective carbon prices remain low. Moreover, rising energy prices led to lower energy taxes in several countries towards the end of 2021. While few energy tax and carbon pricing measures were implemented during the height of the COVID-19 pandemic in 2020, almost all countries implemented tax measures in response to rising energy prices in 2021. Given the huge scale of government responses, the report contains a special feature as its fourth chapter to discuss the tax and non-tax measures implemented, their fiscal cost and how governments can improve the effectiveness of their interventions to balance budgetary costs with longer-term climate change and energy security objectives.

Box 3.10. New carbon pricing systems

Austria

As part of its "Ecological Social Tax Reform Act 2022", Austria enacted a new carbon taxation scheme in 2021 named "*Nationales Emissionszertifikatehandelsgesetz*" (NEHG), which will enter in force on 1 July 2022 (Bundesministerium für Finanzen, 2022[48]).

The scheme will cover emissions from petrol, diesel, heating oil, coal and natural gas consumed in sectors not covered by the European Union emission trading system (transport, buildings, agriculture, waste management and non-ETS industries), similar to the German emission trading system from which it has taken inspiration. During a first phase, the logic will be like a carbon tax as prices will be fixed (with gradual increase from EUR 30 per ton of CO_2 equivalent in 2022 to EUR 55 by 2025) and the supply of allowances will be unlimited (for the sectors that qualify) (Damberger, 2022[49]). Motivated by a desire to avoid carbon leakage, relief will be granted for consumption of diesel in agriculture and forestry, fuels used in the industrial sector (from 65% to 95% discharge) and in cases of hardship for companies. The second phase, starting from 2026, will introduce a market mechanism.

The implementation of this reform should translate into higher fuel prices, e.g., by 6 cents per litre in the case of petrol. However, the true impact of the reform will depend on the pass-through of the tax from the energy providers to final consumer prices (Angela Köppl, 2021[50]).

Compensation measures for private households will be introduced under the form of a climate bonus depending on the place of residence and its connection to the public transport network, which will range from EUR 100 to EUR 200 per year. Furthermore, the reform act also includes measures to reduce other taxes including social security contributions, which will outweigh the revenues raised from the carbon tax reform (Austrian Parlament, 2021[51]). Health insurance contribution of low- and middle-income earners and of pensioners will be reduced, the personal income tax rate in the second and third tax bracket will be lowered, and the family bonus will be increased. Individuals will also benefit from additional environmental reforms; in particular, from an energy tax exemption for electricity self-generated from renewables, as well as from an income tax deduction based on expenditures that increase energy efficiency. Corporations will benefit from a gradual two percentage point cut in the corporate income tax rate and the withholding tax on profit distribution; these rates will be reduced incrementally to 23% by 2024.

Indonesia

Indonesia passed the Law on the Harmonization of Taxation Regulations in October 2021, within which it introduced a carbon tax. The tax will be payable on the purchase of "goods containing carbon" and on activities that produce greenhouse gas emissions. The revenue generated from the carbon tax may be used to finance the country's climate change mitigation and adaptation activities through the national budget. The carbon tax was initially due to enter into force from 1 April 2022, but this date was postponed until 1 July 2022 to facilitate the implementation of the tax.

The minimum carbon tax rate is set at IDR 30 per kilogram of CO_2 equivalent (approximately EUR 1.9 per tonne), less than half of the originally proposed rate of IDR 75 (Ministry of Finance, 2021[52]). While low, according to the law, the tax rate will be set to be "higher than or equal to the carbon market price per kilogram of carbon dioxide or its equivalent", when the cap-and-trade carbon emissions trading system will be operational. For the initial phase beginning in 2022, the carbon tax will apply to coal power plants only. The carbon tax will be levied on the amount of emissions that exceeds a given cap, based on intensity criteria depending on the power plant size. Starting from 2025 onwards, the full implementation of the carbon trading system and an expansion in the number of sectors that are subject to the carbon tax will be considered depending on a number of factors, including economic conditions, the readiness of actors and impact assessments.

Indonesia is the fourth Asian country to implement a carbon-pricing mechanism, after China, Japan, and Korea. Other countries in the region, such as Thailand and Viet Nam, are also considering implementing an emission trading system.

3.4.1. Environmentally related tax revenues vary widely across countries and continue to be dominated by taxes on energy use

Across the Inclusive Framework jurisdictions for which data are available,[30] environmentally related taxes raised revenue amounting to 2% of GDP in 2020, on average, slightly below the revenues in 2010 (2.2% of GDP). These revenues varied significantly across countries, ranging from 0.6% of GDP in Colombia to 3.8% of GDP in Greece in 2020 (Figure 3.22). Between 2010 and 2020, environmentally related tax revenues, measured as a share of GDP, fell in almost three quarters of the countries where data is available (see endnote 30). Denmark, Ireland, Luxembourg, Norway and Türkiye experienced the largest decreases in revenues as a share of GDP (over -0.5 percentage points of GDP). Revenues increased in eleven countries, with particularly sharp increases in Greece, Mexico, and South Africa. In nominal terms, revenues declined in 2020 compared to 2019 in almost three quarters of the countries for which 2020 data are available.[31] Nevertheless, when comparing revenues since 2010, environmentally related nominal tax revenues declined only in Japan, Luxembourg, Mexico, Switzerland, and to a lesser extent, in Denmark.

Taxes on energy use accounted for more than 50% of total environmentally related tax revenues in all but two countries in 2020. On average, taxes on energy use yielded 71% of environmentally related tax revenues. Taxes on energy use are principally fuel excise duties and carbon taxes, where applicable. Brazil (5%) and New Zealand (39%) are the exceptions, partly because of lower fuel excise duties and because they levy other environmentally related taxes that raise a significant amount of revenue. New Zealand, for example, raises notable revenues from road user charges based on the distance travelled by diesel-fuelled cars and diesel-powered heavy vehicles.

Motor vehicle taxes and other taxes on transport are the second largest component of environmentally related tax revenues. Mainly consisting of one-time registration taxes on motor vehicles and annual taxes on users or owners of vehicles, they account on average for 23% of environmentally related tax revenues across the countries covered in the report and range from 2% of environmentally related tax revenues in Estonia to 95% in Brazil.

Figure 3.22. Revenues from environmentally related taxes by country, 2020

Share of GDP (%)

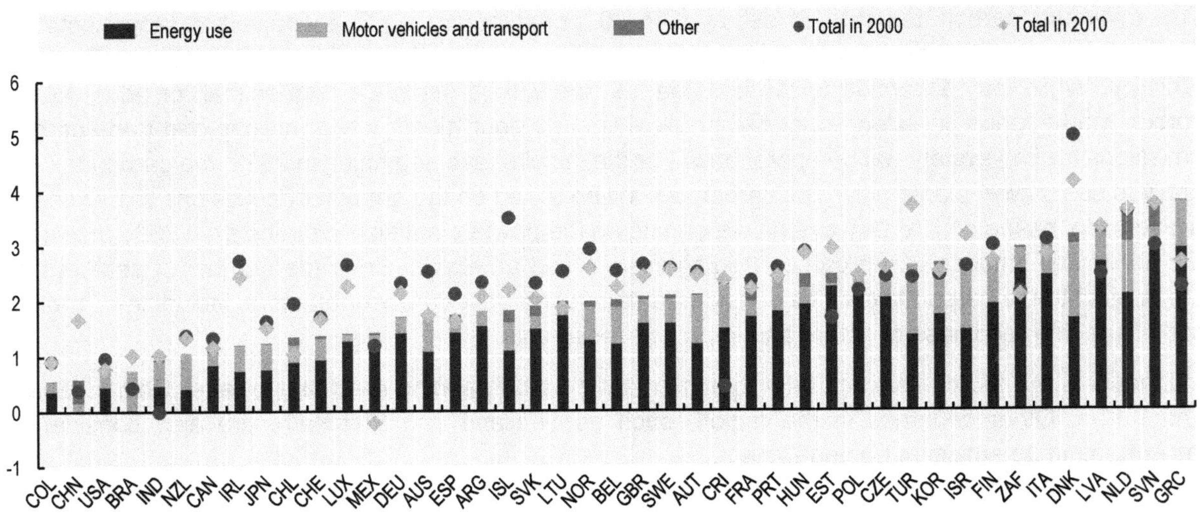

Note: Data for Brazil, Costa Rica, Argentina, China and South Africa are from 2019, data for Australia, Israel and the United Sates are from 2015, while data for Canada, Korea and India are from 2014. Data for the category "other" uses group revenues from pollution and resources tax plus eventually other taxes not specified resulting from adjustments to match the total.
Source: OECD Database on instruments used for environmental policy.

StatLink https://stat.link/0zi8yd

3.4.2. Despite growing coverage and higher values, carbon prices remain low

Almost half of all carbon emissions from energy use are now priced in OECD countries and selected non-OECD Inclusive Framework jurisdictions (49% in 2021 up from 37% in 2018).[32] The OECD calculates effective carbon rates (ECRs), which is a comprehensive indicator measuring positive carbon prices considering fuel excise duties, carbon taxes and prices of tradable emission permits. Relevant exemptions, rate reductions and refunds are also accounted for within the indicator. ECRs are expressed in euros per tonne of CO_2 for all carbon emissions from energy use. The share of carbon that is priced has increased from 37% in 2018 to 49% in 2021, although ECRs remain low for a significant share of carbon emissions (OECD, 2021[53]; OECD, 2021[54]).

On average, countries increased carbon prices between 2018 and 2021. Across G20 countries (not including Saudi Arabia), the average effective carbon rate (the sum of explicit carbon prices and fuel excise taxes) was EUR 19 per tonne of CO_2 equivalent in 2021 (USD 23.75), a modest EUR 2 (USD 2.5) increase from 2018. This increase is mainly the result of higher explicit carbon prices, which have increased to an average of EUR 4 per tonne of CO_2 (USD 5), mainly as a result of the increase in the price from emissions trading systems (up to EUR 3 from EUR 1 in 2018), while the level of carbon taxes continues to be low at less than EUR 1 (USD 1.25) on average (Figure 3.25). Despite recent progress with explicit carbon prices, effective carbon rates continue to be dominated by fuel excise duties of EUR 15 (USD 18.75) on average, which is a slight decrease relative to 2018.

The share of emissions covered by effective carbon rates differs strongly across countries. Moreover, changes are concentrated in specific countries, especially where new explicit forms of carbon pricing have been introduced, which has been the case in Canada (federal carbon pricing backstop system since 2019 and provincial/territorial carbon pricing systems since 2019 or earlier), China (emission trading system for the power sector since 2021), Germany (emission trading system complementary to the EU's since 2021) and South Africa (carbon tax since 2019). As a result, carbon prices have increasingly diverged across the G20 (not including Saudi Arabia), with little change in carbon prices in countries where rates were relatively low in 2018.

Large differences in effective carbon rates continue to exist across sectors. Taxation of carbon emissions from energy use is the highest in road transport, both in terms of coverage (94%) and in terms of effective rates (EUR 88.3 per tonne of CO_2 equivalent; USD 110). The comparatively high effective tax rate on road transport is driven by fuel excises, which represent 96% of the effective carbon rate, whereas carbon taxes, while adopted by a growing number of countries, cover only a very small share of CO_2 (about 1%).

Figure 3.23. Emissions coverage by fossil fuel and sector across G20 countries, 2018-2021

Emissions coverage (%)

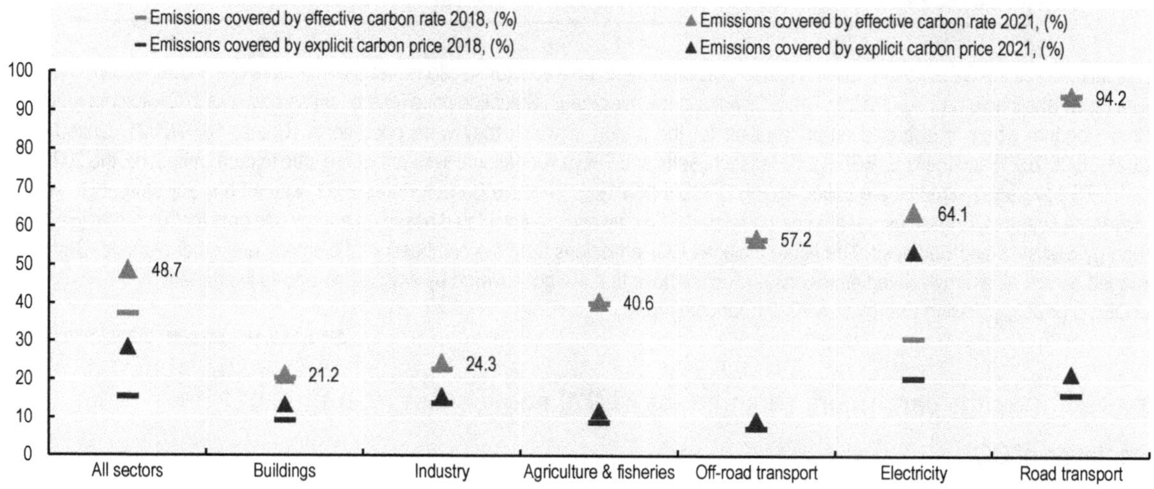

Note: G20 includes all the OECD countries and non-OECD Inclusive Framework jurisdictions that are members of the G20, except Saudi Arabia. Priced means that a positive price applies after correcting for tax reductions and refunds. Taxes are those applicable on 1 April 2021. ETS coverage estimates are based on the OECD's (2021[54]), Effective Carbon Rates 2021, with ad hoc adjustments to account for recent coverage changes. Emissions refer to energy-related CO_2 only and are calculated based on energy use data for 2018 from IEA (2020[55]), World Energy Statistics and Balances. The figure includes CO_2 emissions from the combustion of biomass and other biofuels. Percentages are rounded to the first decimal place.
Source: OECD (2022[56]), Taxing Energy Use 2022 (forthcoming).

StatLink https://stat.link/8vbf5d

Outside of the road sector, carbon emissions from the use of fossil fuels are increasingly priced, but price signals remain weak. As a recent change, electricity is now the second sector with the highest coverage with 64% of emissions priced in 2021, up from 30% in 2018 (Figure 3.23), because of wider coverage of emissions trading systems. Other sectors experienced little change – off-road transport having more than half of its emissions covered, whereas the fossil fuels used in agriculture and fisheries are covered at 41% and industry and buildings are covered at below one quarter.

Figure 3.24. The composition of effective carbon rates by sector in G20 economies, 2021

Percentage of total (%)

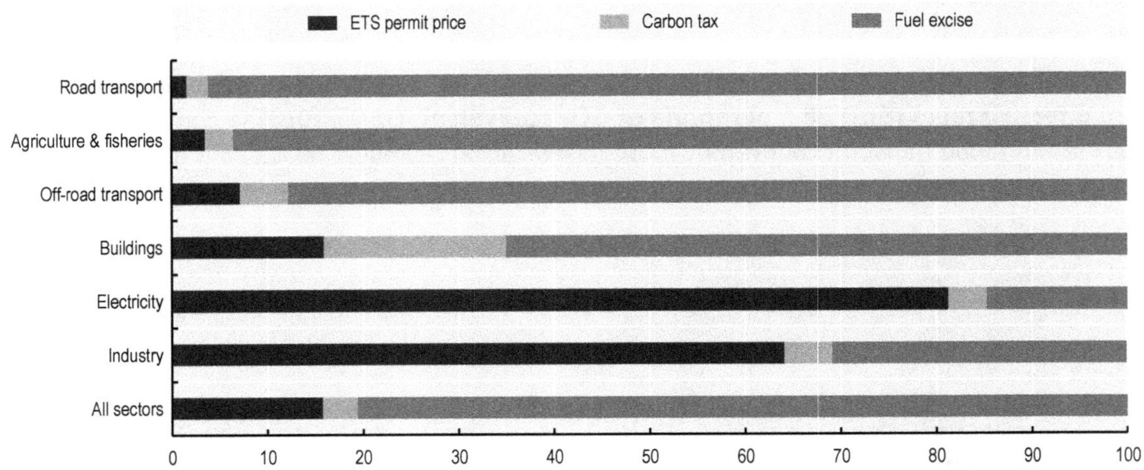

Note: G20 includes all the OECD countries and non-OECD Inclusive Framework jurisdictions that are members of the G20, except Saudi Arabia. Taxes are those applicable on 1 April 2021. The ETS price is the average ETS auction price for the first semester of 2021, except for China and the United Kingdom where it is based on information for the period in which they were operational (China: 16/07/2021, United Kingdom: 19/05/2021-30/06/2021) and the U.S. RGGI and Massachusetts and Tokyo subnational systems where, due to data limitations, the 2020 average was used. ETS coverage estimates are based on the OECD's (2021[54]), Effective Carbon Rates 2021, with ad hoc adjustments to account for recent coverage changes. Emissions refer to energy-related CO_2 only and are calculated based on energy use data for 2018 from IEA (2020[55]), World Energy Statistics and Balances. The figure includes CO_2 emissions from the combustion of biomass and other biofuels. Carbon prices are averaged across all energy-related emissions, including those that are not covered by any carbon pricing instrument.
Source: OECD (2022[56]),Taxing Energy Use 2022 (forthcoming).

StatLink https://stat.link/vfbaxk

Figure 3.25. Average carbon prices and rates in G20 economies, 2018 and 2021

EUR per tonne of CO2

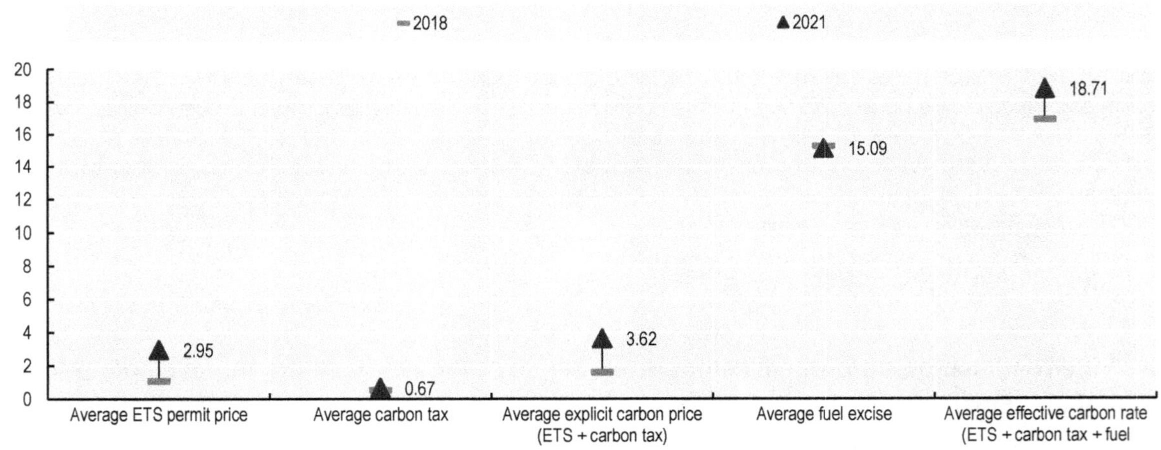

Note: G20 includes all the OECD countries and non-OECD Inclusive Framework jurisdictions that are members of the G20, except Saudi Arabia. Taxes are those applicable on 1 April 2021. The ETS price is the average ETS auction price for the first semester of 2021, except for China and the UK where it is based on information for the period in which they were operational (China: 16/07/2021, UK: 19/05/2021-30/06/2021) and the U.S. RGGI and Massachusetts and Tokyo subnational systems where due to data limitations the 2020 average was used. ETS coverage estimates are based on the OECD's (2021[54]), Effective Carbon Rates 2021 with ad hoc adjustments to account for recent coverage changes. Emissions refer to energy-related CO_2 only and are calculated based on energy use data for 2018 from IEA (2020[55]), World Energy Statistics and Balances. Carbon prices are averaged across all energy-related emissions from G20 countries, including those that are not covered by any carbon pricing instrument. All rates are expressed in real 2021 EUR using the latest available OECD exchange rate and inflation data; change can thus be affected by inflation and exchange rate fluctuations. Prices are rounded to the nearest eurocent.
Source: OECD (2022[56]), Taxing Energy Use 2022 (forthcoming).

StatLink https://stat.link/qemlvj

3.4.3. Phasing-out of preferential sectoral taxes in several countries and the expansion of carbon pricing mechanisms has encouraged transition towards low-carbon economies

Countries have introduced new carbon taxes and carbon pricing mechanisms, increased carbon tax rates, and phased out carbon tax exemptions. First, five countries enacted new carbon pricing mechanisms in 2021 and 2022. The Netherlands introduced a national CO_2 tax for industrial ETS companies on top of the ETS price in 2021, with a price floor at EUR 30 (USD 37.50) per tonne of CO_2 equivalent. Luxembourg introduced a carbon tax in 2021 at a rate of EUR 20 (USD 25) per tonne of CO_2. In 2022, Andorra, Austria and Indonesia will introduce carbon pricing mechanisms, at a rate of EUR 30 (USD 37.50) in Andorra and Austria and a minimum carbon price of EUR 1.9 in Indonesia (see Box 3.10). Second, CO_2 rates were increased in countries where carbon prices were already in place. Ireland increased its carbon tax rate by EUR 7.5 (USD 9.37) per tonne of CO_2 as part of its planned annual rate rises – Ireland has planned for its carbon tax to reach EUR 100 per tonne of CO_2 by 2030. Luxembourg announced that it would increase its carbon tax rate to EUR 25 in 2022 and EUR 30 in 2023. In South Africa, carbon tax rates were increased as part of pre-defined annual revisions, by inflation plus 2%. Denmark also set higher taxes on greenhouse gas emissions in 2021. Canada also announced an updated benchmark, under which the explicit carbon price is set to rise to CAD 170 (USD 136) in 2030. Finally, sectoral carbon tax exemptions declined in 2021. Latvia abolished the exemption for peat in stationary technological equipment, while Norway increased its carbon tax rates and broadened its base by including waste incineration, and LPG and natural gas consumption from its greenhouse industry.

Preferential energy excise treatment is being phased out, mainly in northern Europe. Preferential tax rates for specific sectors can weaken incentives for polluters to reduce their emissions, and their phasing out is a positive step to strengthen carbon taxation. Denmark, Finland, and Sweden all increased their energy taxes rates on heating fuels. In addition, Sweden increased its energy tax by abolishing energy tax reductions for agriculture and increasing rates for certain electricity uses. In 2025, the Netherlands will remove the exemption for mineralogical and metallurgical processes, the reduced rate for greenhouse horticulture, and limit the input exemption for combined heat and power. Latvia abolished the reduced rates for biofuels and Finland introduced an energy tax on biogas used in transportation in 2022. The United Kingdom will remove the entitlement to use red diesel for most business sectors from April 2022, and Belgium will gradually reduce the refund for professional diesel from EUR 248 per 1 000 litres in 2021 to EUR 202 by 2026. Electricity production taxation increased in the Czech Republic in 2021 with the introduction of a solar levy.

A small number of countries announced general increases in their fuel and electricity excise duties in the first half of 2021, before energy prices began to rise significantly. Albania announced that it would equalise the excise duty on LPG by mid-2022, while Israel stated plans to gradually increase excises on coal, fuel oil, LPG and natural gas starting from 2023. South Africa implemented an indexation of fuel excise duties to inflation, while Sweden and Estonia increased their electricity excise duties. Poland raised excise duty rates on certain fuels to align these with minimum taxation levels stipulated by European Commission directives.

Permanent tax reductions and new exemptions are scarcer than in previous years. Denmark and Finland reduced their taxes on electricity to encourage electrification and the Netherlands announced its intention to do so in 2023, in line with OECD recommendations (OECD, 2019[57]). Some sectoral exemptions were also introduced, regarding heating bio-propane in Sweden and for natural gas used for transport in Slovenia until 2025. France again postponed the removal of a tax expenditure on the excise duty on non-road diesel, which is expected to largely impact the building sector (agriculture continues to benefit from a reduced rate under these plans). Finland temporarily increased the exempted volume of peat used for heating due to larger than expected falls in peat use as a result of an increased ETS price.

Few countries have taken measures to align diesel excise with petrol excise. Relative to gasoline, diesel results in higher emissions of harmful air pollutants and CO_2 per litre of fuel (although equipment and technology can reduce non-CO_2 emissions). Nevertheless, the diesel discount is growing in the Czech Republic and Estonia, which reduced the diesel excise duties in 2020 and 2021.

Table 3.11. Changes to taxes on energy use

	Rate increase/Base broadening		Rate decrease/Base narrowing	
	2020	2021 or later	2020	2021 or later
Fuels, sector specific:				
Agriculture	LTU	SWE		
Building		GBR, FRA [4]		
Electricity production		CZE		
Heating	LVA	DNK, FIN, SWE		FIN [1]
Transport	FIN	BEL, FIN [2]		SVN [2]
Fuels, all sectors:	LTU, NLD	ALB, ISR, LVA [2], NDL, POL,	CZE [4], EST [4], GBR [4]	ITA [1]
Carbon tax	CAN, DNK, ISL, IRL	AND, AUT, CAN, DNK, FIN, IDN, IRL, LUX, LVA, NDL, NOR, UKR, ZAF [3]		
Electricity consumption	IRL	SWE	EST[4]	DNK, NLD, FIN
VAT/GST			PRT	CZE, ESP, ITA [1], POL

1. Denotes a temporary measure.
2. Tax related to biofuels
3. Taxes indexed to inflation.
4. A postponed measure.
Source: OECD Annual Tax Policy Reform Questionnaire.

3.4.4. Transport and vehicle tax reforms resumed in 2021, following a slowdown during the height of the pandemic in 2020

Several countries introduced reforms to recurrent vehicle and registration taxes in 2021 to increase the burden on polluting vehicles. Slovenia altered its taxation of vehicles in 2021, introducing a new tax scheme depending on CO_2 emissions, fuel consumption, and European pollution standards, rather than being solely based on the purchase price of vehicles as had previously been the case. Four countries with CO_2 or pollution-based taxes enacted increases in the cost of emissions intensity. Germany raised the CO_2 component of its registration tax in 2021. Norway announced it would implement the same reform as Germany from the beginning of 2022. Sweden raised its vehicle tax for the first three years following the purchase of new cars, light-duty buses and lorries fuelled by petrol and diesel petrol in 2021 and announced that it would raise the tax again by mid-2022. France strengthened its "car malus" for 2021 and 2022 by increasing the price of its vehicle registration tax for the most polluting cars and by introducing a penalty of EUR 10 (USD 12.5) per kilogram on vehicles weighing over 1 800 kg for those vehicles – whether new or imported – that are registered for the first time. Ireland adjusted its graduated vehicle registration tax so that older and more-polluting diesel cars are taxed more heavily. The Netherlands announced that it would reduce its vehicle tax (*Belasting van Personenauto's en Motorrijwielen*) exemption for vans to 0% in three steps over the period 2024-2026.

Several countries have continued to introduce fiscal incentives to encourage investment in, and the purchase of, alternative fuel vehicles. Belgium announced that it would increase corporate income tax deductions for investments in zero-carbon trucks and charging infrastructure from 2022. Allowance rates will then gradually be lowered until 2026. Sweden enhanced the bonus provided for new electric vehicles as part of a plan to simplify its *bonus-malus* system.[33] The Netherlands extended the registration tax and vehicle tax full exemption for electric vehicles until 2024, as did Germany for its registration tax, until 2025. The province of British Columbia in Canada exempted electric bicycles and tricycles from its provincial sales tax.

Some countries that have provided tax incentives for the purchase of electric vehicles for a relatively long period, decided to curtail the provision of these benefits in 2021. Norway, for example, announced that it would reduce the tax registration advantages available for plugin hybrid vehicles for 2022, largely to guard against tax base erosion concerns. Norway has significant experience in providing electric car incentives and has already reached a very low level of fossil-fuel vehicles sales – 35% in 2021, including hybrid vehicles. It has now set a target of 100% zero-emission vehicles sales from 2025. Similarly, Ireland tapered the tax relief it provides for high-value electric vehicles.

There were also several reforms made to other tax bases, such as air travel and road use. Both the Netherlands and Portugal introduced a fee per passenger for air travel in 2021, of EUR 7.45[34] (USD 9.31) and EUR 2 (USD 2.5), respectively, while Belgium changed the tax rate on airline tickets so that rates vary depending on the distance travelled (the highest rate has been imposed on flights of less than 500 km). Norway suspended their air passenger and aviation tax for 2020 and 2021 in response to the COVID-19 crisis. As part of yearly adjustments, the tax on air travel in Germany will decrease in 2022. Relatively fewer changes were made to road taxes, with Sweden announcing plans to introduce a congestion tax in 2022 for the Marieholm Tunnel (in Gothenburg) and the Netherlands planning to introduce a road user charge based on mileage under the form of a motor vehicle tax for both electric and fossil-fuel vehicles.

Several countries temporarily altered excise taxes on vehicles sales in 2021 in relation to the COVID-19 pandemic. The Seychelles introduced a 25% increase in its excise tax rates to discourage the importation of vehicles, while Japan temporarily reduced environmental performance excise taxes to encourage vehicle sales. Canada introduced a tax on the sales of luxury cars (for personal use) and Türkiye increased its special consumption tax on electric vehicles.

Table 3.12. Changes to taxes on motor vehicles and other transport taxes

	Rate increase/Base broadening		Rate decrease/Base narrowing	
	2020	2021 or later	2020	2021 or later
Excise and VAT / GST		CAN, ICE, SYC [1], TUR	KOR [1], MRT [t]	JPN [1], TUR
Vehicle tax		NLD, SWE		PRT, SVN
Registration tax	IRL, LTU	DEU, IRL NOR		
Vehicles running on alternative fuels		SWE	ISR, IRL,	BEL, NDL
Road use		NDL, SWE		
Air travel	AUT	BEL, NLD, PRT	USA	DEU [2]
Other (e.g., company cars, road accidents)				

Note: 1. Denotes a pre-planned annual change. 2. Temporary measures.
Source: OECD Annual Tax Policy Reform Questionnaire.

3.4.5. Recent trends suggest growing interest in taxes on plastic

The taxation of plastics is becoming more common. In 2021, the European Union introduced a "plastics contribution". This new "own resource" aims to raise revenues to finance the EU recovery package implemented following COVID-19 (NextGenerationEU). The tax rate is EUR 0.8ρ per kilogram of non-recycled plastic packaging starting from 2021. As a contribution from Member States to the EU budget, it does not oblige EU member countries to tax plastic to reduce waste. Nevertheless, the new levy may induce some EU members to introduce their own plastic taxes. As from 2022 onwards, Greece will tax single plastic cups and lids. Italy postponed the entry into force of the plastic tax on single-use plastic items to 2023. Spain will introduce a tax on non-reusable plastic packaging in 2023. In the United Kingdom, the "Plastic Packaging Tax" will take effect from April 2022, at a rate of approximately GBP 200 (USD 286) per tonne of plastic packaging with less than 30% of recycled content. This type of tax has proven to be efficient in other forms – the introduction of a five pence charge on use carrier bags in 2015 led to a 95% reduction in the number of bags used in England (UK Government, 2020[58]). Starting from 2021, this charge was increased by 10 pence and was extended to all retailers. Outside Europe, Israel will tax disposable plastic utensils starting from 2022.

No rate decreases nor base narrowing measures were observed in 2021 for other environmentally related tax bases, including taxes on waste, plastic, and chemicals. Despite their adoption remaining limited, countries appear to have greater interest in exploiting these tax bases, both for the positive environmental impact induced by their greater taxation and for their revenue mobilisation potential.

Table 3.13. Changes to other environmentally related taxes

	Rate increase/Base broadening		Rate decrease/Base narrowing	
	2020	2021 or later	2020	2021 or later
Pollution	LVA	LTU		
Plastic	ITA, SWE	GBR, GRC, ISR, ITA [2]		
Waste	LVA, SWE	SWE [1]		

Note: [1] denotes taxes indexed to GDP, [2] postponed measures.
Source: OECD Annual Tax Policy Reform Questionnaire.

3.5. Property Taxes

While there have been fewer property tax reforms compared to previous years, existing reforms put a clear focus on promoting progressivity and fairness in property taxation. Property tax reforms predominantly involved tax increases, through either increases in tax rates or tax base broadening measures. Tax increases were mostly targeted at individuals or entities who use properties predominantly as an investment vehicle as well as higher net worth individuals, who were affected by wealth tax and estate duty, inheritance, and gift tax reforms. Compared to previous years, reforms increasingly focused on promoting the efficient use of the existing housing stock as well as the fairness of property taxation more generally. Only two countries implemented reforms in the area of recurrent immovable property taxes while seven countries made changes to their transaction taxes. Two countries introduced reforms to their wealth tax and estate duties, and inheritance and gift taxes. (Table 3.14).

3.5.1. Property taxes continue to provide a limited source of total tax revenues

Countries impose a variety of taxes on the acquisition, holding and disposal of property. The most prominent property taxes across the countries covered in the report are recurrent taxes on immovable property, which are typically a key source of revenue for local governments. On average across OECD countries and the five selected non-OECD Inclusive Framework jurisdictions (Argentina, Brazil, China, Indonesia, and South Africa), recurrent taxes on immovable property account for 55.8% of total property tax revenue, though governments in developed countries generally show a greater reliance on recurrent taxes on immovable property due to the challenges involved in administering a fiscal cadastre, valuing property, as well as collecting property tax revenue. Transaction taxes are also common across OECD countries and non-OECD Inclusive Framework jurisdictions and account for 27.8% of total property tax revenue. Notably, taxes on financial and capital transactions make up more than half of total property tax revenue in the five-selected non-OECD Inclusive Framework jurisdictions (50.6%) compared to 24.3% across OECD countries. Inheritance, estate, and gift taxes account for a smaller share of total property tax revenue at 5.8% of total property tax revenue. A few countries impose a tax on some measure of total net wealth, which makes up nearly a quarter of total property tax revenue (23.1%), in countries in which they apply.[35] Over time, the share of recurrent taxes on immovable property within total property tax revenue has slightly increased while revenue from net wealth taxes and taxes on financial and capital transactions decreased, though to a lesser extent in non-OECD Inclusive Framework jurisdictions.

Despite growth in property tax revenues in recent years, generally they remain a limited source of total tax revenues across OECD countries and the five selected non-OECD Inclusive Framework jurisdictions. In most countries covered within the Global Revenue Statistics dataset, property taxes remain a comparatively small source of revenue, amounting to 1.8% of GDP across OECD countries and the five selected non-OECD Inclusive Framework jurisdictions (Argentina, Brazil, China, Indonesia, and South Africa). The revenue collected from property taxes varies widely across countries, ranging from 0.2% of GDP in Indonesia to 4.2% of GDP in Canada. Trends in property tax revenues over time also differ across countries, with a majority having seen their property tax revenues rise since 2000. Between 2000 and 2020, 25 countries recorded increases in property tax revenues as a share of GDP, while 18 countries recorded decreases. On average across OECD and the five selected non-OECD Inclusive Framework jurisdictions, absolute property tax revenue as a share of GDP increased by 0.2 percentage points, which marks a 12.5% increase over the past two decades. The largest absolute property tax revenue increases as a share of GDP over the period 2000-2020 were seen in Argentina (1.4 p.p.) and Korea (1.4 p.p.) while Sweden (0.7 p.p.) and Ireland (0.6 p.p.) recorded decreases (Figure 3.26).

Figure 3.26. Property tax revenues as a share of GDP in OECD and partner countries, 2000 and 2020

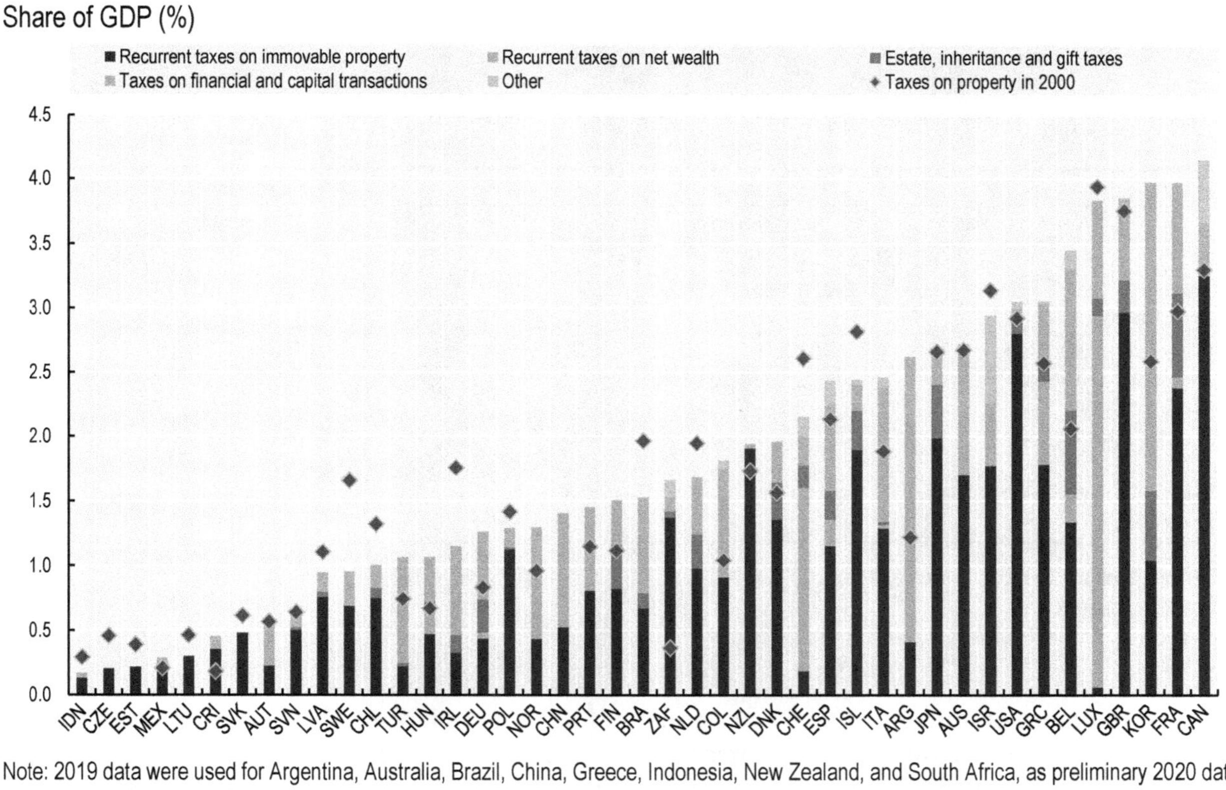

Note: 2019 data were used for Argentina, Australia, Brazil, China, Greece, Indonesia, New Zealand, and South Africa, as preliminary 2020 data were not available at the time of writing.
Source: Global Revenue Statistics Database.

StatLink https://stat.link/6shfml

3.5.2. The number of property tax reforms has declined compared to previous years, while the focus of reforms has shifted towards increasing fairness within property taxation

The latest property tax reforms have generally raised tax burdens on wealthier taxpayers and property investors, with the aim of promoting fairness in property tax systems. Generally, property tax reforms legislated in 2021 have involved increases in tax rates, introduced by six countries, or base broadening measures, implemented by seven countries (Table 3.14). Property tax increases have commonly been targeted at individuals or entities who use properties predominantly as an investment vehicle for rental purposes, with empirical evidence showing that secondary housing is heavily concentrated among high-income and high-wealth households (Millar-Powell et al., 2022[59]). Two countries also introduced measures, which lower property tax burdens, particularly for lower-wealth households. Several property tax reforms implemented in 2022 aimed at promoting the productive use of the existing housing stock, by, for instance, providing disincentives for investors who use property to store wealth. Where governments aimed at increasing property tax revenue, they tried to do so in a progressive manner.

Several countries continued to provide or introduced new property tax relief measures in response to the COVID-19 pandemic and to promote the economic recovery. To promote housing transactions and economic activity more broadly, the United Kingdom introduced a two-stage transaction tax cut in 2021. The tax-free limit was first increased from GBP 125 000 (USD 171 924) of the housing transfer value to GBP 500 000 (USD 687 696) in March 2021 and cut back to GBP 250 000 (USD 343 848) in June 2021. From September 2021, the normal tax rate schedule applied. Chile introduced a property tax deferral for individuals and companies, which allows for the payment of immovable property tax liabilities due in the 2021 tax year to be paid in 2022, subject to certain eligibility criteria. Chile also implemented a 90-day waiver for fines and interest associated with overdue payments of immovable property taxes in March 2021 (until July 2021).

Table 3.14. Changes to property tax rates and bases

	Increase		Decrease	
	2021 or later		2021 or later	
	Base	Rate	Base	Rate
Recurrent taxes on immovable property	CAN [1,2], IRL			
Transaction taxes on movable and immovable property	ARG, DEU	GBR[2,1], IRL, NLD, ISR [2,1]	MLT	
Recurrent taxes on (net) wealth	NOR	ARG, NOR	ARG	
Estate duties, inheritance and gift taxes	GBR, NLD			

1. Denotes a temporary property tax measure.
2. Denotes a new tax.
Source: OECD Annual Tax Policy Reform Questionnaire.

The tax treatment of housing is a key component of housing policy and has wider implications for countries' tax systems and their economies. Housing tax policy affects macroeconomic developments through its effect on housing investments, property prices, housing financing as well as financial stability. Housing tax policies also have important equity implications, as they affect house price developments, investment and savings incentives in the housing market and housing market accessibility more broadly. A recent study by Millar-Powell et al. (2022[59]) examines the tax treatment of housing across 40 OECD countries and non-OECD Inclusive Framework jurisdictions and discusses the implications of housing taxation for efficiency and equity goals (Box 3.11).The study finds that the effective taxation of housing is highly dependent on the investment scenario including the holding period and type of finance (debt or equity), but does not vary much with income or wealth.

Box 3.11. Measuring effective taxation of housing

Measuring and interpreting effective tax rates

Effective Tax Rates (ETRs) are an important tool for measuring the overall impact of the tax system on housing investments. ETRs combine in one indicator the impact of a wide range of taxes and tax design features under different scenarios as well as non-tax factors including for instance inflation. They thereby provide a more complete picture of how the tax system affects prospective housing investments. Marginal Effective Tax Rates (METRs) measure tax incentives to invest in different asset classes. The margin considered is one additional unit of investment (e.g., an additional dollar, euro, yen) in the chosen asset type, financed either through savings (equity-finance) or borrowed funds (debt-finance). METRs measure the difference between the pre-tax and post-tax return, i.e., the difference between what the taxpayer would retain in a world with no taxes and what the taxpayer keeps, divided by the first term (the return in a no-tax world). The paper by Millar-Powell et al. (2022[59]) provides ETR estimates which are comparable across countries and housing investment scenarios.

Housing taxation and economic efficiency

The effective taxation of housing is typically lower for investments involving owner-occupied housing, long holding periods, and debt-finance. Owner-occupied housing is typically tax-favoured compared to rented residential property. The METR is commonly lower for debt-financed compared to equity-financed housing due to mortgage interest relief; in some countries housing investments are subsidised to the extent that they result in negative METRs, which reflects that tax deductions and credits outweigh the housing taxes levied over the holding period by the investor of the housing asset. The METR on housing also decreases with longer holding periods, holding other factors constant, because transaction taxes are spread over the life of the investment, as many countries offer concessionary tax treatment for long-term capital gains, and because capital gains taxes are deferred as they are commonly levied on realisation instead of on accrual.

The primary drivers of differences in METRs across investment scenarios (owner-occupied vs. rented and equity vs. debt-financed) are mortgage interest relief on debt-financed property and income taxes on rental income (but not imputed rental) (Figure 3.27). Mortgage interest relief reduces the financing costs of housing, commonly at the taxpayer's marginal income tax rate, which can reduce the overall tax liability generated by a housing investment. Figure 3.27 shows that mortgage interest relief considerably reduces METRs for debt-financed property, nearly outweighing the combined effect of all other taxes levied over the life of an owner-occupied housing investment on average across the countries considered in the study. The taxation of rental income and the non-taxation of imputed rents on owner-occupied housing, which is widespread practice across most countries in the study, is an important driver of the differences in METRs between rented and owner-occupied housing, respectively.

Figure 3.27. The composition of marginal effective tax rates, all housing investment scenarios, average across 40 countries, 2016

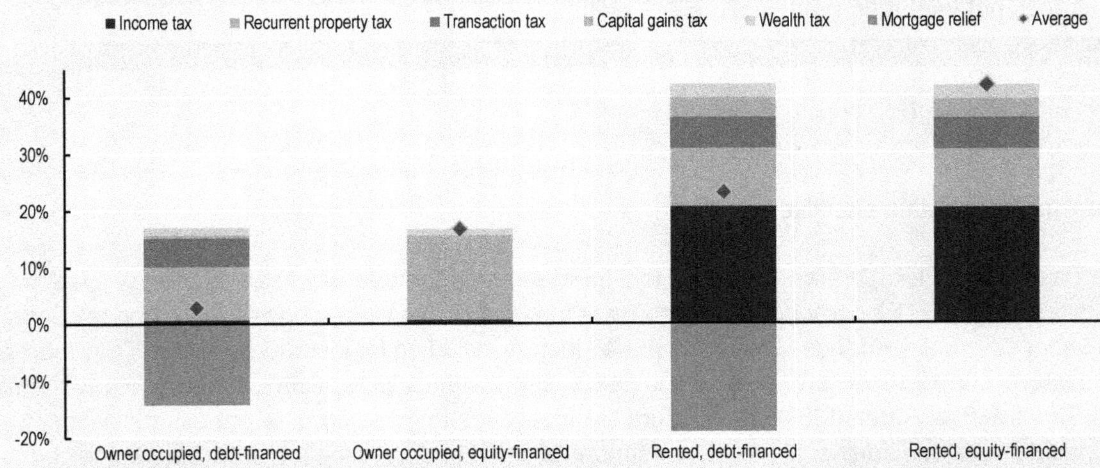

Note: Results are presented for a taxpayer earning 100% of average wage case; assuming inflation at the OECD average level; with a 20-year holding period; and the returns stemming 50% from capital gains and 50% from rent or imputed rent.
Source: Millar-Powell et al. (2022[59]).

StatLink https://stat.link/iy1knf

Housing taxation and equity

METRs are slightly progressive across income levels. The paper finds that METRs are similar for low-income (67% average wage) and average-income (100% average wage) taxpayers, with slightly higher METRs for high-income taxpayers (500% average wage), though there is substantial variation across countries. While the composition of METRs is relatively similar across different income levels, mortgage interest relief can provide greater benefit to taxpayers with higher incomes, particularly in countries where deductions are provided at the taxpayer's marginal income tax rate and tax systems are progressive. Recurrent taxes on immovable property and transaction taxes are found to have slightly progressive effects on average. Given that the share of total housing wealth held by households rises with income (with an even more skewed distribution for second residences), higher-income households are able to derive greater absolute benefits from the favourable taxation of owner-occupied housing.

Source: Millar-Powell et al. (2022[59])

Ireland introduced one of the most significant property tax reforms of the countries covered in the report, revising its recurrent tax on immovable property to promote equity and tax certainty. The Local Property Tax (LPT) reform introduced in July 2021 broadened the tax base by updating the fiscal cadastre, which previously included property values from May 2013 when the LPT was introduced, as well as by bringing new properties, which were previously exempt, into the tax base. At the same time, the reform cut existing property tax rates and widened the tax rate bands, while maintaining its rate schedule structure (which is made up of 20 bands). Despite significant property value increases in some regions since 2013, the reform is expected to decrease or leave property tax liabilities unchanged for most taxpayers. Around one third of the taxpayers are expected to face an increase in their recurrent property tax burden of up to EUR 100 (USD 118) per year while only 3% should face an increase of more than EUR 100. Residential property values are planned to be updated every four years instead of every three which aims to balance the need for timely property value updates with challenges in the tax administration and compliance (taxpayers self-assess the value of their property). With the introduction of the reform, new residential property is regularly added into the tax base, which both aims to maximise tax revenue and increase the equity of the tax system. Properties built between valuation dates are valued with reference to the preceding valuation date and become liable at the upcoming liability date (on an annual basis). The reform also phased out some exemptions, including for first-time buyers. It also increased the income threshold below which taxpayers are eligible for property tax deferral and lowered the interest charged on deferred tax payments from 4% to 3% (Department of Finance - Ireland, 2021[60]).

Canada also introduced a recurrent tax on immovable property on vacant or underused homes held by foreign non-residents to promote a more productive use of the existing housing stock. From January 2022, a nation-wide annual 1% tax will be levied on the property value of homes considered vacant or underused. All property owners (other than owners excluded from the reform, such as Canadian citizens or permanent residents) are required to file an annual return for each property they own. The tax aims to raise revenues to support the government's investments in making housing more affordable. In addition, by increasing the costs of holding vacant homes, the tax aims at increasing housing supply and promoting housing market accessibility (Department of Finance - Canada, 2021[61]).

Several countries introduced reforms to their property transaction taxes, some of which were specifically targeted at property investments by larger-scale real estate investors. In addition to its recurrent property tax reform, Ireland also introduced a 10% stamp duty in May 2021, which applies to individuals or entities purchasing ten or more residential properties (excluding apartments) on a cumulative basis within a 12-month period (the tax applies to all properties purchased within this 12-month period). In comparison, the standard stamp duty rate for residential property is 1% on properties valued up to EUR 1 million (USD 1 182 741) and 2% on properties valued in excess of EUR 1 million. By reducing the incentive to bulk buy residential property, including by institutional investors, the stamp duty aims at promoting opportunities for individual buyers (KPMG, 2021[62]). Germany amended its Real Estate Transfer Tax (RETT) Act, which has tightened the real estate transfer tax rules for investors and made certain business structures, previously used to reduce tax liabilities, less attractive. In particular, the amendment aims to prevent transfer tax avoidance through certain share deals (i.e., the transfer of shares or interests in a real estate holding corporation or partnership, which does not trigger the RETT). In the Netherlands, the real estate transfer tax for non-owner-occupied real estate will be increased from 8% to 9% in January 2023, following an increase from 6% to 8% in 2021. Malta introduced a transaction tax exemption for eligible properties applying to the first EUR 750 000 (USD 887 005) of the property's transfer value. These properties have also been exempted from capital gains taxes. Israel temporarily updated its transfer tax rates and the tax brackets that these apply to for owners of more than one residential apartment; the same measure was implemented between 2015 and 2020 to reduce house price inflation. From November 2021 to the end of 2024, an individual buyer of a single residential apartment will pay an 8% purchase tax (up from 5%) for the part of the value of the apartment in excess of NIS 2 073 190 (USD 641 850) and up to NIS 5 348 565 (USD 1 655 900) (the third purchase tax band), and a 10% rate for the part of the value in excess of this. Previously, an 8% rate applied for the part of the apartment value between NIS 5 348 565 (USD 1 655 900) and NIS 17 828 555 (USD 5 519 680) and a 10% rate for the value thereafter. The reform has been introduced with the aim of curbing the demand for properties by residential real estate investors and thereby promote housing affordability.

Changes to existing wealth taxes were introduced in Argentina and Norway, both of which have increased the tax burden on the wealthiest. Argentina increased the progressivity of its wealth tax schedule by including two additional bands at the top.[36] While net wealth over ASR 18 million (USD 189 492) used to be uniformly taxed at a rate of 1.25%, the reform added a band for net wealth between ASR 100 million (USD 1 052 734) and ASR 300 million (USD 3 158 202), which is taxed at 1.50%, and a band for net wealth above ASR 300 million, which is taxed at 1.75% (IBFD, 2022[63]). The reform narrowed the wealth tax base, however, by raising the tax exemption threshold and by introducing additional exemptions. In Norway, the net wealth tax rate was raised from 0.85% to 0.95% for those with a net worth above NOK 1.7 million (USD 197 905) (the tax-free threshold was increased from NOK 1.5 million) while net wealth above NOK 20 million (USD 2 328 289) is taxed at a rate of 1.1%. The reform also decreased the valuation discount (e.g., a factor by which the taxable base is reduced) for primary residences with a property value of above NOK 10 million (USD 1 164 144) from 75% to 50% as well as valuation discounts for secondary residences and farming permits.[37] The valuation discount of shares and operating assets and associated debt was changed from 55% to 75%.

The Netherlands and the United Kingdom introduced reforms broadening their inheritance and gift tax bases. Taking effect in 2023, the Netherlands will abolish the tax exemptions for gifts used for home purchases, improvements, or maintenance, applicable to transfers from parents to their children. The gift tax exemption is reduced from EUR 106 671 (USD 126 164) to EUR 27 231 (USD 32 207) in 2023 before it is abolished in 2024. In the United Kingdom, exemption thresholds for inheritance tax including both the Nil-Rate Band, the Residence Nil-Rate Band[38] and the Nil-Rate Band taper have been frozen at the level of the 2021/22 tax year until 2026 (thresholds are commonly adjusted for inflation on an annual basis). The Nil-Rate Band and the Residence Nil-Rate Band are maintained at GBP 325 000 (USD 447 003) and GBP 175 000 (USD 240 694) respectively while the Nil-Rate Band taper (threshold after which the tax relief is gradually reduced) is maintained at GBP 2 million (USD 2 750 786).

Several countries have introduced reforms to the taxation of crypto assets, which involved a mix of property and income tax changes. The taxation of crypto assets, crypto transactions and income derived from crypto exchanges has become an increasingly important topic on governments' policy agendas (see Box 3.12). Argentina broadened the base of its tax on debits and credits on bank accounts to include transactions related to crypto assets and crypto currencies (IBFD, 2021[64]). A 0.6% tax is levied on crypto exchanges carried out by intermediaries located in the country. Austria and Hungary also introduced taxes on income derived from crypto currency transactions (see Section 3.1 for further information).

Box 3.12. Crypto assets: tax policy and transparency implications

Crypto-asset regulation is high on the political agenda, notably among OECD countries. Whereas the financial stability implications and the anti-money laundering and counter terrorism financing issues related to crypto assets have been addressed, the tax implications have been largely unexplored until recently.

Against this background, two main directions have been developed for the OECD's work on tax and crypto assets. The first relates to transparency, with the establishment of a Crypto-Assets Reporting Framework. The second is policy-related, with prospects for expansion.

A Crypto-Assets Reporting Framework

The crypto-asset market is characterised by a new set of intermediaries that are frequently not subject to tax reporting requirements. Furthermore, detention and transfer of crypto assets across jurisdictions poses a risk that they will be used for illicit activities or to evade tax obligations. The OECD/G20 Common Reporting Standard (CRS), published in 2014, is a key tool in ensuring transparency on cross-border financial investments and in fighting offshore tax evasion. However, the current scope covered by the CRS does not provide tax administrations with adequate visibility on when taxpayers engage in tax-relevant transactions in, or hold, crypto-assets.

Therefore, the OECD is developing the Crypto-Asset Reporting Framework ("CARF"), complementing the CRS, and designed to ensure the collection and exchange of information on transactions in crypto-assets. The CARF has been designed around three key building blocks and some due diligence procedures to be followed. The first building block is a definition to establish the scope of crypto assets to be covered. The second defines the intermediaries subject to data collection and reporting requirements. The third building block defines the transactions within the scope of the reporting requirements.

The taxation of virtual currencies

In response to growing interest in the taxation implications of virtual currencies, the OECD published a report: *Taxing Virtual Currencies: An Overview of Tax Treatments and Emerging Policy Issues* in November 2020 (OECD, 2020[65]). Including detailed information on the tax treatment of virtual currencies in more than 50 jurisdictions, it is the first comprehensive analysis of the approaches and policy gaps across the main tax areas for such a large group of countries.

This report aims to support policy makers in their efforts to determine the appropriate tax treatment of virtual currencies. It provides a cross-country comparison of tax laws and guidance regarding virtual currencies and highlights emerging issues for policy makers.

The OECD is also in the early stages of examining the tax policy implications of non-fungible tokens (NFTs), following-up on its work on the tax treatment of virtual currencies. Preliminary analysis suggests that governments should consider whether the regulation of NFTs, including their tax treatment, should be similar or different to that of crypto assets. The objective of this work is to understand countries' challenges and options in taxing NFTs and related crypto-assets and will lead to a new analysis following-up on the 2020 Taxing Virtual Currencies report.

Source: G20 Finance Ministers and Central Bank Governors (2022[66]); OECD (2020[65]).

References

Angela Köppl, S. (2021), *CO2-Bepreisung in der Steuerreform 2022/2024*. [50]

Austrian Parlament (2021), *Eco-Social Tax Reform Act 2022 Part I*, https://www.parlament.gv.at/PAKT/VHG/XXVII/ME/ME_00158/. [51]

Baker McKenzie (2022), "2022 updates to Sweden's tax treatment of stock options for startup employees and board members — qualified employee stock option", https://www.bakermckenzie.com/en/newsroom/2022/01/2022-updates-sweden-tax-treatment (accessed on 14 March 2022). [11]

Baker McKenzie (2022), *Mexico: A deep dive into the 2022 Mexican tax reform*, https://insightplus.bakermckenzie.com/bm/attachment_dw.action?attkey=FRbANEucS95NMLRN47z%2BeeOgEFCt8EGQJsWJiCH2WAUTleh6%2BAJHrsOy%2Bhtpcv8m&nav=FRbANEucS95NMLRN47z%2BeeOgEFCt8EGQbuwypnpZjc4%3D&attdocparam=pB7HEsg%2FZ312Bk8OIuOIH1c%2BY4beLEAeWbySatahRJM%3D. [24]

Bundesministerium für Finanzen (2022), *Ökosoziales Steuerreformgesetz 2022 Teil I*, https://www.ris.bka.gv.at/Dokument.wxe?Abfrage=BgblAuth&Dokumentnummer=BGBLA_2022_I_10. [48]

Celani, A., L. Dressler and M. Wermelinger (2022), "Building an Investment Tax Incentives database: Methodology and initial findings for 36 developing countries", *OECD Working Papers on International Investment*, No. 2022/01, OECD Publishing, Paris, https://doi.org/10.1787/62e075a9-en. [28]

Damberger, R. (2022), *Austria's ecological tax reform: a model for other EU Member States?*, http://kluwertaxblog.com/2022/02/03/austrias-ecological-tax-reform-a-model-for-other-eu-member-states/. [49]

de la Feria, R. and M. Walpole (2020), "The Impact of Public Perceptions on General Consumption Taxes", *British Tax Review*, Vol. 67/5, pp. 637-669, https://ssrn.com/abstract=3723750. [36]

Department of Finance - Canada (2021), *Budget 2021 - Part 4: Fair and Responsible Government*, https://www.budget.gc.ca/2021/report-rapport/p4-en.html#254 (accessed on 11 March 2022). [61]

Department of Finance - Ireland (2021), *Minister Donohoe announces changes to Local Property Tax*, https://www.gov.ie/en/press-release/a9a5a-minister-donohoe-announces-changes-to-local-property-tax/# (accessed on 11 March 2022). [60]

EBANX (2021), *A study on the state of cross-border e-commerce in Latin America*. [41]

European Commission (2021), *Plastics own resource*, https://ec.europa.eu/info/strategy/eu-budget/long-term-eu-budget/2021-2027/revenue/own-resources/plastics-own-resource_en#:~:text=As%20of%201%20January%202021,non%2Drecycled%20plastic%20packaging%20waste. [47]

European Social Policy Network (2021), *Hungary will exempt young people from personal income tax as of January 2022*, http://file:///C:/Users/ramm_a/Downloads/ESPN%20-%20Flash%20report%202021%20-%2050%20-%20HU%20-%20July%202021%20(1).pdf (accessed on 13 March 2022). [12]

G20 Finance Ministers and Central Bank Governors (2022), *Communiqué - G20 Finance Ministers and Central Bank Governors Meeting*. [66]

González Cabral, A., S. Appelt and T. Hanappi (2021), "Corporate effective tax rates for R&D: The case of expenditure-based R&D tax incentives", *OECD Taxation Working Papers*, No. 54, OECD Publishing, Paris, https://doi.org/10.1787/ff9a104f-en. [67]

IBFD (2022), "Argentina Amends Progressive Rate of Personal Assets Tax", https://research.ibfd.org/#/doc?url=/data/tns/docs/html/tns_2022-01-05_ar_1.html (accessed on 11 March 2022). [63]

IBFD (2022), "Budget Law for 2022: Italy Amends Individual Income Tax Rates and Earned Income Credits", https://research.ibfd.org/#/doc?url=/linkresolver/static/tns_2022-01-14_it_3%23tns_2022-01-14_it_3 (accessed on 13 March 2022). [3]

IBFD (2022), "COVID-19 Pandemic: Tax Authorities Extend Once More Reduction of Social Security Contributions for Employers in Health Care Sector", https://research.ibfd.org/#/doc?url=/data/tns/docs/html/tns_2022-01-10_ar_1.html (accessed on 14 March 2022). [23]

IBFD (2022), *Netherlands Clarifies Compensation in Case of Unduly Taxed Savings and Investment Income*, https://research.ibfd.org/#/doc?url=/data/tns/docs/html/tns_2022-03-03_nl_2.html (accessed on 15 April 2022). [17]

IBFD (2021), "Argentina Considers Salaries Paid to New Workers as Training Expenses for Purposes of Incentive Regime for Knowledge-Related Economic Activities", https://research.ibfd.org/#/doc?url=/data/tns/docs/html/tns_2021-12-09_ar_1.html (accessed on 14 March 2022). [22]

IBFD (2021), "Argentina Introduces Income Tax and Personal Assets Tax Exemptions to Promote Investment in Domestic Currency", https://research.ibfd.org/#/doc?url=/data/tns/docs/html/tns_2021-08-06_ar_1.html (accessed on 11 March 2022). [64]

IBFD (2021), "Chamber of Deputies Approves Income Tax Reform Bill", https://research.ibfd.org/#/doc?url=/data/tns/docs/html/tns_2021-09-03_br_1.html (accessed on 14 April 2022). [7]

IBFD (2021), *COVID-19 Pandemic: Uruguay Introduces Temporary Personal Income Tax Measures*, https://research.ibfd.org/#/doc?url=/data/tns/docs/html/tns_2021-05-20_uy_1.html (accessed on 14 April 2022). [16]

IBFD (2021), *COVID-19 Pandemic: Vietnam Approves Income Tax and VAT Relief for 2021*, https://research.ibfd.org/#/doc?url=/linkresolver/static/tns_2021-10-22_vn_1 (accessed on 14 April 2022). [14]

IBFD (2021), "Government Proposes New Rules on Taxation of Crypto Currency", https://research.ibfd.org/#/doc?url=/linkresolver/static/tns_2021-05-26_hu_2%23tns_2021-05-26_hu_2 (accessed on 11 March 2022). [19]

IBFD (2021), "Lithuanian Government Plans To Increase Tax-Exempt Amount of Income", https://research.ibfd.org/#/doc?url=/data/tns/docs/html/tns_2021-10-18_lt_4.html (accessed on 13 March 2022). [5]

IBFD (2021), "Ministry of Finance Issues Draft Bill Introducing Carbon Tax, Reduced Tax Rates for Individuals and Taxation of Cryptocurrencies", https://research.ibfd.org/#/doc?url=/linkresolver/static/tns_2021-11-11_at_1%23tns_2021-11-11_at_1 (accessed on 15 March 2022). [20]

IBFD (2021), *New Government makes Changes to Budget for 2022*, https://research.ibfd.org/#/doc?url=/data/tns/docs/html/tns_2021-11-16_no_1.html (accessed on 14 April 2022). [18]

IBFD (2021), "Turkey Launches Public Consultation on Earnings Exemption for Social Content Creation and Mobile App Development", https://research.ibfd.org/#/doc?url=/data/tns/docs/html/tns_2021-12-29_tr_1.html (accessed on 14 April 2022). [10]

IEA (2020), *World Energy Statistics and Balances*, http://www.iea.org/statistics/topics/energybalances. [55]

IRS (2022), *Changes to the earned income tax credit for the 2022 filing season*, https://www.irs.gov/newsroom/changes-to-the-earned-income-tax-credit-for-the-2022-filing-season (accessed on 13 March 2022). [9]

KPMG (2021), *10% stamp duty for bulk purchasers of homes*, https://home.kpmg/ie/en/home/insights/2021/05/government-10-per-cent-stamp-duty-bulk-purchase-homes.html (accessed on 11 March 2022). [62]

KPMG (2021), "Norway – Budget 2022 Has Several Measures Affecting Individuals", https://assets.kpmg/content/dam/kpmg/xx/pdf/2021/12/fa21-317.pdf (accessed on 13 March 2022). [6]

Mastercard and Kaiser Associates (2019), *Mastercard Gig Economy Industry Outlook and Needs Assessment: The Global Gig Economy, Capitalizing on a ~$500B Opportunity*. [44]

Millar-Powell, B. et al. (2022), "Measuring effective taxation of housing: Building the foundations for policy reform", *OECD Taxation Working Papers*, No. 56, OECD Publishing, Paris, https://doi.org/10.1787/0a7e36f2-en. [59]

Ministry of Finance (2021), *UU Nomor 7 Tahun 2021*, https://peraturan.bpk.go.id/Home/Details/185162/uu-no-7-tahun-2021. [52]

OECD (2022), *Crypto-Asset Reporting Framework and Amendments to the Common Reporting Standard*, OECD, Paris, https://www.oecd.org/tax/exchange-of-tax-information/public-consultation-document-crypto-asset-reporting-framework-and-amendments-to-the-common-reporting-standard.pdf. [21]

OECD (2022), *Tax Policy and Gender Equality: A Stocktake of Country Approaches*, OECD Publishing, Paris, https://doi.org/10.1787/b8177aea-en. [8]

OECD (2022), *Taxing Energy Use 2022 (forthcoming)*. [56]

OECD (2021), *Carbon Pricing in Times of COVID-19: What Has Changed in G20 Economies?*. [53]

OECD (2021), *Corporate Tax Statistics - Third Edition*, https://www.oecd.org/tax/tax-policy/corporate-tax-statistics-third-edition.pdf. [26]

OECD (2021), *Effective Carbon Rates 2021: Pricing Carbon Emissions through Taxes and Emissions Trading*, OECD Publishing, Paris, https://doi.org/10.1787/0e8e24f5-en. [54]

OECD (2021), *Revenue Statistics in Asia and the Pacific 2021: Emerging Challenges for the Asia-Pacific Region in the COVID-19 Era*, OECD Publishing, Paris, https://doi.org/10.1787/ed374457-en. [33]

OECD (2021), *Tax Policy Reforms 2021: Special Edition on Tax Policy during the COVID-19 Pandemic*, OECD Publishing, Paris, https://doi.org/10.1787/427d2616-en. [27]

OECD (2021), *Taxing Wages 2019-2020 - Taxing Wages in Selected Partner Economies*, OECD, Paris, https://www.oecd.org/tax/tax-policy/taxing-wages-in-selected-partner-economies.pdf (accessed on 2 May 2022). [1]

OECD (2021), *Taxing Wages 2021*, OECD Publishing, Paris, https://doi.org/10.1787/83a87978-en. [2]

OECD (2021), *The Impact of the Growth of the Sharing and Gig Economy on VAT/GST Policy and Administration*, OECD Publishing, Paris, https://doi.org/10.1787/51825505-en. [45]

OECD (2020), *Consumption Tax Trends 2020: VAT/GST and Excise Rates, Trends and Policy Issues*, OECD Publishing, Paris, https://doi.org/10.1787/152def2d-en. [34]

OECD (2020), *Tax Policy Reforms 2020: OECD and Selected Partner Economies*, OECD Publishing, Paris, https://doi.org/10.1787/7af51916-en. [30]

OECD (2020), *Taxing Virtual Currencies: An Overview Of Tax Treatments And Emerging Tax Policy Issues*, OECD, Paris. [65]

OECD (2020), *Taxing Wages 2020*, OECD Publishing, Paris, https://doi.org/10.1787/047072cd-en. [15]

OECD (2019), *Tax Policy Reforms 2019: OECD and Selected Partner Economies*, OECD Publishing, Paris, https://doi.org/10.1787/da56c295-en. [37]

OECD (2019), *Taxing Energy Use 2019: Using Taxes for Climate Action*, OECD Publishing, https://doi.org/10.1787/058ca239-en. [57]

OECD (2017), *International VAT/GST Guidelines*, OECD Publishing, Paris, https://doi.org/10.1787/9789264271401-en. [39]

OECD (2017), *Mechanisms for the Effective Collection of VAT/GST*. [38]

OECD (2015), *Addressing the Tax Challenges of the Digital Economy, Action 1 - 2015 Final Report*, OECD/G20 Base Erosion and Profit Shifting Project, OECD Publishing, Paris, https://doi.org/10.1787/9789264241046-en. [42]

OECD (2015), *Countering Harmful Tax Practices More Effectively, Taking into Account Transparency and Substance, Action 5 - 2015 Final Report*, OECD/G20 Base Erosion and Profit Shifting Project, OECD Publishing, Paris, https://doi.org/10.1787/9789264241190-en. [25]

OECD (2015), *Transfer Pricing Documentation and Country-by-Country Reporting, Action 13 - 2015 Final Report, OECD/G20 Base Erosion and Profit Shifting Project*, OECD Publishing, https://doi.org/10.1787/9789264241480-en. [29]

OECD/AUC/ATAF (2021), *Revenue Statistics in Africa 2021*, OECD Publishing, Paris, https://doi.org/10.1787/c511aa1e-en-fr. [31]

OECD et al. (2022), *Revenue Statistics in Latin America and the Caribbean 2022*, OECD Publishing, Paris, https://doi.org/10.1787/58a2dc35-en-es. [32]

OECD et al. (2021), *Revenue Statistics in Latin America and the Caribbean 2021*, OECD Publishing, Paris, https://doi.org/10.1787/96ce5287-en-es. [40]

OECD et al. (2021), *VAT Digital Toolkit for Latin America and the Caribbean*, OECD, Paris, https://www.oecd.org/tax/consumption/vat-digital-toolkit-for-latin-america-and-the-caribbean.pdf. [43]

Panteghini, P. and S. Pellegrino (2022), "Italy's 2022 Tax Reform Targets Personal Income Tax And Child Benefits", https://www.taxnotes.com/tax-notes-international/international-taxation/italys-2022-tax-reform-targets-personal-income-tax-and-child-benefits/2022/01/31/7d41t (accessed on 13 March 2022). [4]

Sveriges Riksdag (2021), *Temporarily reduced tax for earned income for 2021 and 2022*, https://www.riksdagen.se/en/news/2021/okt/13/temporarily-reduced-tax-for-earned-income-for-2021-and-2022/#:~:text=In%20the%20case%20of%20earned,500%2C000%2C%20it%20will%20be%20reduced. (accessed on 13 March 2022). [13]

Thomas, A. (2020), "Reassessing the regressivity of the VAT", *OECD Taxation Working Papers*, No. 49, OECD Publishing, Paris, https://doi.org/10.1787/b76ced82-en. [35]

UK Government (2020), *Plastic carrier bag sales slashed by more than 95% since 5p charge introduced.* [58]

World Health Organisation (2017), *WHO report on the global tobacco epidemic, 2017: monitoring tobacco use and prevention policies*, Geneva: World Health Organization, https://apps.who.int/iris/handle/10665/255874. [46]

Notes

[1] In addition to all OECD members, the report covers the following Inclusive Framework jurisdictions that responded to the questionnaire in 2022: Albania, Andorra, Argentina, Armenia, Bosnia and Herzegovina, Brazil, Brunei Darussalam, Bulgaria, Cabo Verde, the Cook Islands, Croatia, Georgia, Honduras, Kenya, Malaysia, Malta, Mauritius, Monaco, Morocco, Nigeria, Pakistan, Peru, Romania, Saudi Arabia, Senegal, Seychelles, South Africa, Togo, Ukraine, the United Arab Emirates, Uruguay, and Viet Nam.

[2] Where the text references an average across OECD and selected non-OECD Inclusive Framework jurisdictions, this represents the unweighted average for all OECD countries, as well as Argentina, Brazil, China, Indonesia, and South Africa, unless otherwise specified.

[3] Notably, the PIT & SSC revenue trends described in the earlier parts of Section 3.1 are not the result of changes to PIT and SSC measures described towards the end of Section 3.1 – the tax revenue data are from 2020 while the tax reforms information covers the following year, 2021.

[4] Comparable data was not available for Costa Rica, who joined the OECD in May 2021, at the time of writing.

[5] Conversions refer to the OECD official 2021 exchange rates and not purchasing power parity rates. See https://data.oecd.org/conversion/exchange-rates.htm#indicator-chart for more detail.

[6] Throughout this section, thresholds and the monetary amounts of tax relief will be provided on an annual basis, unless stated otherwise.

[7] These tax rates are paid on top of Canada's federal tax rates. Canada's federal tax rates for 2021 were: 15% on the first CAD 49 020 (USD 37 700) of taxable income; 20.5% on the portion of taxable income over CAD 49 020 up to CAD 98 040 (USD 75 415); 26% on the portion of taxable income over CAD 98 040 up to CAD 151 978 (USD 116 906); 29% on the portion of taxable income over CAD 151 978 up to CAD 216 511 (USD 166 550) and 33% of taxable income over CAD 216 511.

[8] At the time of writing, the IMF had not published an official exchange rate for the Nigerian Naira to United States Dollar for 2021. The 2020 exchange rate of NG 358.81:1 USD has therefore been used.

[9] Preliminary CIT revenue data for 2020 were not available for Australia, Greece, or New Zealand.

[10] The OECD Corporate Tax Statistics Database provides statutory CIT rates for all OECD countries as well as the following additional Inclusive Framework jurisdictions: Argentina; Brazil; Bulgaria; China; Croatia; Hong Kong, China; India; Indonesia; Peru; Romania; Saudi Arabia and South Africa.

[11] The OECD uses the canton of Zurich as a basis for its combined CIT rate for Switzerland.

[12] Not all firms are subject to this 25% tax rate, however. From the start of 2021, Türkiye lowered the corporate income tax rate by 2 percentage points for five accounting periods (from the accounting period of their initial public offering) for corporations whose shares are offered to the public for the first time to be traded on the Borsa Istanbul Equity Market, and who are subject to a corporate tax rate of at least 20%. Financial leasing companies, factoring companies, financing companies, payment and electronic money institutions, authorized foreign exchange institutions, asset management companies, capital market

institutions, insurance and reinsurance companies and pension companies are excluded from qualifying for this lower rate.

[13] Türkiye also announced in 2021 that it would apply a 23% tax rate to corporate income for the year 2022.

[14] Ontario's Regional Opportunities Investment Tax Credit only applies to up to CAD 500 000 (USD 400 000) of property, and therefore largely targets SMEs.

[15] The measures discussed in this paragraph refer to those that apply to R&D and innovation related expenditure and income. General CIT measures, e.g., accelerated depreciation on investments, that is not specifically targeted to R&D or innovation, even though it may have an indirect effect, is not discussed as an R&D and innovation-related policy.

[16] See the German Finance Ministry's Combating Tax Avoidance and Unfair Tax Competition Act at https://www.bundesfinanzministerium.de/Content/EN/Downloads/Resources/Laws/act-combating-tax-avoidance-and-unfair-tax-competition-and-amending-further-acts.pdf?__blob=publicationFile&v=2.

[17] Tax revenue data for taxes on goods and services were selected for all OECD countries and five non-OECD inclusive framework members (Argentina, Brazil, China, Indonesia and South Africa). Notably, the country coverage of the tax revenue data (43 countries) differs from the tax policy reform trends (71 countries). The latter is based on responses to the OECD's annual tax policy reform questionnaire, which includes all OECD countries. See the Introduction of the report and endnote 9 for more detail.

[18] The United States is the only OECD country that employs a retail sales tax rather than a value added tax as its principal consumption tax. Its retail sales tax is not a federal tax but is rather tax imposed at the state and local government level.

[19] The United States is the only OECD country that employs a retail sales tax rather than a value added tax as its principal consumption tax and is therefore not included in VAT comparisons. The non-OECD Inclusive Framework jurisdictions referred to are Argentina, Brazil, China, Indonesia, and South Africa.

[20] Comparisons of changes between 2019 and 2020 were not possible for Australia, Japan, and New Zealand as these had not published preliminary 2020 VAT revenue data at the time of writing. The USA does not operate a federal VAT and was therefore not included in this VAT analysis.

[21] VAT rate data were used for 36 OECD countries and for Saudi Arabia. Comparable data were not available for Costa Rica or for partner countries (Argentina, Brazil, China, Indonesia, and South Africa) at the time of writing. The USA does not operate a federal VAT.

[22] The zero VAT rate applied to hotels and tourism services was later extended until the end of 2022. The VAT rate previously applied to restaurants (food and beverage services) was the 8% reduced rate, while airline tickets and related services had previously been subject to the standard 19% rate. The 5% reduced rate on airline tickets and related services will remain in place until 31 December 2022.

[23] This measure was extended, retrospectively, at the end of April 2022.

[24] There have since been discussions in the Estonian parliament to extend the period during which the reduced rate will be applicable to January 2023.

[25] Italy has since extended the temporary cut in its VAT rate on domestic and industrial use gas until 30 June 2022. The 10% reduced VAT rate was previously applied to sales of natural gas up to 480 cubic

metres a year, and the standard 22% VAT rate was applicable for consumption above this amount. The VAT rate on domestic gas use had previously been 22%.

[26] These measures were then extended as part of the Polish government's second "anti-inflation shield" package of measures. From 1 February 2022 until 31 July 2022, the VAT rate for natural gas was reduced to 0% and to 5% for district heating.

[27] In December 2021, the Spanish government announced that it would extend this measure until the end of April 2022. A further extension, until the end of June 2022 was later approved.

[28] The VAT digital toolkit for Latin America and the Caribbean is the OECD's most well-established digital toolkit.

[29] In Poland, changes to the taxation of tobacco products and their substitutes were legislated in 2021, and will take effect as of 1 January 2022 (e.g., an increased excise tax rate on heated tobacco products) and in subsequent years (e.g., the increase in the excise tax rate on cigarettes, rolling tobacco and raw tobacco).

[30] Environmentally related tax revenue data covers all 38 OECD countries and four non-OECD Inclusive Framework jurisdictions (Argentina, Brazil, India, and South Africa). 2020 data were available for all but nine of the 42 countries. Data for 2019 was used for Argentina, Brazil, Costa Rica, and South Africa; 2015 data for Australia, Israel, and the United Sates; and 2014 data for Canada, India, and Korea. Data for the category "other" uses group revenues from pollution and resources tax plus eventually other taxes not specified resulting from adjustments to match the total.

[31] Environmentally related tax revenue data for 2020 were available for 32 of the 38 OECD countries. Data were not available for Australia, Canada, Costa Rica, Israel, Korea, and the United States.

[32] Effective carbon rates data are available for 37 OECD countries and six non-OECD Inclusive Framework jurisdictions (Argentina, Brazil China (People's Republic of), India, Indonesia, and South Africa). At the time of writing, 2021 data on effective carbon rates were only available for Argentina, Australia, Brazil, Canada, France, Germany, India, Indonesia, Italy, Japan, Korea, Rep., Mexico, South Africa, Türkiye, the United Kingdom and the United States.

[33] Sweden operates a *bonus malus* system whereby it seeks to reward vehicles that emit relatively small amounts (up to 60 grams per kilometre) of CO_2, with a maximum *bonus* of SEK 70 000 (USD 8 140), while burdening vehicles that emit relatively large amounts of CO_2 with higher vehicle tax for the first three years: *malus*.

[34] This will rise to EUR 7.95 (approximately USD 9.94) in 2022.

[35] Note that "Recurrent Taxes on Net Wealth" include taxes levied on individuals and corporate entities

[36] Note that Argentina levies a permanent tax on net wealth ("*Impuesto sobre los bienes personales*" (ISBP) discussed in this report, which is different to the one-off wealth tax which was introduced in addition to the ISBP

[37] For example, a property with a market value of NOK 5 million (USD 582 072) would have had a taxable value of NOK 1.25 million (USD 145 518) before the reform while the taxable value after the reform would be NOK 2.5 million (USD 291 036).

[38] Besides a basic allowance (Nil-Rate Band) of GBP 325 000 (USD 447 003), the United Kingdom provides an additional tax-free threshold ("Residence Nil-Rate Band") for residences with certain qualifying characteristics, which are passed on to direct descendants.

4 Special Feature: Policy responses to rising energy prices

This chapter is a Special Feature, which provides an overview of the measures adopted by OECD countries and Inclusive Framework jurisdictions in response to rising energy prices, as well as some policy recommendations in the event that prices remain elevated. The Special Feature is based on a joint Policy Brief produced by the Centre for Tax Policy and Administration, the Economics Department, the Environment Directorate and the Trade and Agriculture Directorate.

4.1. Introduction

Energy prices have been soaring since early 2021 due to a combination of supply and demand factors. These include long-term trends such as underinvestment in natural gas and clean energy supply, and short-term developments like reductions in natural gas spot delivery by Russia and a strong recovery in demand in the aftermath of the COVID-19 slump (IEA, 2021[1]). Russia's invasion of Ukraine has put further strain on already tight energy markets and increased uncertainty over the near-term development of supply. Russia has cut off energy supply to several countries, and others have introduced embargoes on Russian energy imports.

The International Energy Agency (IEA) predicts that high prices of petroleum and gas products are here to stay. This is despite the fact that steadily rising oil supply volumes from the Middle East and the United States, along with slower economic growth, are expected to mitigate oil and gas supply constraints due to the Russian supply disruption.[1] Volatility of energy prices has also been extremely high. As a result, the energy crisis is now contributing to rising inflation pressures across the world (OECD, 2022[2]) (Figure 4.1).

Energy users have few options to cut demand drastically in the very short run, meaning that concerns over energy affordability and the cost of living loom large.[2] Price shocks have had significant adverse effects on households and businesses, which has prompted governments to respond (Boone and Elgouacem, 2021[3]). This Special Feature takes stock of the responses and considers their respective merits and drawbacks.[3] It also highlights the challenges of providing well-designed income support, including for the transition to carbon neutrality.

Support measures can be classified in several ways, but a key distinction is between income support – i.e., transfers to households and businesses – and price support measures, which seek to reduce energy prices paid by consumers. Income support can be delivered through transfers or vouchers to households and firms. In times of crisis, income support measures already in place can be extended to a wider population or the amount of existing transfers can be increased.

Price support measures can take the form of, for instance, price controls, reduced electricity excise taxes and network fees, value added tax (VAT) and fuel excise tax reductions or exemptions, and rebates at the pump. Both income support and price control measures can be targeted, either through means-testing or by restricting the benefit of the measures to certain specific categories of energy consumers based on some criteria, such as energy consumption, income, or residence.

Figure 4.1. Relative contribution of factors to headline inflation rates in the euro area and the United States

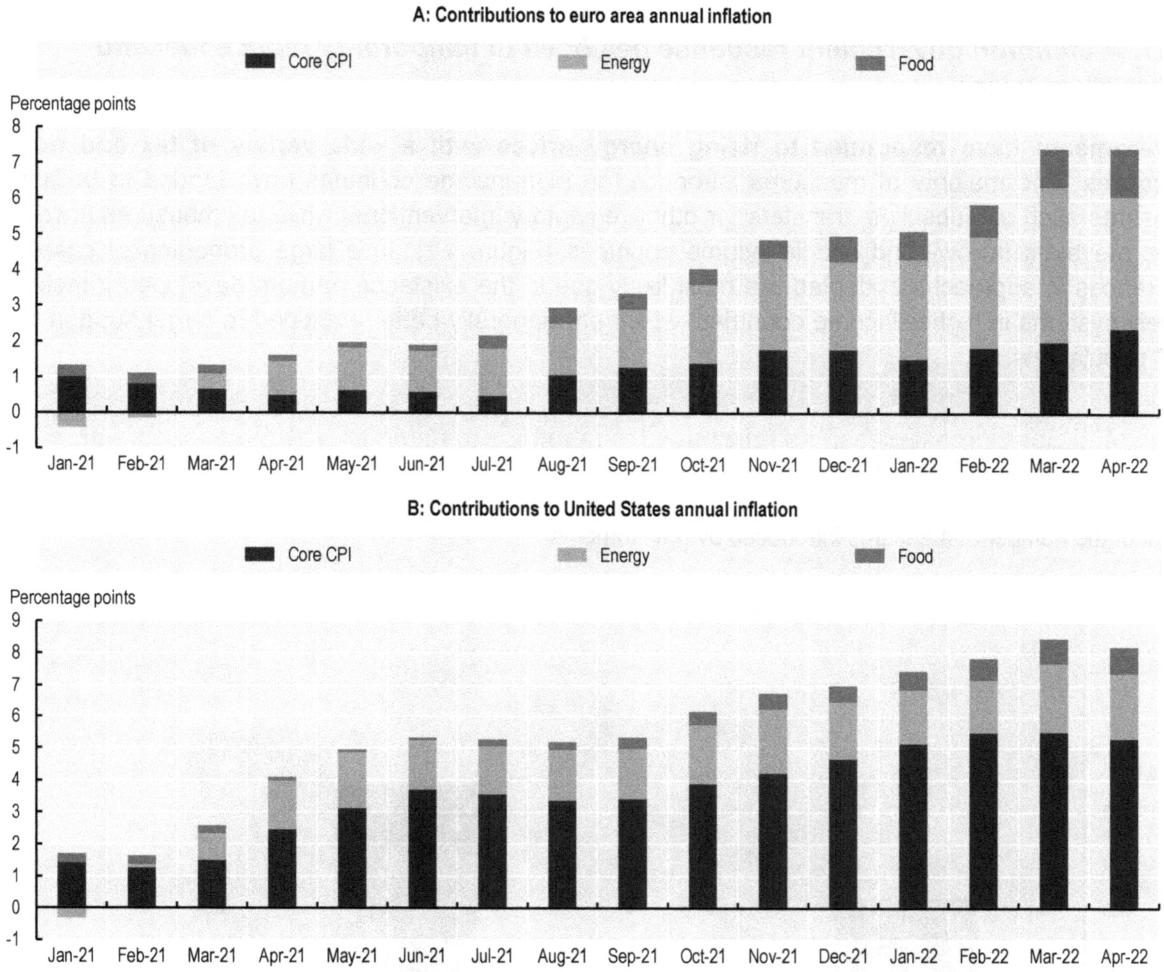

Source: OECD (2022[4]); OECD Eurostat Harmonised Indices of Consumer Prices, OECD Consumer Price Indices.

StatLink https://stat.link/w4jbs8

The key message of this Special Feature is that governments will need to shift from policies that directly seek to limit price increases to those that cushion their impact through targeted income support. This approach will ensure that the support provided is fair and effective, while limiting its effects on government budgets and maintaining price signals to encourage the transition to carbon neutrality. However, even the most sophisticated fiscal systems may not be fully geared to the task, calling for action to improve their capacity to target specific groups. In addition, broad access to alternative energy sources is a prerequisite for an effective and publicly acceptable longer-term strategy to shift away from fossil fuels.

4.2. Government support measures

This Chapter draws on data collected by the OECD on government support measures implemented in 89 jurisdictions, including 74 member jurisdictions of the OECD/G20 Inclusive Framework on Base Erosion and Profit Shifting[4] since the onset of the energy crisis in the third quarter of 2021.

As of 30 May 2022, the information collected covered over 350 measures designed to cushion the impact of rising energy prices in the short run. Some governments have also estimated the fiscal costs of the key measures, in terms of either resources spent or revenue foregone.

4.2.1. A common government response has been to temporarily reduce fuel and electricity excises

Governments have responded to rising energy prices with a wide variety of tax and non-tax measures. The majority of measures introduced in high-income countries have tended to be non-tax measures such as subsidies, transfers, or other regulatory interventions, while tax measures have been more prevalent in low- and middle-income countries (Figure 4.2). In a large proportion of cases, the differences in approaches adopted are most likely due to the existence of more developed transfer and benefit systems in higher-income countries, which are generally better equipped to target support to "at-risk" populations.

Figure 4.2. Government measures introduced in response to rising energy prices, September 2021 to May 2022

Count of the number of measures introduced by governments

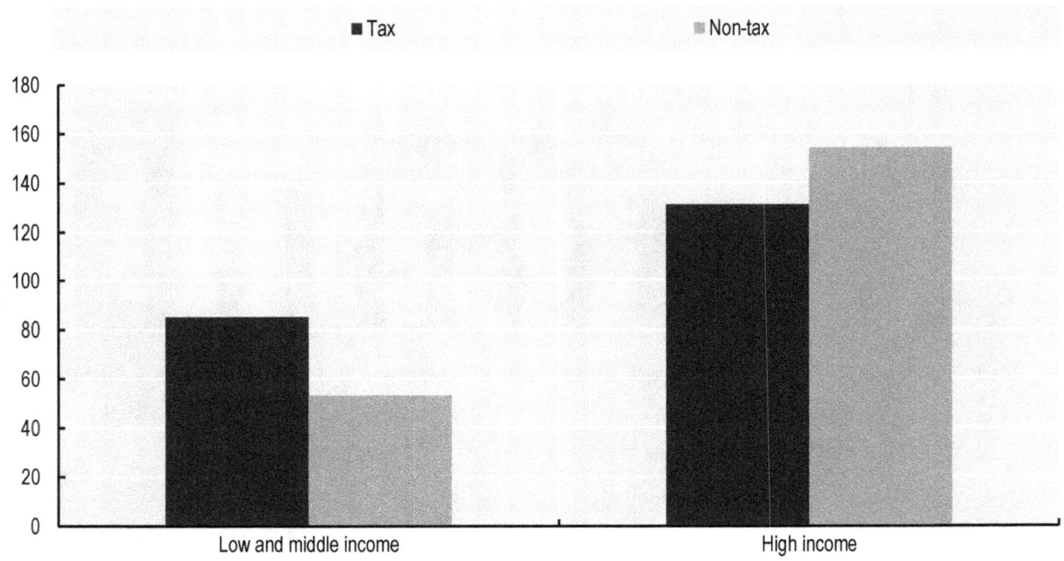

Note: Measures up to date as of 25 May 2022. Country income status reflects World Bank classifications.
Source: OECD Working Party 2 Delegate responses.

StatLink https://stat.link/in1sw4

Temporary indirect tax reductions have been the most common form of tax measure implemented by countries. Reductions in environmentally related taxes, largely cuts in excise taxes on petroleum products, were the most frequently introduced measure to cushion the impact of rising prices, followed by decreases in the VAT/GST rate on fuel products, and lower import duties (Figure 4.3). Subsidies and cash transfers have been the most common non-tax measures implemented, with lower-income households being the primary target of both types of measures and businesses receiving some subsidy support in a small number of countries.

Figure 4.3. Tax measures introduced in response to rising energy prices, September 2021 to May 2022

Count of the number of tax measures introduced by governments

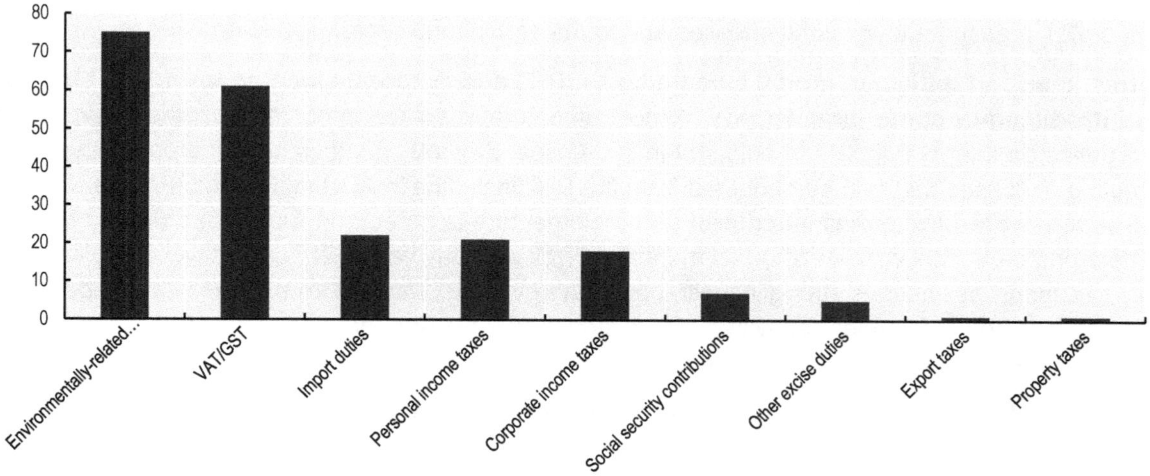

Note: Measures up to date as of 25 May 2022.
Source: OECD Working Party 2 Delegate responses.

StatLink https://stat.link/e0pd9t

Excise taxes were cut in 73 of the 89 jurisdictions covered by the database, mainly for petroleum products. The largest cuts in excise duties per litre of gasoline were implemented in Germany (EUR 0.30 for three months starting from June 2022), Italy (EUR 0.25 from March 2022 until at least 8 July 2022), Ireland (EUR 0.20 for petrol and EUR 0.15 for diesel for six months starting from March 2022), Korea (KRW 264 (EUR 0.23) for three months from May 2022) and Belgium (EUR 0.175 from 19 March 2022 until at least the end of December 2022).[5] A number of countries initially implemented excise tax cuts for short periods of around a month when they were first introduced, but with energy prices remaining high, these measures were often extended (in some cases, on several occasions) and many countries also increased the size of the excise tax cut. Some countries temporarily removed excise duties on tax altogether while others provided tax credits on fuel duties or decided against planned increases. Other environmentally related tax measures included lowering excise taxes on electricity, delaying new taxes (and rises to existing taxes) on coal, and providing excise duty holidays for the purchase of electric vehicles.

VAT reductions on energy products have also been a common policy response, mostly in European countries and most frequently for electricity and natural gas products. As Europe was one of the first regions to experience rising energy prices, EU countries were among the first countries to introduce VAT cuts. Similar to the excise duty cuts, most cuts to VAT were announced as temporary measures, but in several cases have been increased or extended, in some cases on several occasions. In June 2021, Spain reduced the VAT rate on energy bills from 21% to 10%; the measure has been extended several times since. Then in October 2021, Italy cut its VAT rate on the use of natural gas supplies for "civil and industrial uses" to 5%, before Cyprus announced reductions in the VAT rate on electricity and gas (from 19% to 5% for vulnerable groups, and to 9% for all other households) and the Czech Republic announced a VAT exemption in November 2021. Several other European countries followed suit in early 2022, including Belgium, Estonia, Lithuania, North Macedonia, and Poland. Türkiye also reduced the VAT rate on electricity used in residents and agricultural irrigation from 18% to 8% from March 2022. Outside of Europe, in March 2022 Barbados capped the VAT payable on gas and diesel (in US dollars) for six months and the

Costa Rican government introduced a VAT exemption for purchases of electrical energy intended for distribution. From April 2022, El Salvador temporarily reduced the VAT rate on fuels and Kenya halved the VAT rate on automotive fuels to 8% as part of its 2022 budget. Other VAT measures have included temporary VAT holidays for the purchase of electric bicycles and cars (Barbados; British Columbia, Canada[6]) and greater flexibility with respect to VAT repayments for businesses. Some countries have targeted VAT measures towards businesses and to the agricultural sector, including Greece.

Reforms to import duties, personal income taxes (PIT) and corporate income taxes (CIT) have also been introduced in some jurisdictions. Almost all natural resource importing countries have reduced import duties on energy supplies to help soften price rises. Several countries have increased the value of commuting expenses that can be deducted from the PIT, including in Austria, Finland, France, Germany, and Sweden, while Mexico has introduced a complementary tax credit on fuel excise duties, which fuel importers and producers can use to offset monthly CIT or VAT payments. CIT credits were also introduced in Italy to support businesses struggling with rising energy costs, ranging from 12-25% depending on the energy-intensity of companies' activities. In Austria, the government introduced a 50% reduction in advance PIT payments to ease the PIT burden for entrepreneurs.

Subsidies and transfers have been central to policy packages, particularly in higher income countries. Targeted support to vulnerable groups has been more commonplace relative to the tax measures described above, with subsidies often directly deducted from energy bills and cash transfers often targeted to poorer and more vulnerable groups. Cash transfers were provided in over a third of the 81 countries covered and of all the cash transfer measures introduced, three quarters were targeted at specific households. In a handful of countries, governments have sought to reduce petroleum prices directly through subsidies, whether through ad hoc refunds to customers (e.g., France) or through pre-existing petroleum price stabilisation funds (such as in Chile, Kenya, and Thailand). For electricity and heating fuels, subsidies benefitting all households were distributed in several countries. Examples include a EUR 100 (USD 118) heating voucher deducted directly from the electricity bill for all households in Belgium (and EUR 225 (USD 281) for households using heating oil), a 10% discount on electricity bills in Cyprus, and a subsidy covering 80% of the cost of energy bills above NOK 0.70 (USD 0.08) per kilowatt-hour in Norway. Some countries also reduced charges and regulatory fees on electricity tariffs.

Several countries provided additional incentives to save energy. Public transport subsidies were provided in Austria, Germany, Ireland, New Zealand, and Singapore. In some countries, these subsidies were available to all households, while in others, they were restricted to poorer families only. Belgium, Portugal, and the United Kingdom were among the countries to provide VAT exemptions or reduced VAT rates for the purchase of energy-saving and renewable energy products, such as solar panels, solar water heaters and heat pumps. Energy efficiency subsidies were introduced in Luxembourg, the Netherlands and Romania, among others.

A small number of European countries have also announced plans to implement windfall profits taxes to support the cost of the measures they have introduced. Bulgaria and Romania announced windfall profits taxes on its nuclear power plant, and for energy producers on revenues exceeding EUR 91/MWh, respectively, from October 2021. In March 2022, Italy imposed a 10% windfall profits tax (*contributo solidaristico straordinario*) on energy companies and intermediaries that experienced a year-on-year increase in earnings of at least EUR 5 million between October 2021 and March 2022. Italy then raised the tax rate to 25% at the beginning of May 2022. Following suit, in May, Greece imposed a 90% windfall tax on the additional profits made by electricity power generators from October 2021 to June 2022 and the United Kingdom announced an *Energy Profits Levy*, whereby a 25% tax rate will be applied to the "extraordinary" profits made by oil and gas companies up until 2025. The measure will include an investment allowance that oil and gas companies can use to reduce the tax base on which the levy applies if they reinvest these profits in the United Kingdom.

4.2.2. *The cost of measures introduced by governments has been significant*

Data show that the cost of the support delivered so far is significant. The aggregate fiscal cost of measures provided since October 2021 and ending by December 2022[7] – i.e. summing the fiscal cost of measures for which an estimate is available – amounts to a total of USD 246 billion of which USD 169 billion has come in the form of support for fossil fuels (left-hand side of Figure 4.4).[8] This means that in a period of over 15 months, governments will have rolled out additional support in the order of magnitude of the regular annual support measures for fossil fuels being provided prior to the energy price hikes (USD 201 billion in 2019 and USD 182 billion in 2020).[9]

Figure 4.4. Cost of government responses to the energy crisis, October 2021 to December 2022

USD Billions

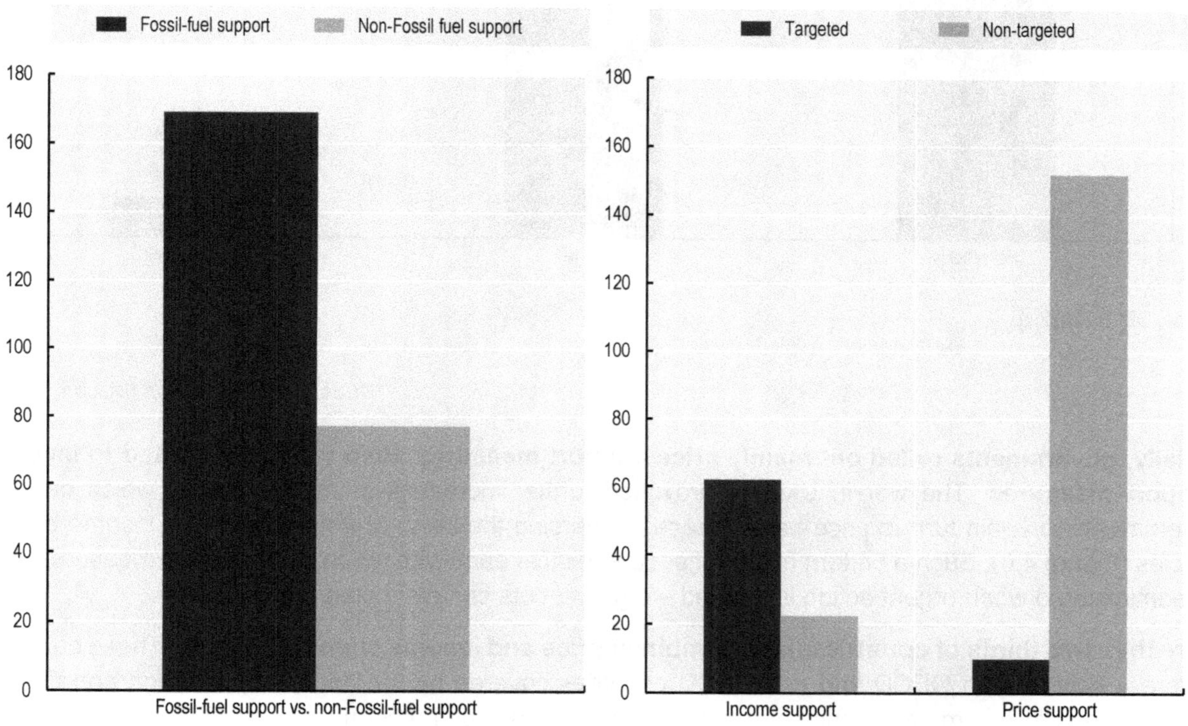

Note: (1) Measures classified as income support are those that provide lump-sum transfers to households or businesses to help alleviate energy cost increases. Price support includes all measures that reduce the post-tax energy price for all energy sources. These include price controls, reduced electricity charges and network fees, VAT and excise tax reductions, and compensation to distributors for selling energy products at reduced prices. Targeted measures are ones provided to specific groups, such as vulnerable households or businesses. Non-targeted measures apply to all consumers with no eligibility conditions. (2) Information on 284 measures was collected for 42 OECD and key partner economies, with 137 measures providing an estimated fiscal cost for a total of USD 246 billion between October 2021 and December 2022. (3) Fossil-fuel support measures imply a change in relative prices of energy sources that encourage the use of fossil fuels.
Source: OECD (2022[4]).

StatLink https://stat.link/r9ibvp

Governments' responses have focused largely on price control – which tends to support rather than curb demand. Income support measures account for 34% of the total value of support provided through policies covered by the database (right-hand side of Figure 4.4). Most of these, 73%, have been targeted. By contrast, price support – 66% of the amount of total support provided – is in large part non-targeted (94%).[10] In terms of counts of individual measures, most support has been directed towards households, and to a lesser extent, firms (Figure 4.5).

Figure 4.5. Targeting of government support measures, March 2021 to May 2022

Count of the number of measures

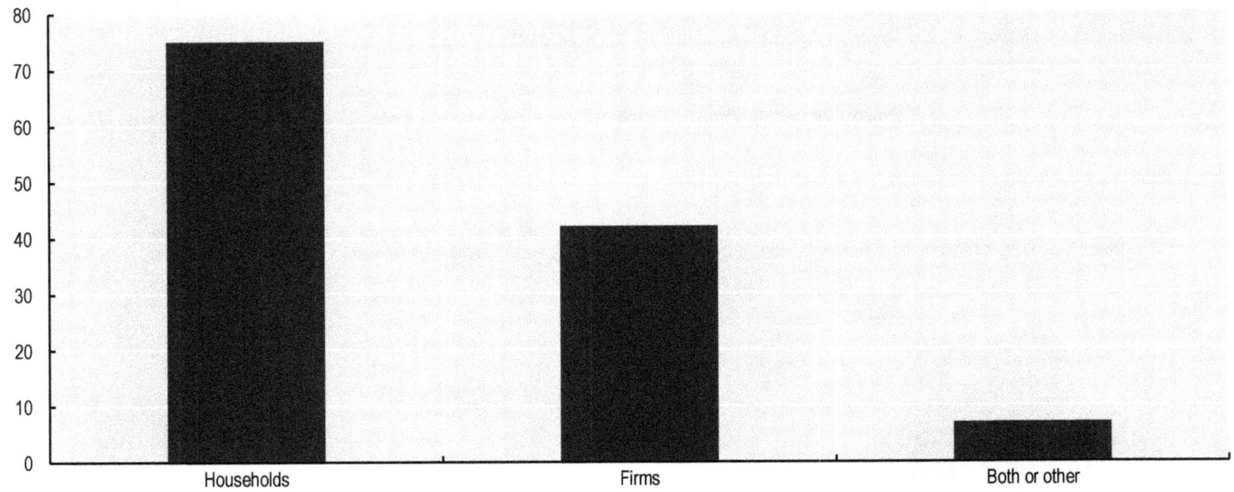

Source: OECD (2022[4]).

StatLink https://stat.link/5zd84u

Initially, governments rolled out mainly price support measures, then gradually shifted to income support measures. The war in Ukraine provoked further increases in energy prices, which caused governments to again turn to price-based polices, reversing the trend of a rising share of income-based policies (Figure 4.6). Such a pattern might reflect the relative ease with which price support measures can be administered when urgent action is needed – e.g., tax cuts can be implemented rapidly.

More than two thirds of countries have combined price and income support policies. These patterns generally hold in both OECD and non-OECD countries covered by the database, although non-OECD countries tend to rely more on price support measures. This may reflect a lack of capacity to administer sophisticated targeted income support programmes, particularly in emerging economies where informality is high and alternative energy sources are less developed (see Section 4.3).[11]

Figure 4.6. Relative share of income and price support measures, October 2021 to May 2022

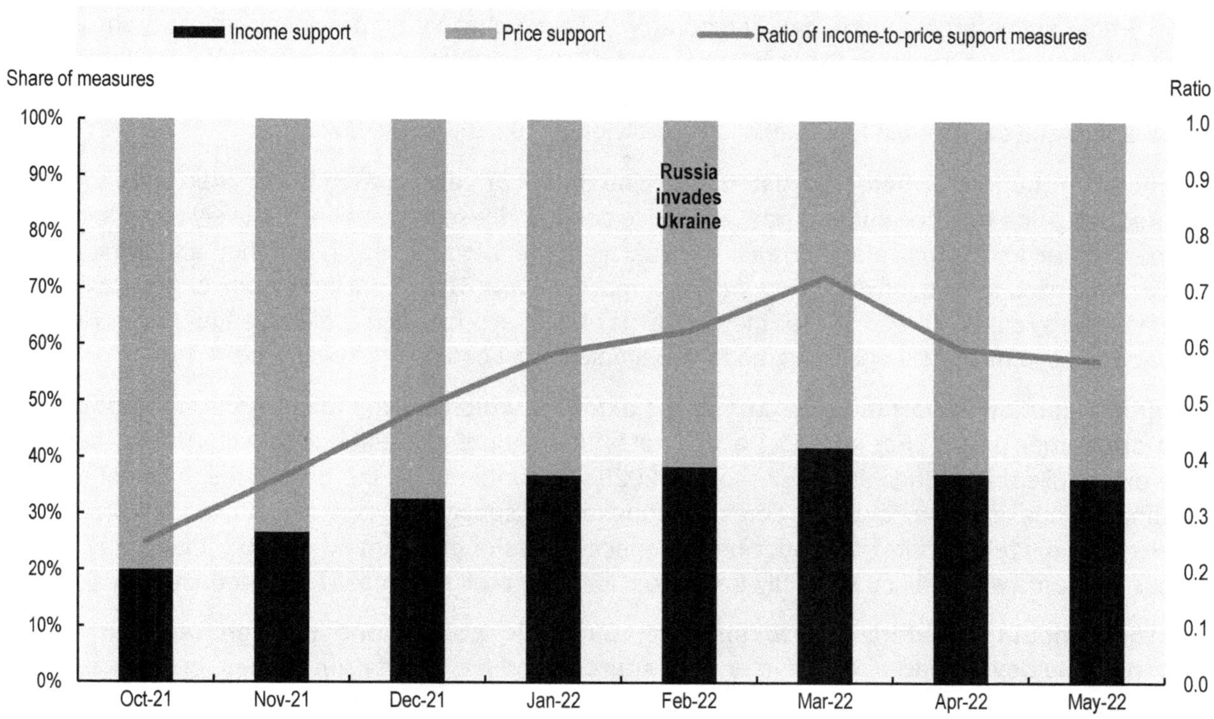

Source: OECD (2022[4]).

StatLink https://stat.link/ut0b4e

4.3. Policy observations

Approaches to delivering support differ in their administrative ease, effectiveness, and alignment with other policy objectives. To the extent that energy prices continue to remain high, support should strike a balance between effectiveness, budgetary and implementation costs, focusing on the strongest needs, and ensuring synergies with longer-term climate change and energy security objectives.

To this end, there are several reasons why countries should move away from price support measures, which for the most part contribute to raising fossil fuel subsidies:

- Price controls fix or cap the price of energy below market prices. While they are relatively simple to implement, they tend to be untargeted and benefits can accrue disproportionately to large energy consumers, who often have higher incomes.
- Price controls may also dampen price signals, limiting the incentive for energy savings or switching away from fossil fuels.
- When end-user energy (e.g., electricity, natural gas, and gasoline) prices are capped at below cost recovery, they can cause large losses further upstream in the energy supply chain thereby discouraging new infrastructure investments and ultimately exacerbating supply shortages (Guenette, 2020[5]). Even if governments compensate energy suppliers for their losses to ensure the continuation of their operations, implicit government guarantees typically weaken incentives for operational improvements. They can hence jeopardise the medium-term goals of ensuring energy

security and the transition to carbon neutrality. Despite their limitations, one advantage of price controls is that they also benefit individuals that fall outside of formal government welfare systems

- Price support measures can temporarily relieve inflationary pressures as they help lower inflationary expectations (Agénor and Knight, 1992[6]; Aparicio and Cavallo, 2021[7]). However, they do not allow for demand to adjust to supply constraints, which could exacerbate commodity shortages and sustain future inflation (Vaitilingam, 2022[8]; Neely, 2022[9]).

Energy tax reductions, whether targeted at excise duties or value-added taxes, also seek to reduce the effective price that consumers pay. Like price controls, these policies are relatively quick and simple to implement and communicate and reach individuals in the informal sector. But they also weaken price signals and hence the incentives to reduce consumption levels. Unlike price controls, energy tax cuts do not affect energy suppliers who still sell their products at market prices and avoid revenue losses. However, fiscal revenues immediately decrease, and the budgetary cost can be high over time.

In addition, caution is warranted regarding the extent to which energy tax reductions translate into lower consumer prices. For instance, a VAT rate cut does not guarantee a consumer price cut of the same extent (Benzarti, Carlonie and Kosonen, 2020[10]). Furthermore, the pass-through of tax cuts into consumer prices may be lower in times of constrained supply, as is the case today (Marion and Muehlegger, 2011[11]). Apart from reducing the effectiveness of government support, there may also be fairness concerns when tax cuts directly translate into larger profits for fossil fuels producers.

Countries should therefore aim to support vulnerable populations through targeted income support, while developing alternative energy sources and transportation modes. In contrast to price support, income support measures – e.g., temporary means-tested transfers – do not mute price signals, thereby encouraging energy savings and fuel switching, resulting in less GHG emissions while providing a financial lifeline to consumers (Pototschnig et al., 2022[12]; Bethuyne et al., 2022[13]).

While income support still has a fiscal cost, better targeting of support measures can allow for a more sustainable policy response if high prices persist. However, given that targeted interventions rely on government social databases to identify beneficiaries, some countries may face challenges in administering or implementing them in practice. First, in countries where social benefit systems are not very well developed or have a hard time reaching many of those potentially in need, e.g., due to high informality or lack of institutional capacity, targeting may be challenging. But even in countries where social benefits systems are more sophisticated, effective targeting would still require more than simply increasing existing transfers. Innovations in transfer mechanisms may be needed to ensure that groups that are most vulnerable to the energy price shock are reached. Digital delivery methods for transfers may be required, to bank accounts and via mobile applications, for example, especially in countries with high informality rates. These methods were used to target informal workers in emerging economies in particular during the COVID-19 crisis (OECD, 2020[14]).

Evidence for Germany shows that existing social and fiscal systems are not entirely capable of addressing the additional burden of higher energy prices in a finely targeted way, and additional fine-tuned measures may be needed to avoid social hardship while limiting budgetary costs (Kalkuhl et al., 2022[15]). The reason for such limited effectiveness is that existing systems do not account for the highly heterogeneous impact of price increases across households, which is driven by many factors. Income is one factor among others: the additional cost of higher energy prices is estimated to reach 6% of the overall consumption expenditure for the poorest decile compared with 2.8% for the richest groups (Kalkuhl et al., 2022[15]). Other factors, however, including housing location and quality, and household composition and access to energy and public transport all determine the degree of a household's financial vulnerability to energy price shocks (Flues and Thomas, 2015[16]; Blake and Bulman, 2022[17]). Therefore, as the case of Germany shows, support based on income alone may not be adequate.

Targeting is also important when providing support to firms. Governments should focus on companies that were previously solvent but are suffering from liquidity and solvency problems deriving directly from the crisis (OECD, 2021[18]). Such approach will mitigate the risk of keeping inefficient firms alive, which could restrict competition, dampen domestic productivity growth, and even distort international markets (OECD, 2020[19]). However, support should be time-limited even as energy costs remain high, as firms will need to adapt over time. More generally, government support to firms should also be transparent, proportionate, and non-discriminatory (i.e., applying objective and transparent criteria for determining firms' eligibility) (OECD, 2020[19]).

The unfolding energy crisis highlights social and political challenges of coping with energy price increases, similar to those anticipated as part of the transition to carbon neutrality (ECB, 2022[20]; IEA, 2021[21]). In addition, persistently high energy prices resulting from the consequences of the war in Ukraine highlight that fossil fuels have become a less reliable source of energy, prompting concerns over energy security, particularly in Europe. In this new geopolitical context, synergies between climate policy and energy security policy should be exploited over the medium term, as pursuing the transition to carbon neutrality can help reduce dependence on fossil fuels. For this reason, interventions that blunt price signals and dampen incentives to reduce fossil-based energy use should be phased out while building capacity to better address household vulnerabilities to price shocks and accelerating the development of alternative sources of energy. This can be done, for instance, by supporting energy efficiency improvements and ensuring that networks and infrastructures are adapted to zero carbon technologies. Over time, investing in capacities for energy users to adapt their energy consumption and shift to alternative fuels should be a common priority for climate, energy, and social policies.

References

Agénor, P. and M. Knight (1992), "Credibility Effects of Price Controls in Disinflation Programs", *IMF Working Papers, 1992*, Vol. 083/A001, https://www.imf.org/en/Publications/WP/Issues/2016/12/30/Credibility-Effects-of-Price-Controls-in-Disinflation-Programs-833. [6]

Aparicio, D. and A. Cavallo (2021), "Targeted Price Controls on Supermarket Products", *The Review of Economics and Statistics* 103(1), pp. 60-71, https://doi.org/10.1162/rest_a_00880. [7]

Benzarti, Y., J. Carlonie and T. Kosonen (2020), *What goes up may not come down*, pp. 4438-4474. [10]

Bethuyne, G. et al. (2022), *Targeted income support is the most social and climate-friendly measure for mitigating the impact of high energy prices*, https://voxeu.org/article/targeted-income-support-mitigate-impact-high-energy-prices. [13]

Blake, H. and T. Bulman (2022), "Surging energy prices are hitting everyone but which households are-more-exposed?", *Ecoscope*, https://oecdecoscope.blog/2022/05/10/surging-energy-prices-are-hitting-everyone-but-which-households-are-more-exposed/. [22]

Blake, H. and T. Bulman (2022), "Surging energy prices are hitting everyone, but which households are more exposed?", *ECOSCOPE*, https://oecdecoscope.blog/2022/05/10/surging-energy-prices-are-hitting-everyone-but-which-households-are-more-exposed/. [17]

Boone, L. and A. Elgouacem (2021), *At the cross-roads of a low-carbon transition: what can we learn from the current energy crisis?*, https://oecdecoscope.blog/2021/10/22/at-the-cross-roads-of-a-low-carbon-transition-what-can-we-learn-from-the-current-energy-crisis/. [3]

ECB (2022), *Looking through higher energy prices? Monetary policy and the green transition*, https://www.ecb.europa.eu/press/key/date/2022/html/ecb.sp220108~0425a24eb7.en.html. [20]

Flues, F. and A. Thomas (2015), *The distributional effects of energy taxes*, OECD Publishing, https://doi.org/10.1787/5js1qwkqqrbv-en. [23]

Flues, F. and A. Thomas (2015), "The distributional effects of energy taxes", *OECD Taxation Working Papers*, No. 23, OECD Publishing, Paris, https://doi.org/10.1787/5js1qwkqqrbv-en. [16]

Guenette, J. (2020), *Price Controls: Good Intensions, Bad Outcomes*, World Bank, https://openknowledge.worldbank.org/handle/10986/33606. [5]

IEA (2021), *Net Zero by 2050*, https://www.iea.org/reports/net-zero-by-2050. [21]

IEA (2021), *What is behind soaring energy prices and what happens next?*, https://www.iea.org/commentaries/what-is-behind-soaring-energy-prices-and-what-happens-next. [1]

Kalkuhl, M. et al. (2022), *Effects of the energy price crisis on households in Germany - Socio-political challenges and policy options*, Mercator Research Insitute on Glboal commons and climate change, https://www.mcc-berlin.net/fileadmin/data/C18_MCC_Publications/2022_MCC_Effects_of_the_energy_price_crisis_on_households.pdf. [15]

Marion, J. and E. Muehlegger (2011), *Fuel tax incidence and supply conditions*, pp. 1202-1212, https://doi.org/10.1016/j.jpubeco.2011.04.003. [11]

Neely, C. (2022), *Why Price Controls Should Stay in the History Books*, https://www.stlouisfed.org/publications/regional-economist/2022/mar/why-price-controls-should-stay-history-books. [9]

OECD (2022), *OECD Economic Outlook, Interim Report March 2022: Economic and Social Impacts and Policy Implications of the War in Ukraine*, OECD Publishing, https://doi.org/10.1787/4181d61b-en. [2]

OECD (2022), *Why governments should target support amidst high energy prices*, https://www.oecd.org/ukraine-hub/policy-responses/why-governments-should-target-support-amidst-high-energy-prices-40f44f78/. [4]

OECD (2021), *COVID-19 emergency government support and ensuring a level playing field*, https://www.oecd.org/coronavirus/policy-responses/covid-19-emergency-government-support-and-ensuring-a-level-playing-field-on-the-road-to-recovery-1e5a04de/. [18]

OECD (2020), *Government support and the COVID-19 pandemic*, https://www.oecd.org/coronavirus/policy-responses/government-support-and-the-covid-19-pandemic-cb8ca170/. [19]

OECD (2020), "Supporting livelihoods during the COVID-19 crisis: Closing the gaps in safety nets", *OECD Policy Responses to Coronavirus (COVID-19)*, OECD Publishing, Paris, https://doi.org/10.1787/17cbb92d-en. [14]

Pototschnig, A. et al. (2022), *Consumer protection mechanism during the current and future periods of high and volatile energy price*, https://fsr.eui.eu/publications/?handle=1814/74376. [12]

Vaitilingam, R. (2022), "Inflation, market power, and price controls: Views of leading economists", *VoxEu*, https://voxeu.org/article/inflation-market-power-and-price-controls-igm-forum-survey. [8]

Notes

[1] The reason is that global refinery maintenance and capacity constraints are exacerbating dislocations caused by the war in Ukraine, thereby leading to tightened markets of petroleum products. See https://www.iea.org/reports/oil-market-report-may-2022 for further discussion.

[2] This is not to say that nothing can be done. For instance, the IEA has designed a 10-point plan to decrease oil use by 6.2% within a four-month time window. See https://www.iea.org/reports/a-10-point-plan-to-cut-oil-use.

[3] The Special Feature is based on the OECD's policy brief Why governments should target support amidst high energy prices (OECD, 2022[4]).

[4] The Inclusive Framework jurisdictions covered by the data include all OECD countries, as well as: Argentina, Barbados, Benin, Brazil, Bulgaria, Burkina Faso, Cameroon, China, Croatia, Cyprus, Egypt, Gabon, Ghana, Gibraltar, Honduras, India, Indonesia, Isle of Man, Ivory Coast, Kazakhstan, Kenya, Morocco, North Macedonia, Pakistan, Paraguay, Peru, San Marino, Senegal, Seychelles, Singapore, South Africa, Thailand, Trinidad and Tobago, Ukraine, Uruguay, and Viet Nam. The 15 jurisdictions covered by the data that are not Inclusive Framework members are: Algeria, Bangladesh, Chad, El Salvador, Ethiopia, Fiji, Guyana, Lesotho, Madagascar, Moldova, Mozambique, Niger, Philippines, Tanzania, and Zimbabwe.

[5] The equivalent amounts in US dollars are: EUR 0.30 = USD 0.36; EUR 0.25 = USD 0.30; EUR 0.23 = USD 0.29; EUR 0.20 = USD 0.24; EUR 0.15 = USD 0.18.

[6] In the case of the Canadian province of British Columbia, an exemption from its provincial sales tax was introduced for the purchase of electric bicycles and tricycles.

[7] The fiscal cost of measures covering several years has been annualized. Estimates were provided by governments for a subset of 137 measures included in the database (from 32 countries).

[8] The total cost estimate is the aggregate of country-level estimations that can employ different methodological approaches, i.e., accrual vs. cash accounting. Additionally, price-based measures can have off-budget and below-the-line implications that are difficult to assess in the short run.

[9] This amount is extracted from the OECD Inventory of support measure for fossil fuels, which is a database that identifies, documents, and estimates more than 1 300 individual policy measures supporting the production or consumption of fossil fuels. It covers approximately the same countries as the database discussed in this Special Feature. See https://www.oecd.org/fossil-fuels/ for more information.

[10] Patterns are the same when considering the number of measures included in the database instead of their fiscal cost. Income support measures account for 38% of all policies covered by the database, with

78% being targeted. Price support measures account for 62% of all measures and are largely non-targeted (77%).

[11] The amount provided through price support measures in OECD countries accounts for 65% of the total against 100% in non-OECD countries. Non-OECD countries covered by the database include Argentina, Bulgaria, Brazil, China, Indonesia, India, Romania, and South Africa.

www.ingramcontent.com/pod-product-compliance
Lightning Source LLC
Chambersburg PA
CBHW061218240926
51846CB00006B/1271
* 9 7 8 9 2 6 4 3 2 2 2 1 9 *